DESERT HEART

Chronicles of the Sonoran Desert

DESERT HEART

Chronicles of the Sonoran Desert

William K. Hartmann

FISHER
BOOKS

Publishers: Bill Fisher
                Helen Fisher
                Howard Fisher
                Tom Monroe, P.E.

Editors: Bill Fisher
                Howard Fisher
                Clara Gualtieri
                Elizabeth Shaw

Art Director: David Fischer

Published by: Fisher Books
               PO Box 38040
               Tucson, Arizona 85740-8040
               (602) 292-9080

Library of Congress
Cataloging-in-Publication Data

Hartmann, William K.
Desert heart : chronicles of the Sonoran Desert / by William K. Hartmann.
p.   cm.
Includes bibliographical references.
ISBN 1-55561-025-0
1. Sonoran Desert—History. 2. Natural history—Sonoran Desert.
3. Sonoran Desert—Description and travel. 4. Hartmann, Willliam K.-
-Journeys—Sonoran Desert. I. Title.
F787.H37   1989
979.1'7—dc20   89-35286
                                                        CIP

ISBN 1-55561-025-0

© 1989 Fisher Books
Printed in the United States of America

*Frontispiece: Playa floor of summit crater, Phillips Buttes.
November 29, 1987.*

To Gayle Hartmann,
    for outdoorsmanship and esoteric information

to Amy Hartmann,
    with thanks for Van Dyke and Thoreau
    and for singing when having fun

to Julian Hayden, Bill Broyles, and T.E.L.,
    with thanks for help,
    and for proof that scholars can be adventurers,
    and vice versa

to Maurice Jarre and Ralph Vaughn Williams,
    for providing the music

and to I'itoi,
    who got there first.

Nonfiction by the same author

The New Mars with Odell Raper

Astronomy: the Cosmic Journey

Moons and Planets

The Grand Tour with Ron Miller

Out of the Cradle with Ron Miller and Pamela Lee

Cycles of Fire with Ron Miller

Contents

Acknowledgments

MANY FRIENDS HAVE HELPED with my desert travels, inspired me, and taken interest in my writing. During my travels in the Pinacate area I have enjoyed the companionship and assistance of many friends, including Diane Boyer, Georgie Boyer, Bill Broyles, Dale Cruikshank, Floyd Herbert, Paul Hirt, Peter Kresan, Dan Lynch, Jay Melosh and his students, Pete Nisbet, Godfrey Sill, Sarah Vetault, Charles Wood, and especially Ranger Fernando Lizarraga who has worked tirelessly to preserve the spirit of the Pinacates.

I am grateful to members of the Tucson Writing Group and other friends of writing for many helpful discussions, ideas and criticisms. These include Linda Dietrich, Gayle Hartmann, Roger Howlett, Carolyn Leigh, Paula McBride, Tom Miller, Nafie Nielsen, Elaine Olsson, Alan Oshiki, Dave Thayer and Margaret Wilder. In the same vein, thanks to Steve Cox and Barbara Beatty of the University of Arizona Press; Joe Wilder of the Journal of the Southwest; L. D. Clark, Lawrence Clark Powell, Bernard Fontana and David Laird of the University of Arizona; and Carlos Nagel of Friends of Pronatura. Paintings by Pete Nisbet and photographs by Jody Forster and Peter Kresan gave additional inspiration.

Pinacate scholars Julian Hayden and Bill Broyles gave invaluable advice, information, and encouragement. I acknowledge helpful conversations with the late explorer, Ronald Ives. Peter Steer, of the University of Arizona Library, went beyond the call of duty in locating the Pinart diary materials. Thanks to Dominique Spaute for her good cheer and enthusiasm in translating Pinart's diaries, handwritten in French. In addition to helping with field trips and Spanish translations, Gayle Hartmann checked some of the sites and shared information during her work on the Cabeza Prieta Wildlife Refuge Management Plan. Alix Ott assisted with some early stages of word processing.

Special thanks to Howard and Bill Fisher, Joyce Bush, Karen McGraw, Daisy the Dog and the rest of the staff at Fisher Books for their faith, assistance and hospitality, and to Josh Young and David Fischer for the superb design work.

All photos are mine unless otherwise credited. Some of the black-and-white negatives, especially the more recent ones, were printed by Jim Abbott and others by Joshua Young, Jr., whom I thank for their fine work.

William K. Hartmann

Preface

One begins by admiring the Hudson River landscape and ends by loving the desolation of [the] Sahara.
J. C. Van Dyke
The Desert, 1901

THIS BOOK DEVELOPED OVER THREE DECADES as I pursued my own involvement with the Sonoran Desert, and especially the eerie Pinacate lava and dune country of its heartland. My first involvement, and the early drafts, began in the sixties when I came to Arizona from Pennsylvania (hardly anybody in Arizona was *from* Arizona) as a graduate student in planetary astronomy at the University of Arizona. My friends and I learned about the Pinacate domain from a locally produced geological guidebook. We made treks there to appreciate the alien landscapes of other planets. It was an opportunity to study giant craters, and to feel what it was like to stand in them. Soon I found myself experiencing a special response to this paradoxically lush and desolate realm. Such a response was absent in the more barren acres around Tucson, where last century's grazing, this century's development, and the dropping water table have left a landscape less fertile to the imagination.

Two decades and a second draft later, in the eighties, I chanced upon a quote that explained to me what I had been doing in the evolving manuscript. Novelist N. Scott Momaday wrote:

> *Once in his life a man ought to concentrate his mind upon the remembered earth . . . He ought to give himself up to a particular landscape in his experience, to look at it from as many angles as he can, to wonder about it, to dwell upon it. He ought to imagine that he touches it with his hands at every season and listens to the sounds that are made upon it. He ought to imagine the creatures there and all the faintest motions of the wind. He ought to recollect the glare of moon and all the colors of dawn and dusk.*[1]

There is a benefit to such a project. It was expressed by Mary Austin, the great naturalist-writer of the early 1900s, who had a phrase for every phenomenon in the Southwest.[2] As she explored and wrote about any area, she said, "I . . . annex to my own estate a very great territory to which none has surer title."

1

The project of writing about a region brings me to the question: what is meant by "the land"? The acres of exposed geology? No, it is something more ephemeral and dynamic: the interaction of wind, water, soil, season and history. Mary Austin said:

> By Land, I mean all those things common to a given region, such as . . . the flow of prevailing winds, the succession of vegetal cover, the legend of ancient life; and the scene, above everything the magnificently shaped and colored scene.[3]

These are the aspects of *land* that the newcomer to the Southwest is missing. These are the aspects supernaturally manifested in the heart of the Sonoran Desert.

For me, the desert heart is Momaday's bit of remembered earth—which I want to examine from as many angles as I can. During my sporadic passages through that landscape, covering a quarter of a century of scrambles up summits and down crater walls, along Indian trails, making mental transpositions to the sands of Mars, struggling to meet its photographic challenges, pursuing old books in library stacks, and studying the latest orbital photos, I find this country ever more fascinating. It is always ready to yield another unexpected mystery . . . and sometimes an answer.

As I researched the history of the area, I read the American naturalists of a century ago and I was struck by the joy and optimism that characterized their relation with the land. Even their warnings of negative trends were expressed in a problem-solving spirit. I returned to the environmental writings of today and found many of them imbued, in dramatic contrast, with a kind of negativism that is hard to pin down. Sometimes it is despair. Sometimes it is just plain orneriness. I have come to identify myself as an environmental activist. My planetary consciousness blossomed on seeing the first pictures of finite, fragile Earth from the cameras of astronauts bound for the moon. It became a practical

reality when I published research on Tucson's air pollution and served on a county air-pollution panel in the '70s. But I felt dissatisfied with the late 20th-century-environmentalist paradigm and with much of late 20th-century American life in general. So, as I put together this book, I tried to view larger problems from the special perspective of the Sonoran Desert experience.

I began to feel it is important for all of us to expand the number of facets to which we respond as we look at the land. To respond not only to the flowers and the dawn light on the hills—the glorious superficialities that grace photographs in nature calendars—but also to the adventures that happened here in the past: the characters who passed through, the unseen geologic forces that molded the mighty shapes. The poems and novels and paintings the place engendered. The spirits that humans have given the land and the spiritual flowers that the land has given back to us.

Perhaps this view of the landscape, enriched by its own history, both natural and social, could arise only at this special moment, in this special century, this culture. For a contrasting view, listen to the Arabs encountered by English adventurer-writer, C. M. Doughty, as recently as 1877, as he rode across the wastes of Saudi Arabia. One day, Doughty and his party encountered a lost ruin. The air of mystery aroused Doughty's excitement. "What are these ruins?" he asked his Arab companions. Their answer: "Works remaining from the creation of the world. What profit is there to inquire about them?"[4]

For much of history, people have lived in their landscapes with such passive acceptance, such inertia. Things just *are*. Why bother to ask questions? Why seek the evolution of a land? Why be interested in a past that can't be changed? Why dream of what could happen in the future, when Celestial Fates determine all?

My answer: to enrich life; to gain a sense of place; to preserve something intangible as well as tangible.

To succeed requires exercising four abilities. The first three are what Lawrence Clark Powell, in his book on classic books of the Southwest, called "the old Three S's that crop up whenever I write about literature . . . seeing, sensing, saying."[5] To these I add a fourth: knowing. I add this because the more you know, the more you can see and sense. As Thoreau wrote, "there is just as much beauty visible to us in the landscape as we are prepared to appreciate—not a grain more."[6]

Thus, the first chapters of this book introduce the pioneers of the region, the Daniel Boones of the Southwest, who seem strangely absent from our children's education. Chapter 4 sketches the 1700s—a lost century in the Southwest, about which not one in a thousand of Tucson's citizens can tell you anything. Chapters 5 and 6 recount some true tales of the roughest part of the Old West. Chapters 7 and 8 focus on the extraordinary geology and archaeology of the central Sonoran Desert, where volcanoes erupted and ancient cultures died before our time. Chapter 9 recounts my own adventure rediscovering a lost diary of a traveler in the 1880s, and following its leads. Chapter 10 and the Epilog reflect on the current state of affairs in this changing, yet timeless, land.

Your visit to the desert could take one of many forms. You may find yourself on the road to Rocky Point. Or spending a month of your retirement in a camper at Organ Pipe Cactus National Monument. Or zooming across the bridge above the ancient Colorado River crossing on Interstate 10. Or pressing down dusty trails into the black heart of the Pinacates on a camping trip. You might even find yourself doing some armchair traveling at home in a suburb of some vast, twinkling metropolis. Whatever beckons you, I hope this book introduces you to a unique piece of our continent, increasing your delight in an amazing, forgotten desert region.

William K. Hartmann
Tucson, August 1989

1. Introduction: The Lure and the Lore

[It is a place which] you discover to be not so much a landmark . . . as a symbolic focus for many vanished streams of human interest . . .

Mary Austin
The Land of Journeys' Ending, 1924

A FORGOTTEN COUNTRY straddles the international border where Arizona, Mexico and the Colorado River meet. It includes the most desolate desert landscapes of North America but also contains some of the continent's most striking geologic features. It is known to only a handful of people. It is the heartland of the Sonoran Desert.

Arizona tilts toward this region. The land drops to the west and south from the high plains of New Mexico where the Rocky Mountains peter out. The steepest parts of the drop are known as the Mogollon Rim, a range of cliffs that slashes diagonally across the state from southeast to northwest. On the northeast side are high fir forests and meadows. To the southwest are the bright, forbidding, cactus-strewn badlands of the desert.

Driving west from Tucson, toward the Colorado River, you drop imperceptibly downhill, from the margins of the Sonoran Desert into its fierce heart. As you follow this route, you notice a change as you enter the desert's heart. The desertscape becomes clean, to use the word that T. E. Lawrence applied to the similar deserts of Arabia. Clean. It means you are leaving behind the brown pall that hangs over Tucson and over Tucson's out-of-control rogue uncle, Phoenix, and over the sprawling weed-cities sprouting along the corridor between them.

It's an insidious thing, this air pollution of Southwestern cities. When you're in the city, you don't notice it, and you think what a fine day it is; ah, life in the Southwest! But then you drive away from town, and the day is somehow brighter, the colors clearer. There is an edge to things, out in the desert.

As you strike into the heart of the Sonoran Desert, you begin to leave behind the patches of bladed ground and refuse and remains of failed housing developments. Those tacky, wonderful, run-down stores appear, run by the kinds of people who prefer being out in "the country," away from the zoning ordinances of the city. Ammo, minerals, gas. Back east, they'd be selling live worms—only here, there's no place to fish.

In an hour you pass Kitt Peak, part of a range sacred to the desert's Indian natives, now housing the mountaintop white temples of the Anglo astronomers. The observatories are like computer rooms in the Anglo's industrial plants. Everything is tidy and dustless, with things in their place, functioning. But now, in contrast,

Previous page: The Pinacate beetle in defensive posture. November 4, 1972.

Desert marigolds north of MacDougal Crater, with basalt hills in background, on the northwest Pinacate flanks. April 6, 1977.

you enter the old land still held by Native Americans—the *Reservation,* as we call it. Until the 1980s, they were called the *Papago Indians.* Then they readopted their ancient name, Tohono O'odham, the Desert People, the name I will use except when citing older documents.

The Desert People. They may be descendants of the prehistoric Hohokam, whose thousand-year-old ruined cities, ball courts, temple platforms, canals and painted potsherds are being overrun unknowingly by the uncomprehending promoters of Tucson and Phoenix, who arrive from Dallas or somewhere with bank loans to build new industrial parks like the ones they just built in Baltimore. They never heard of the Hohokam and they think the Sonoran Desert is just an extension of summer back home. And inside their buildings, it is—you push a button and the air conditioner comes on. You turn on the faucet and water comes out.

But out on the Reservation, the Tohono O'odham smile cryptically. They don't have the glitzy cars and salaries of the city Anglos. They don't even have quiet because Air Force jets stray from the aerial gunnery range farther west and roar over their villages. But they know the desert and how to live in it. Not as comfortably as the Anglos, perhaps, but with more stability. The Anglo cities may be a transient phenomenon, a passing fad. Take away the Safeways and the 7-11's and the Anglo cities would collapse. But the Tohono O'odham could last another thousand years, thank you very much. The Indians' big city, Sells, is not as clean as the desert, but at least it hasn't turned its air brown.

From here on to the west, the land is neglected, hence beautiful. Here are purple basalt hills, distant mountains blue with the pure air, flowers not struggling but adapted and minding their own business. Soon the land turns more forbidding, but stays just as beautiful. The flowers and shrubs become tougher, the land is drier, you can see farther, the ranges are stranger and more jagged, and tracts of dunes appear.

At last you have to decide whether you want to turn

The saguaro "met and surmounted all the conditions that . . . menace . . . the vegetative type. Passing, I salute it in the name of the exhaustless Powers of Life." Mary Austin. The Land of Journeys' Ending, *1924.*

Saguaro and blooming palo verde. Tucson, May 22, 1973.

north through Ajo and reenter the 20th century, or head south into the desert heart. You have to make this choice at a fork in the road, at a little settlement to which the few residents, tough as catclaw, have given the name "Why." If you go south, you head directly toward the border and Organ Pipe Cactus National Monument.

Sitting exactly on the border is a little Anglo community. It is named *Lukeville,* but a little road sign put up by its sardonic inhabitants announces it as *"Gringo Pass."* This is the gateway to the ancient Mexican hamlet of Sonoita, on an arroyo charitably called the *Sonoita River.* Through Gringo Pass rumble the campers and boat trailers to enter Sonoita and pick up highway Mexico 8, the road south to the popular seaside town of Puerto Peñasco, or Rocky Point.

Another road, Mexico 2, goes east and west out of Sonoita. East, it heads back into the pleasant, civilized country of central Sonora, with its leafy river valleys and picturesque mission towns. The latter were founded by Father Eusebio Kino when he, almost single-handedly, pushed the frontier through this country in the late 1600s. West out of Sonoita, Mexico 2 runs a few hundred meters south of the slanting Arizona-Sonora border.

This is the way toward desolation's heartland: naked mountain ridges of contrasting volcanic-brown basalt lavas and brilliant, crumbling granites; Alice-in-Wonderland plant life of spindly ocotillos, stands of stately saguaros, drifting sand dunes; and finally, the green broad ribbon of the Colorado River winding through barren hills. Buses and trucks roar along this road in a hurry to get to the other end—the comforts of San Luis, its American sister Yuma, and the promised land, the megalopolis—Los Angeles.

North of the speeding buses, north of the slanting borderline, the most aridly forlorn piece of the United States bakes in the sun. It is a strip unexpectedly called the *Cabeza Prieta National Wildlife Refuge*, bordered on its north by the Barry M. Goldwater Air Force Range where silver jet fighters slice the sky and blast imaginary targets, in training for what no one wants to imagine.

There are almost no natural water supplies along this road. Hundreds of people have died in this country, simply by getting stranded in it. The road goes where it does because this is the only direct corridor from Old Mexico to California. To the south are lavas and a wasteland of dunes. To the north are waterless valleys and arid rocky ridges. But hidden in the rugged hills along this route are natural "tanks," or water catchments in the rocks, where ponds of water survive from year to year. Centuries ago, the Indians knew them and showed them to the first European explorers. A trail grew along this stretch of land, from Sonoita to the Colorado. It was called *El Camino del Diablo*, the Devil's Highway. For years after the California gold rush of 1849, it was littered with the bones of those who lacked perseverance or luck. Today there are shiny cartridges ejected from a skyland beyond the speed of sound.

The land survey that transferred parts of this country to the United States placed the border along the same route; it is the slanty stretch of Arizona border that bends north instead of continuing on the east-west line of the Arizona and New Mexico borders to the east. A lonely line of white cairns on bright hillsides marks a line that exists only on maps and gets little attention. Beyond the Colorado River are the dunes and scrublands of the Colorado Desert, a different country, with different rocks and different vegetation, but the same cleanness and bright clarity.

The Sonoran Desert has a dark core at its center. Travelers on Mexico 8 or Mexico 2 go right by it, but most of them never notice it. It is the historic, volcanic core of the desert's wasteland: the forgotten volcanoes of the Pinacate Mountains, where Earth overflowed her banks. Here in this border country, then, is the black heart of the Sonoran Desert—and the heart of the matter.

Showing up on astronaut's orbital photos as a black blotch in the midst of the tan desert, the Pinacates are a mountain mass of dark lavas spreading over an oval patch roughly 35 by 25 miles. On the northern edge is Mexico 2 and the border, across which the northernmost lava tongues spill onto the dry sands of the Cabeza Prieta National Wildlife Refuge in the United States. To the east of the lavas, Mexico 8 runs south to the coast and the Sonoita River struggles in the same direction, getting lost in the desert before it can reach the sea. To the south, the sands run down all the way to Puerto Peñasco and the Gulf of California, as serene and dry a seashore as you will find anywhere. To the west, a trackless sea of dunes called the *Gran Desierto*, stretches to the Gulf and to the mouth of the Colorado River. The total depth of the sand is unknown, but the relief from dune crest to trough runs to nearly 600 feet in some areas.[1]

Biologically, each mountain range, including the Pinacates, forms an extraordinary environmental niche. For example, while the 4,500 square kilometers of Gran Desierto dunes support 75 species of plants, the 78

Astronauts' photos from the Space Shuttle in 1982 show much of the Sonoran Desert's heart. Dark patch, right center, is the Pinacate volcano complex, with Gran Desierto dunes stretching up the coast to its west. The bay southwest of the Pinacates is Adair Bay. Fishing port of Puerto Peñasco is at the hook on its east end. Mouth of Colorado River is at upper left. Width of two photos is about 150 miles. (NASA photos.)

Late afternoon sun on hills along Interstate 8, near Gila Bend.
January 17, 1980.

Twisted lava squeezeups, Ives Flow, southern Pinacate flank.
November 29, 1985.

square kilometers of the tiny granitic Sierra del Rosario range, west of the Pinacates, support 105 species, a concentration 68 times as great. The Pinacate range is like a secret preserve of desert plants and animals.

Fifty thousand years ago the Pinacates were some of the most violent volcanoes to erupt in the Southwest. Explosions and collapses opened half a dozen extraordinary craters, approaching a mile across and ranging up to hundreds of feet deep, unique on the North American continent. Lavas spilled out of its central vents to make jagged flows that look as if they could have formed yesterday. Geologically speaking, they did. The lavas piled into a dark, low mountain dome rising 3,960 feet above sea level—and nearly as far above the adjacent coastal desert.

The Pinacates country also forms a historic core to the region because the lavas and surrounding sands blocked the travelers who tried to open the northern frontier from Spanish Mexico. Only during the years of the California gold rush, around 1850, did it see really heavy travel—with hideous results. It was such a godforsaken place that people left it alone afterwards, with the result that the volcanic heartland of the Sonoran Desert is nearly pristine.

The Pinacates form the hub of a vast wheel. Surrounding it like a latticework of spokes are the playas, arroyos, and ridges of the open desert. Surrounding them at a radius of about 100 miles is a rim made of rivers. To the east are the fertile Magdalena and Altar valleys of Sonora and the Santa Cruz valley of Arizona; to the north is the Gila River; to the west is the broad Colorado. The thrust of history was counterclockwise around this wheel: up from Mexico, pushing, pushing to the north and west, trying to open the way around the north end of the Gulf to California; trying to get past the obstacle of the Pinacates, the Gran Desierto, the Cabeza Prieta; the Sonoran Desert's savage core.

Hence the string of white, Sonoran missions leading north to Tucson, Kino's triumph, a booming Ameri-

MacDougal Crater, about 3/4 mile across, seen from the air. White granitic range beyond the crater is the Hornaday range; most other, darker peaks are volcanic cones. Infrared photo, ca. 1963.

can Sunbelt city. Tucson has changed from a vigorous Hohokam farming village a thousand years ago, to Kino's mission center of San Xavier del Bac in 1700, and then to a Spanish garrison, a cow town, and finally a metropolis. Tucson has grown in the American way: too fast for its own good, outstripping its own water supply, so the shady cottonwood and mesquite groves that once graced its riverbanks are now gone.

Back in the desert, sudden summer showers loosen black rocks and fill the washes with transient, gushing torrents. When the rains have stopped, the sun plays on

Plants gain a foothold. Crack in welded cinders, west of Cerro Colorado Crater, northeast Pinacate flanks. January 11, 1970.

an hour through the same landscape to get to them. But once you enter the Pinacate lavas, something is different. The spatial scale of variety is small—yards. That is part of its strange charm. There is a fierce intimacy. Volcanoes form enclaves where variety occurs on a human scale. A path encountered leads not in a line for miles toward a vanishing point, but around the next corner, behind a cinder cone, into some unexpected cavity. The lava cannot seem to flow without forming nooks for soil, crannies for flowers, folds and crenulations, vesicles, cracks filled with seeds.

Because the Pinacate country formed an obstacle to civilization's advance, it became a last, hidden fastness of the pristine Sonoran Desert—reason enough to celebrate this peculiar landscape. As more and more people flock to the Sonoran Desert Sunbelt, they seem to know less and less about it. More accurately, the *sense of place* declines, because new citizens come too fast, and try to convert the desert to Cleveland before they can learn about the presence and pace of this alien land.

Sense of place. A good phrase. *Sense* refers to comprehending what is around you by direct sensory inputs, by observation, by blocking out the mental preconceptions that would fool you into thinking this can be Ohio. *Place* refers to the sum of the geography, geology, climate, botany, history and archaeology that make the land, which is more than the soil under your feet.

Down in the Pinacates, the earth falls away suddenly into caves and craters; black and reddish-brown lava flows form nearly insurmountable barriers that run for miles; beige sands, dazzling in the sun, bank against ashy cinder cones that rise like purple anthills.

To the Jesuit padre, Juan Salvatierra, the Pinacate Volcanoes and the deserts around them showed the "condition of the world in the general conflagration." Salvatierra crossed the lavas with Kino in 1701, and someone in their party discovered "a big hole of such depth that it caused terror and fear."

the dry and dusty playas, heating them until the air next to the ground gets hot and starts to rise and swirl. Then ghostly dust devils walk across the land and the wind whistles through the prickly chollas and through holes worn in rocky outcrops. This happens whether or not human beings pay attention.

Out on the flat, tan desert, the spatial scale of variety is large. You see mountains 60 miles away and drive

Pinacate Peaks from the southwest, in the dune fields west of Moon Crater.
April 8, 1977.

One-hundred thirty-five years later, frontier law officer, customs agent, and colorful personality Jefferson Davis Milton, put it more succinctly: "Hell must have boiled over at Pinacate." The little stinkbug known as the Pinacate beetle, *Eleodes armata*, "the little bug that stands on his head," elevates his rear and threatens with foul perfume any adversary that sufficiently upsets him. It is his name that attaches to the volcanic mountain complex.

There were earlier names. A 1951 traveler and popular writer, Wilson McKenney, reported that the local Indian name for the mountains was *Tjuktoak,* or Black Mountain. Carl Lumholtz, the naturalist-explorer who published an account of the region in 1912, also mentions the term Black Mountain, although he and other writers use mainly the term Pinacate.[2] Earlier, around 1700, Father Kino assigned the name Santa Clara on his maps. His maps were subsequently forgotten.

When the Pinacate lavas were erupting, they piled up in a broad, dome-like mass, forming the present, 40-mile-wide volcano. Such a form is known as a *shield volcano,* because it is shaped like an ancient warrior's shield. The shield is dotted with smaller individual vents—cinder cones and twisted spatter cones called *hornitos*. In some regions, explosive eruptions emptied underground magma chambers and widened vents, leading to collapses that created yawning pits, the craters that provide some of the most extraordinary sights.

The central Pinacates still manifest geologic adolescence. Fewer erosive agents have been active here. A ghostly aura of violent creation permeates vents that look like they formed yesterday. Great rafts of balanced lava, 20 feet across, still teeter underfoot. If nature rules, hundreds of millenia will transpire before this place loses its supernatural strangeness.

As recently as 1957, a hitherto unmapped major crater was discovered here. But the era of major discoveries is drawing to an end. Photos from high altitude and from space allow armchair explorers to examine features

Badilla crater (foreground), with the Pinacate Peaks in the distance, showing the shield-like profile of the mountain mass. Light windblown dust blankets the crater floor. In mid-distance, behind the cinder cone at right, is Sykes Crater. Aerial photo, September 14, 1972.

that were not even mapped two decades ago. Today, the sense of otherworldliness persists, however, in the names and stories that drift across the years to us—Quitobaquito, the hotspring campsite; I'itoi's cave at the Pinacate summit, sacred shrine of the Tohono O'odham; Cabeza Prieta, the "black-head" Mountains formed by basalt cascading across granite slopes; Kino's lost "Spring of the Moon;" "spirit candles" of St. Elmo's fire, reported on the peaks at night; and the persistent rumors of ruined missions and lost gold that all the Southwest's strange sites engender.

Journal entry. Toward the Pinacates. February 8, 1985.
A group of us, hikers from Tucson, are heading for the Pinacates. Normally, the car ride is a forgettable part of a camping trip but today I am reexperiencing the special quality of winter desert light and air, fused together. Sunlight seems to suffuse everything.

Dry, tan, soft grass grows to the edge of the road just as green furry moss creeps to the sidewalks and rock walls of cloudlands. This tan grass, like the pinker dry soil, is lighter in color than the scrubby, leafless black mesquite bushes and green palo verdes. They bathe in the soft light reflected from the ground—a soft, skin-colored glow.

The sky is a full blue dome overhead, blue down to the horizon, and offers cleaner, brighter vistas than the sky in the city, which is mushed in by a pall of purple smog that is almost invisible, but robs us of clarity and happiness. Even though the sun is bright and the sky is blue, the winter light of the desert has a soft quality, unlike the glare of the summer desert sun. The reason is that the sun is lower, only about $40°$ high as we approach noon, instead of the $83°$ maximum altitude of summer. So the sunlight beam travels through about 60 percent more air and dust than in June.

Now there are high, pale cirrus clouds scattered about in this blue sky, almost as thin and blue as the sky itself, but a touch pinker than the sky color, picking up the fleshy pink of the ground reflected off their bottom surfaces.

The temperature is a pleasant 70F. Winter in the desert. The hillsides, reddish-brown weathered-basalt heaps, are splotched by green palo verdes and forested by the upright toothpicks of light, yellow-grey-green saguaros. Clean skies and clean light and clean rocks and clean plants; we are on our way to the Pinacates.

15

2. The Quest:
Tales of the Spanish Pathfinders

READING OF THE FIRST SPANIARDS to penetrate the Sonoran Desert, you begin thinking that they were, somehow, superhuman. Each story of fantastic deeds leads to a story still more fantastic. Tough men, walking, walking, across lavas and dunes, all the way to the Colorado River and back, with no maps.

The counterclockwise swing of European exploration around the northern end of the Gulf of California was triggered in 1536 by the conclusion of a bizarre odyssey, a journey-by-accident, involving four lost explorers who wandered in the wilderness for eight years. Without plan or compass, they forged the first link between the modern-day border and the seat of European power at that time, the conquered Aztec metropolis that is now Mexico City.

It happened this way. In 1528, the son of a distinguished Spanish family, Alvar Nuñez Cabeza de Vaca, signed up for an expedition that was attempting to repeat Hernán Cortés' recent triumph. All they needed to do was to find another rich Indian nation to plunder. Unfortunately, they made the mistake of looking for culture along the coast of the Gulf of Mexico. Finding none, they tried to work their way around the Gulf with one party on land and the other at sea. They got separated. Disaster struck. Indians wiped out most of the expedition on the Texas coast, capturing de Vaca, two white companions, and a dark-skinned Moorish servant named Esteban, who some writers refer to as black.

During their first few years of captivity, they were virtual slaves. But wily, good-hearted de Vaca and his comrades established themselves as shamans and healers. Soon they were working their way westward from tribe to tribe, bartering and establishing good will. For eight years they wandered and survived, crossing the plains of west Texas, probably part of New Mexico, perhaps a bit of Arizona, and finally turning south across Sonora and Chihuahua. On foot! Many a seasoned traveler cringes at *driving* across west Texas, let alone wandering in it for years! They accumulated a band of several hundred Indian disciples who would travel with them for a few villages, then return home, only to be replaced by others from the next village.

Finally, this ragtag band stumbled into Spanish slave raiders working northward out of the Mexican town of Culiacán, nearly 500 miles south of the present Arizona-Sonora border. Culiacán was the northern

Previous page: The role of Melchior Díaz was recreated in historically authentic costume, along with the fateful lance, during celebration of the 50th anniversary of the Cabeza Prieta Wildlife Refuge, near his original route, at Tule Well in the Tule Mountains. April 1, 1989.

Dawn in camp under a palo verde tree southeast of Elegant Crater; east Pinacate flank. February 19, 1989.

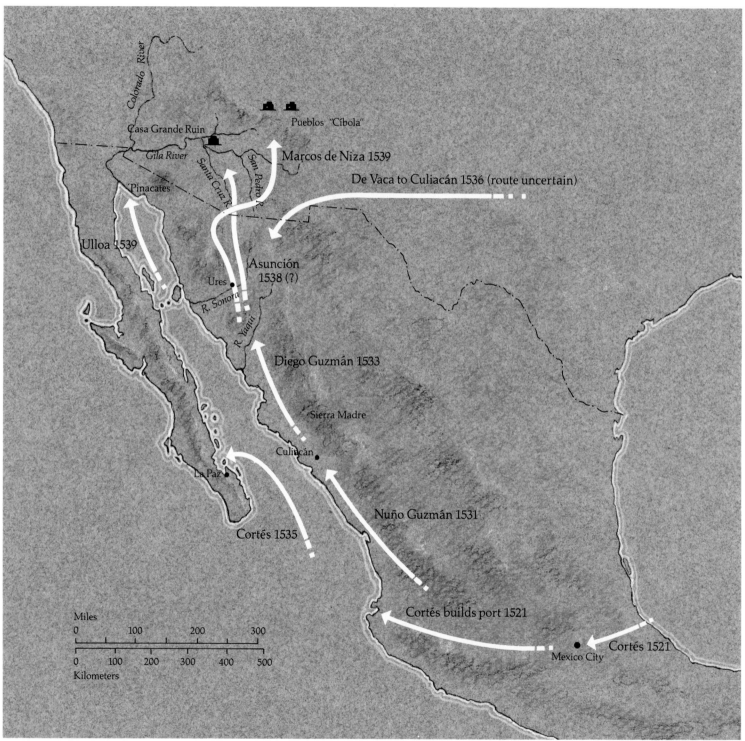

Colorado River

Casa Grande Ruin

Gila River

Santa Cruz R.

San Pedro R.

Pinacates

Pueblos "Cíbola"

Marcos de Niza 1539

De Vaca to Culiacán 1536 (route uncertain)

Ulloa 1539

Ures

Asunción 1538 (?)

R. Sonora

R. Yaqui

Diego Guzmán 1533

Sierra Madre

La Paz

Culiacán

Nuño Guzmán 1531

Cortés 1535

Cortés builds port 1521

Cortés 1521

Mexico City

Miles
0   100   200   300

Kilometers
0   100   200   300   400   500

Early Spanish explorations.

frontier of New Spain in 1536, ruled by a notorious trafficker in Indian souls, Nuño Beltrán de Guzmán. De Vaca and his companions went on to the comforts of civilization in Mexico City, where de Vaca sensibly wrote a book about his adventures, still fascinating after four and a half centuries.[1] Esteban reappeared a few years later in another hair-raising quest, as we will see.

De Vaca's eight-year journey had three consequences. First, it closed a tenuous loop across a continent, between the Spaniards of Florida and those of Mexico. Second, it probably gave the Mexican state of Sonora its name, because de Vaca and his companions tried to teach the Indians something of Christianity, and a corruption of Mary's title, *Señora*, stuck as a place name. Third, and most important, de Vaca brought rumors of great cities, said by the Indians to lie somewhere north of de Vaca's path.

De Vaca's rumors fell on receptive ears. In Mexico City, the avaricious young conquistadors who had conquered the Aztecs were all too ready to believe another fabulous empire lay beyond the horizon. Strangely enough, his rumors affirmed still earlier rumors of gold to the north.

A peculiar medieval tale, with roots perhaps as far back as 1150, claimed that when the Moors captured Spain, seven bishops and their followers escaped by sea to the west, reaching an island called *Antilia*, and founding settlements that came to be called *The Cities of the Seven Bishops*, or *The Seven Cities of Antilia*.[2] After 1492, many believed that one of Columbus' islands was Antilia, hence the name Antilles. The Seven Cities had eluded explorers so far, but might exist somewhere in the uncharted north, consistent with de Vaca's rumor.

In another development, the name *California* had come into use as early as 1510-21, as the result of a novel, *The Adventures of Esplandian,* published in Toledo. It told of a Pacific Island, California, beyond the New World, peopled by beautiful Amazons. Their queen was Califia. They were rich in gold, silver and jewels.

Even the wildest tales of gold gained credence in 1519, when the adventurer Hernán Cortés, with his small band of soldiers, entered the fabulous Aztec capital, Tenochtitlán. Montezuma, in all his barbarous finery, came out to greet them and lead them into the city. Cortés' soldiers stared in wonder, reporting that the bustling market was larger and better laid out than any they had seen "in Constantinople, and Rome and all over Italy." One soldier, Bernal Díaz, in his vivid chronicle of Cortés' campaign, describes how Montezuma and his priests led Cortés and his soldiers up the 114 steps of the great pyramid. With great deference, Montezuma remarked to Cortés, "You must be tired . . . after climbing up this great temple of ours." Brash Cortés replied that neither he nor his soldiers ever got tired from anything. Cortés soon seized the disillusioned Montezuma and, after near-disasters, captured the entire city on August 13, 1521, becoming at age 36 the conquerer of an astoundingly wealthy nation. Within years, Tenochtitlán had been virtually destroyed by the Europeans, and replaced by the smaller settlement of Mexico City.

Now they could start the search for more riches. Cortés himself wrote to the King of Spain about the rumored "island of Amazons or women only, abounding in pearls and gold, lying 10 days' journey from Colima," a coastal district west of Mexico City. Entrepreneur that he was, Cortés in 1522 began the new quest, founding a town on the west coast of Mexico to build ships for a fleet to explore the Pacific and its coastline. The first naval expeditions were disasters. Of three ships that set out in 1527, two were lost at sea and a third was captured by the Portuguese.

Cortés' stock fell. The times were rife with intrigue. Pressure on Cortés mounted. One of Cortés' own lieutenants, the notorious Guzmán, began trying to undermine Cortés' position by starting his own search for riches to the north. By 1530, Guzmán "had in his possession"[3] an Indian who testified that as a boy he had gone with his father on trading expeditions to the northern realm, where there were seven large towns and streets of silver workers. The seven cities were supposed to be 40 days' journey north from the Indian's native village. Guzmán's army of 400 Spaniards and a reported 20,000 friendly Indians started on an intended march of 600 miles, but they erroneously thought they had to cross the rugged Sierra Madre, backbone of Mexico. When they were defeated by the steep ridges and canyons in 1531, they stayed to found Culiacán, the important coastal town across from the tip of Baja California. Already they were halfway from Mexico City to the Sonoran Desert. Culiacán became Guzmán's private empire, center of his slave-trading business and staging area for many northward sorties to explore the land and raid Indian villages.

Cortés had to strike out in this direction too, but luck was still not with him. Naval expeditions that he sent to explore along the coast in 1532 and 1533 ended in mutinies. However, one of the mutinous parties reached the south tip of Baja California in 1533 or 1534 and returned (after the slaughter of some of their party by Indians) to tell of pearls in the Bay of La Paz. Could this be the famous kingdom of Queen Califia?

During that same period, in 1533, came news that supported the dream of wealth throughout the Americas. Francisco Pizarro conquered the Inca empire in Peru, capturing treasures beyond belief.

Cortés decided to do it right this time and lead the explorations himself. In May, 1535, he landed at the Bay of La Paz and took possession of the arid land for the King of Spain. He called it *Santa Cruz* and established a colony. More pearls were found, adding economic incentive for the project. But supplying the colony from across the Gulf proved too difficult. By 1536, 23 colonists had starved to death and the colony was abandoned.

This was the year in which de Vaca and his companions wandered into Culiacán with their story of wealthy cities on the mainland to the north. Here was fuel for the combustible mixture of speculation and intrigue! All eyes shifted toward the northern frontier. A chaotic, four-year stampede began.

Treacherous Guzmán and his nephew, Diego, had already probed as far as the Yaqui or Mayo rivers, in the southern reaches of the Sonoran Desert, about three-fourths of the way up the coast from Mexico City (see map, page 18).[4]

De Vaca reported that along the river valleys east of the Sonoran Desert (near the present-day junction of Arizona, New Mexico, and Sonora) he had seen turquoise, fine deerskin clothes, and other goods bartered from inhabitants of mysterious great cities farther north. Surely this was proof of the long-rumored Seven Cities of Antilles!

The seven cities, of course, turned out to be the pueblos of New Mexico, with whom Indians from central Mexico had established trade routes centuries earlier. But instead of dusty adobe towns, the over-fired imaginations of the Spaniards conjured exotic cities where the kitchen utensils were made of gold. Here we see a perfect example of a preconception confounding the use of language. The concept, the *gestalt*, of seven rich settlements was already a ghost lurking behind any rumors from the north. How could one speak to any Spaniard of Mexico City in 1536 of undiscovered cities without conjuring a mental image of such wealth as had already been found among the Aztecs and Incas? How easy it is for us to see it—and how impossible for them to realize the disappointment they were heading for!

A POWERFUL DRAMA of competing personalities emerges from the still-preserved documents of the period. In Mexico, the king's representative was the viceroy (i.e., the vice-*roi* or vice-king). Cortés aspired to this post, but his string of naval failures discredited him. Much to his dismay, the king appointed one Antonio Mendoza in 1537. Mendoza was faced with hordes of young adventurers and older captains flooding Mexico City, impatient to go north, conquer, and get rich. Who

Dusk near Dragoon, Arizona. Asunción, Fray Marcos and Coronado may have crossed southern Arizona near here. September 20, 1986.

ever his plan, Mendoza acted with great caution. A letter of his, written between November 1538 and September 1539, indicates that in 1537 he set to work trying to launch a party organized around the survivors of de Vaca's odyssey, but this failed and caused Mendoza some embarassment with the crown.

Some documents refer cryptically to a northward probe in 1538. These accounts[5] refer to a journey by Fr. Juan de la Asunción, possibly with a second friar, Fr. Pedro Nadal, who departed in January, 1538, and traveled some 600 to 800 miles north of Culiacán until they were stopped by a large river, allegedly at latitude around 33°. Some authors, including Spanish writers as early as the 1700s, speculated that this river was the Colorado, which flows south from the Grand Canyon and enters the Gulf at about 32° latitude. That is unlikely, because a trip to the Colorado does not match what Asunción and Nadal reportedly saw. Besides, it would have taken them through the ferocious heart of the Sonoran Desert, a difficult journey at best. Other writers thus dismiss the trip as myth. More likely, Asunción and Nadal's journey was a real event.[6] Probably they were led along the Indian trading routes that others were to follow in the next few years, reaching the headwaters of the Santa Cruz or San Pedro near the present border, and tracing them north to the great Gila River, in central Arizona, the river which stopped them. According to the later authors, Asunción and Nadal reported that they saw multistoried buildings and people who wore shell jewelry and beads, and when they were stopped by the large river, the people there told them that even greater cities lay ten days' journey farther north. These facts agree with a possible discovery of the Gila. In the next years, Fray Marcos de Niza and Coronado confirmed that Cíbola lay about 15 days' journey through an uninhabited region north of the Gila. All along the middle Gila at that time were ruins of the multistoried adobe buildings of the Hohokam Indians. (The only surviving example today, after 4-1/2 centuries, is the "great

should lead the great venture north? Cortés, conquerer of the Aztecs, was falling into disrepute. Another contender could have been Guzmán, already halfway to the north, but his sleazy operations had by now attracted so much attention that he had been arrested. Another contender was a 28-year-old conquistador who had been appointed to replace Guzmán as governor of the new northern province, Francisco Vazquez de Coronado.

While Mendoza wrestled with this problem, he decided to seek more information about the north. He needed somebody who could quietly reconnoiter. Whomever he picked would become the first European to probe north into the present-day border country. At this point, the historical records become cryptic. What-house" of Casa Grande National Monument) Thus, little-known Asunción and Nadal were likely the first Europeans to cross northward into the present-day American Southwest.

The reason Asunción and Nadal are so little known is that Mendoza probably sent them in secret, so that the story came out only a few years later, by word of mouth. (This is consistent with Mendoza's action the next year, when he sent his next team north with instructions to report only in secret.)

Whether or not Mendoza had a secret report from Asunción and Nadal, he acted decisively in the fall of 1538. He commissioned not a vast expedition by the chafing conquistadors, but a quiet reconnaissance by a mere three Europeans: the Franciscan friar Marcos de Niza, a lay brother, and the black survivor of de Vaca's odyssey, Esteban. Taking Indian guides, they were to travel north in search of the seven cities, with instructions to stay near the coast and report on the nature of the coastline. Marcos de Niza, or Marcos of Nice, was an interesting man. A few years earlier, he had been disillusioned in Peru by the slaughter of the Indians. He was an advocate of the Indians' rights and was highly recommended by his bishop, who knew him personally and wrote in 1537 that "this father is a great religious person, worthy of credit, of approved virtue and of much religion and zeal, and whom the friars in Peru elected *custodio*." He was described as skilled in cosmography and navigation. Seemingly, he was responsible and well regarded. Yet he was about to become one of the most vilified explorers in history—a friar denounced as a fraud!

Still extant in the archives are the instructions that Fray Marcos received from Mendoza on November 20, l538, and the *relación* that Fray Marcos wrote upon his return the following year. The instructions told him to "... take much care to observe the people ... if they live in communities ... the quality and fertility [of the soil], the temperature, ... minerals and metal ... You shall

Gulf of California coast near Puerto Peñasco, looking north toward Pinacates (skyline, left). This is the latitude where the coastline begins to run west, a region reported on by Marcos de Niza. May, 1975.

arrange to send information by Indians ... And if God, Our Lord, is so served that you find some large settlement, where [we might] establish a monastery ... you shall send information by Indians or return yourself ... Send such information with all secrecy, in order that whatever is necessary can be done without commotion ..."

Fray Marcos left from Culiacán, apparently on March 7, 1539 (there has been some controversy about the date). His lay brother colleague fell ill after a few days and returned. Fray Marcos and Esteban continued north, on foot, with their Indian guides.

In late summer, Fray Marcos returned to Culiacán without Esteban. According to eyewitnesses, he was secretive about his results when he reached Culiacán, but once he reached Mexico City and after his report was certified on September 2, 1539, gossip spread like wild-

"The sun falls fierce and hot as a rain of meteors."
J. C. Van Dyke, The Desert, 1901.

Cholla cactus and sun, Growler Mountains, Arizona. November 4, 1972.

fire about what he said he had seen.

His report told an astonishing tale of adventure and violence. Along the way, the local Indians were exceedingly friendly, celebrating Fray Marcos' announcement of Mendoza's promise of freedom from slave raiding. He had traveled north to the latitude where the seacoast turned west, some tens of miles south of the present border. Here, he had made a side trip toward the coast to confirm this. Throughout the trip, his Indian admirers went before him, preparing camps along the well-established Indian trading trails. Esteban had gone a few days ahead, with instructions to make inquiries, wait for Fray Marcos, and send back a cross if he received news of settlements ahead. It was to be a small cross if small settlements; large, if large. Esteban sent back big crosses! In a region corresponding to present-day Sonora, Fray Marcos said he traveled along valleys where Indians wore good cotton clothes and abundant turquoise jewelry. These Indians confirmed the existence of the larger cities ahead, large and powerful settlements of a region called *Cíbola*. Contrary to Fray Marcos' instructions, Esteban did not wait, but pushed ahead across a 15-day-long uninhabited region toward Cíbola. Fray Marcos entered this region some days later. Then, on the threshold of triumph, disaster struck! A few days from Cíbola, some of the Indians who had gone with Esteban came staggering back along the trail, bloody and frightened. They reported that Esteban had brazenly entered Cíbola, ignoring warnings from the chief of Cíbola to turn back, and trusting instead to his previously proven charisma as a shaman. But after housing him for a night outside the city, the Indians of Cíbola killed him!

Fray Marcos reported that he stealthily approached to within sight of the city of Cíbola, which he said "is situated on a plain at the skirt of a round hill. It has the appearance of a very beautiful town, the best that I have seen in these parts. The houses are of the fashion that the Indians had described to me, all of stone, with their stories and terraces . . . [It] is bigger than the city of Mexico."

In the safety of his hidden vantage point, Fray Marcos built a large cairn of stones surmounted by a small cross and claimed the lands for Spain. Prudently, he decided that a safe return was of greater service to Mendoza than martyrdom in the footsteps of Esteban. So he turned and fled as fast as he could, he said, "more with fear than with food."

To the conquistadors in Mexico City Fray Marcos' report was eyewitness proof of the legends about another fabulous empire in the north: The Seven Cities of Cíbola! All that was needed now was an expedition to conquer them.

But wait! The story of Fray Marcos is one of the most peculiar in the annals of American exploration. While some historians treat Fray Marcos as the pioneer

". . . the first pure draughts of desert air and the nakedness of space, pure as a theorem, stretching away into the sky drenched in all its own silence and majesty . . ." Lawrence Durrell, Balthazar, *1958.*

Sunrise west of Yuma, in the region penetrated by Díaz. June 1, 1986.

who first reported on the American Southwest in a detailed fashion, others label him a liar! Most agree that he made it as far north as southeastern Arizona. But many say that it was impossible for him, in the time available, to have made it all the way to Cíbola, now known to be the pueblo of Zuni. (Zuni lies near the western border of New Mexico, a little more than half-way up the state from the present Mexican border.) The same historians add that Fray Marcos *certainly* lacked time to make a side trip to see where the coast turned west. The question of whether he could have made this trip is of special interest here, because it would have taken him into the Sonoran Desert heartland.

Before we can assess whether Fray Marcos told the truth, we need to continue with other events of 1539. In that same year, a second expedition was sent north, this one by sea, consisting of three ships under Francisco de Ulloa. This one reached the north end of the Gulf of California and entered the mouth of the Colorado River, about 75 miles west of the Pinacates. This expedition made the important discovery that Baja California was not an island.

A third important expedition of that year came when Mendoza promptly sent out a party to follow Fray Marcos' footsteps, within months of Fray Marcos' return. On November 20, 1539, a colorful soldier named Melchior Díaz set out from Culiacán with 15 horsemen. He traveled 300 or 400 miles north—about two-thirds the length of the gulf—to a populated region of central Sonora. There the Indians confirmed Fray Marcos' descriptions of Cíbola.

Stouthearted Díaz returned with this news and was fated for a further harrowing Sonoran Desert adventure, as we will soon see.

Meanwhile, during the fall, Cortés and Coronado had been jockeying for leadership of the proposed grand army to conquer Cíbola. In September, Coronado petitioned a royal court to block Cortés' proposed expedition. In response, by March of 1540, Cortés was off to the Council of the Indies, petitioning to block Coronado! But Coronado was already at Compostela, on the coast west of Mexico City, assembling his expeditionary forces. By March he had already moved his army north to the jumping-off point at Culiacán. Cortés had been outflanked and the ill-fated conquest of the rich northern *terra incognita* fell to Coronado and his army.

The great expedition of Francisco Vasquez de Coronado constituted the 16th-century version of our Apollo moon program—a massive voyage into the unknown. There were 225 cavalrymen and 60 foot soldiers, five friars including Marcos de Niza himself, nearly 1,000 Indian guides, scouts, and servants, and some 1,500 cattle, horses and mules. They moved into a land vast and silent with only scattered villages. They faced hot days and cold nights. There would be river valleys lined with luxurious green trees, surrounded by arid, brown countryside. But they were willing to suffer any hardships of the trail. They were going to be rich.

IN SPITE OF TANTALIZING CLUES in several chronicles of the expedition, Coronado's exact route is uncertain—an exciting challenge for desert buffs. My own surmise is that they were somewhat east of Fray Marcos' route in the Sonoran Desert region. Fray Marcos had been ordered to stay near the coast. Also, he had been interested in the Indians (heathen souls to be "saved"), and had tended to go from one populated valley to the next. Coronado preferred the most direct route.

Especially in the northern Sonora and border regions, where Fray Marcos said he made the side trip to the sea, Coronado's army was probably many miles to the east. This would explain one mystery: at a stopover in southern Arizona, Fray Marcos seemed confused; he apparently estimated they were much closer to the sea than they really were, and Coronado wrote ruefully in a letter to Mendoza that at this point, he and his men "all became very distrustful, and felt great anxiety and dismay to see that everything was the reverse of what [Fray Marcos] had told Your Lordship." Coronado's remark was Monday morning sour grapes—in a letter written by Coronado in Cíbola, after the army arrived and found, much to their dismay, that it was not a fabulous kingdom of gold.

Nonetheless, the letter and Fray Marcos' confusion have been cited as evidence that Fray Marcos never had been as far north as Arizona. But our reconstruction explains the situation: if Coronado diverged slowly eastward from Fray Marcos' route, Fray Marcos would necessarily have been uncertain about how much farther east from the sea they really were.

As soon as Coronado's army reached and conquered Cíbola, vilification of Fray Marcos began in earnest. One of Coronado's soldiers later wrote that on the day when Coronado and the advance guard approached Cíbola, "when they saw the first village . . . such were the curses that some hurled at Friar Marcos that I pray God may protect him from them . . ." Cíbola turned out to be a group of stone-built, multiterraced pueblos with prosperous, cultured inhabitants, a small amount of turquoise and other jewelry, and no gold. Fray Marcos, Coronado's trooper wrote, "had been wrong in everything that he said." Such was the calumny that Fray Marcos fled once again from Cíbola back to Mexico City, while Coronado's army was doomed to wander as far as Kansas, unsuccessfully seeking some rich kingdom to conquer. The ultimate failure of the expedition led to a century and a half of neglect of the northern frontier desert country.

Nonetheless, Fray Marcos and Coronado touched the Sonoran Desert country in two important ways. First, Fray Marcos gave us our first written record of Indian life in the Sonoran Desert border region—the valleys that historians agree he *did* reach. Second, Coronado sent his captain, Melchior Díaz, west to locate the coast. This became the first clearly recorded trip across the Sonoran Desert heart—a trip ultimately fatal to Díaz.

BEFORE WE RECOUNT those adventures, we need to address the loose ends about mysterious Marcos de Niza. First of all, we observe that Fray Marcos was a victim of gestalt psychology at work. When he said that the Indians along the way had told him of rich cities to the north, and that the cities had stone, multistoried buildings much grander than the rude adobe huts of the Sonoran and southern Arizona Indians, and that the Indians of the region wore jewels of turquoise, he was telling the absolute truth. But the words were heard by men in Mexico City who already had an image in their minds of the wealth of the Aztecs. So the true words of Fray Marcos were transmogrified into a fantasy. Eyewitness accounts from Mexico City in late 1539 testify to the pandemonium as rumors spread about Fray Marcos' discovery of the legendary seven wealthy cities. Some historians have ridiculed Fray Marcos for stating that Cíbola was as large as Mexico City (which the conquistadors took to be a comparison with the Aztecs' Tenochtitlán); but turn-of-the-century historian Adolf Bandelier, calling Fray Marcos "the most maligned man in history," concludes that Fray Marcos was making a comparison not to Tenochtitlán, which he had not seen, but to the rude Spanish town that replaced it, which Fray Marcos had known since arriving in 1536 or 1537—a town that was indeed about as big as the Zuni pueblos.

As for whether Fray Marcos actually reached Cíbola, there is no question that at least Esteban made it all the way. Coronado recorded stories of his fate among the Zuni Indians, and even in the 1800s ethnographers recorded tales at Zuni of the ancient murder of a black Mexican, accompanied by Mexican Indians who were chased away.[7]

The strongest arguments against Fray Marcos revolve around time: did he have time to go to Zuni and back, and also make the side trip to a point where he could see where the coast turns west? Some historians assert that he couldn't have traveled fast enough because of the rough country. Taking into account the days he rested and giving him a few extra days to approach the sea, he needed to cover around 20 to 25 miles per day while on the trails, both northward and southward. This is not unreasonable. Fray Marcos, indeed, specifically says he averaged about 30 miles a day on the first three days when he fled from Cíbola. Perhaps these figures sound extreme because most of us do not spend our lives walking. But they are not extreme. One hiker, who claimed not to be particularly practiced, made a 12-day walking trip from Boston to New York City, averaging nearly 22 miles a day, and did "almost" 30 miles on three of his days. Similarly, geographer Ronald Ives cites records of parties carrying wounded soldiers on stretchers, sustaining rates of travel of 25 miles a day and more in level desert country.[8]

Modern hikers in good condition often cover even greater daily distances on back-country trails. Thanks to modern archaeological studies, such as those of Charles Di Peso in 1974, we know that the Indians had much better trail systems through the region than earlier critics assumed. And Fray Marcos noted that the enthusiastic Indians made camps for him in advance when he was on the trail. Thus, contrary to the impression given by many historian-critics, Fray Marcos was not bushwhacking through unknown country.

As for other details of Fray Marcos' report, Cíbola *did* exist at the foot of a hill, the buildings *were* of stone, the Indians *did* wear turquoise. Thus, while some historians claim outrageous fabrications in Fray Marcos' narrative of his trip, it is actually hard to put a finger on a single sentence in his narrative that is overtly untrue.

Yet as early as 1540, Cortés joined in the debunking, even *before* knowing the outcome of Coronado's journey. Speaking of Fray Marcos' 1539 report of Cíbola, Cortés wrote, "I deny that [Fray Marcos] had seen or discovered it; instead, what the friar says [comes] solely through the account which I gave him . . . Stating what he had neither seen nor saw is nothing new, because many other times he has done this . . . as is well known

in . . . Peru . . ." This last is one of the strongest claims against Fray Marcos, because it asserts that he already had a reputation of exaggerating before he made his Cíbola trip. Yet can it be trusted? Cortés was hardly unbiased; he was trying to establish his claim over that of Coronado. It is a toss-up whether to side with Cortés or with the bishop who called Fray Marcos *virtuous*.

Moving to the present, we encounter statements such as historian Carl Sauer's in 1937: ". . . it is time that the [narrative of Fray Marcos] be classed where it belongs, as a hoax devised in the interest of Mendoza's *Realpolitik*." Sauer is very sure of himself. Yet, look at what Sauer and other critics would have us believe: a man concocts an elaborate hoax, knowingly ballyhoos a false picture of a northern bejeweled Babylon, and then arranges to go with an army of expectant soldiers to the very spot where he surely knows they will discover his grand lie. This action makes no sense. The prudent thing for a hoaxer to do would have been to accept Mendoza's thanks and fade into the woodwork as the army was leaving. It is easier to accept that Fray Marcos believed what he reported, which was, in the details that we can check, literally correct, and that the conquistadors misunderstood it, than to believe that pious Fray Marcos was a cunning fraud.

If we accept that Fray Marcos really did make the trip all the way to Cíbola-Zuni, and reported what he thought he saw and what the Indians told him of the place, then we face the question of the trip west to the sea. Here, a second piece of modern evidence comes into play. Archaeologist Julian Hayden has discussed evidence that the Arizona Indians of this period had routes to the sea which they followed to collect salt and seashells (much prized in their jewelry).[9] One such trail passed directly through the Pinacate lavas, according to Hayden's interpretation of petroglyphs of shells, pecked on the rocks at one Pinacate water tank. Furthermore, a century and a half after Fray Marcos, Father Kino and his colleagues were guided on similar trips to the coast when they, too, were trying to see where the coastline turned west. Note that the objective (contrary to the implication of historian-critics) was not to reach the actual beach, where only a few miles of coastline might be seen, but to reach a spot, such as a mountain near the coast, from which the lay of the coastline might be perceived. For example, Kino was guided in 1694 from a region that would have been along Fray Marcos' route, down the Altar River to a mountain just west of present-day Caborca, where he could see the coast. The point where the coast turned abruptly west is only about 65 miles from that mountaintop. And if the Altar valley is one of those mentioned in Fray Marcos' cryptic account of his travels in populated valleys, his narrative might make much better sense than some historians claim. He could have made a few-day side trip down the Magdalena and Altar rivers for a mountaintop survey west of Caborca, just as Kino did 155 years later. Having completed his objective of convincing himself of where the coast turned, he would not have wasted time retracing his steps to the east, but would have struck out northeast, directly toward Cíbola, up the Altar and across the Santa Cruz headwater country. We can hardly be so cavalier as historian Cleve Hallenbeck, who wrote in 1949 that Fray Marcos' "claim of having visited the coast . . . is also demonstrably false . . . [He] made inquiry of the Indians and then deliberately falsified what they told him." Historians such as Sauer and Hallenbeck show a striking tendency to deduce *their* favorite route that Fray Marcos *should* have followed (typically 150 miles or so inland), and then brand him a liar for not having followed it. Instead of being vilified, this maligned explorer should probably be celebrated throughout Southwestern schools as being the first European to enter and write about the region from the southeastern Sonoran Desert to western New Mexico.

There is another tantalizing bit of history in the Fray Marcos story: Fray Marcos mentions in his narrative that he had submitted a second document giving the

Featureless dunes and cinder cones of the Gran Desierto separate the Gulf of California coast from more clement landscapes farther east. Cinder cone west of MacDougal Crater. April 25, 1964.

names and details of the villages along his route. If only we could find that document! Perhaps it is moldering in a box in some archive in Mexico City or a nearby mission, where, according to researchers, many historic files have yet to be cataloged.

AS FOR THE FIRST EUROPEAN PENETRATION through the *heart* of the Sonoran Desert, we have much more detailed information—and one more tale of adventure. From the start, Viceroy Mendoza had been interested in naval support for Coronado's massive land expedition. Hence, Fray Marcos' instructions to reconnoiter the coast. Naval support was preposterous if we look from today's perspective at the appalling stretch of desert that lay between the Gulf and Coronado's route through eastern Arizona. Fray Marcos' own narrative showed that he required three and a half to four weeks of travel to go from his purported coastal viewpoint all the way to Cíbola. Nonetheless, a seaborne task force under Hernando de Alarcón sailed up the Gulf toward the mouth of the Colorado in 1540. These ships penetrated even farther upriver than de Ulloa's 1539 party. In those days, the waters of the river were not siphoned off for agriculture and distant cities; the Colorado was a broad throughway at a time when river valleys, not interstates, were the important routes.

The idea was for Alarcón to rendezvous with some of Coronado's party. Alarcón reached his most northern point roughly halfway between the Colorado's mouth and present-day Yuma, at about the same time that Coronado was subduing Cíbola 400 miles to the east. Indian communication along the intervening Gila River was good; Indians interviewed by Alarcón knew of the huge expedition to the east, and of the fate of Esteban at Cíbola the previous summer. But direct contact with Coronado seemed impossible. Alarcón turned back after leaving a cache and a sign posted on a tree:

ALARCÓN CAME THIS FAR. THERE ARE LETTERS AT THE FOOT OF THIS TREE.

Meanwhile, Coronado, who was making his temporary base in Cíbola, sent out numerous splinter expeditions, including one that discovered the Grand Canyon. Now he sent his popular captain, Melchior Díaz on such a trip. Díaz and his men were to go west, to see if they could locate the head of the Gulf, and find any trace of Alarcón and his supply ships.

Melchior Díaz, now destined to be the first European known to have crossed the Pinacate border country, is one of the most attractive figures to emerge from the gloom-shrouded conquest of the New World. His men praised him and the Indians revered him for his efforts to protect them from the outrages of the slavers. He had risen rapidly from obscurity to a position of some authority and fame.[10]

Díaz began by dropping back south to a staging area called *Corazones* ("Hearts"), about 140 miles south of present-day Nogales. The area had been named by de Vaca because natives fed his party there with deer hearts. It had become a famous jumping-off site on the new frontier, but its exact location, near the present Mexican town of Ures, has been lost.[11] From here, Díaz set out for the coast with a mounted party of 25 men and a number of sheep.

Díaz departed Corazones in the fall of 1540 and entered a dry country, pleasant at that time of year. Rivers, as always, provided thoroughfares, but they shrank as the party proceeded northwest. Unbeknownst to Díaz, the Colorado River was more than 300 miles away across a vicious wilderness.

Díaz' exact route is a mystery, intriguing for several reasons. As he followed the coast, counterclockwise around the Gulf's head, his route was blocked by the Pinacate Peaks and lava flows. He faced a choice, to bear to the right, passing east of the peaks, putting the mountains between him and the Gulf and Alarcón's sought-for ships; or bearing left between the mountains and the sea. He could have skirted the west edge of the lavas, where there were several water tanks, but as the Indians no doubt told him, he could not easily travel closer to the Gulf because of a 20- to 100-mile belt of barren dunes bordering the beach—the Gran Desierto. Geographer-historian Ronald Ives, who published an account of this trip,[12] concluded that Díaz went around the east and north sides—route A on the accompanying map, because this route was the first choice of Kino 150 years later, and would provide more forage than the drier country closer to the sea. But because Díaz was trying to explore the coast, he may as plausibly have chosen the western route, B, where he could espy the Gulf from hilltops, and where small villages existed, as recorded 159 years later by the great explorer, Father Kino.

A free translation of two old sources, synthesized, gives this account of the first part of the trip:

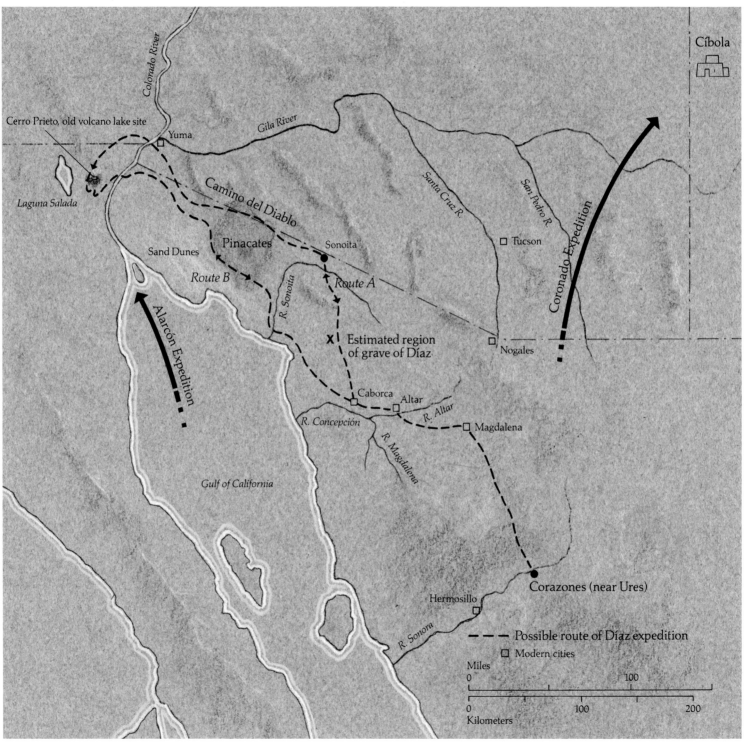

Two possible routes of the Díaz expedition, 1540-41, in relation to
Coronado and Alarcón expeditions.

Captain Melchior Díaz decided to search out the southern sea. He took twenty-five of the best men and left Corazones in search of the sea, crossing some mountains and traveling toward the west and somewhat north, led by guides. They walked until they came to the sea. They were along its banks for some days, in the land of Indians who lived on corn that they harvest and fish from the sea. Having walked with difficulty about 350 miles, they found themselves in the province of giant Indians, very tall and burly. They reached a large and very deep river that could accommodate ships.

The texts are somewhat unclear as to where the sea was reached. The giants were the Yuma Indians, long known for their stature; and the deep river was the Colorado. The difficulty must have been greatest in the dry desert west and northwest of the Pinacates. Díaz and his men were almost surely guided along parts of the famous trail that later became known as the Devil's Highway. This trail leads from water tank to water tank, and eventually to the Yuma crossing, along the jagged granitic ridges and flat sand basins of southwesternmost Arizona. Ives reconstructs that they averaged about ten miles per day prior to reaching Yuma.

When Díaz' party reached the Colorado, they heard news from the Indians that ships had reached a point three days to the south. Excitedly, they pressed on to this spot and located Alarcón's sign, still tacked to its tree. (In those days it was possible to travel a quarter of a continent's width and find a particular sign tacked to a particular tree—Indian communications were that good!) Here they unearthed a pot at the foot of the tree. Alarcón's letters were still fresh:

In the year 40, Francisco de Alarcón arrived with three ships . . . Having stayed many days without news, they left because their ships were being eaten by shipworms.

Melchior Díaz was not about to be stopped by this setback. The party was about 15 leagues (about 37 miles) upstream from the mouth of the river. Díaz now decided to cross the river and set out in search of the ocean, rumored to lie to the west. A strange episode ensued. West of the river, they came to a bizarre scene: here were "beds of burning lava. None of the group could cross them, for it would be like going into the sea to drown. The ground resounded like a drum, as if there were lakes underneath." This infernal spot has been identified by Ives and others as a volcanic hotspring about 20 miles southeast of the California-Baja border towns of Calexico and Mexicali, about 100 miles west of the Pinacates. It lies at the foot of a black cinder cone known as Cerro Prieto.

The strange quality of the ground is caused by a thin crust of turf overlying hot mud produced by hotsprings in the temporarily dormant volcanic area. The ground might support a man in some areas, but not a horse. In 1906, explorer-writer George James visited a second similar area some 50 miles to the north, now covered by the Salton Sea. He described it "as if a lot of tiny devils were playing at making volcanoes: watery mud . . . bubbled and gurgled . . . Black, ill-smelling, and fearsome it was."[13] Similar areas are known in Yellowstone National Park.

Until the first decade of this century, the area of mud volcanoes and rubbery ground south of Calexico was called *Volcano Lake*. But in the canal building that preceded irrigation in the Colorado River valley, Volcano Lake and its environs were altered almost beyond recognition. Today this strange site is dominated by irrigated farmland and a steam-venting geothermal power station that utilizes the hot springs.

Díaz' journey through dunes, across the Colorado, and into this infernal area reminds us that the genre of fantastic quest fiction, from *The Odyssey* to Tolkien's Ring trilogy, derives from ancient truth! ("And on the next day, he entered an enchanted new kingdom . . .")

As we zip in air-conditioned cars from one Rodeway Inn to its clone 400 miles away, it is hard to remember that until a hundred years ago, each new day of travel brought a new adventure. From Ulysses to Díaz, wandering travelers *did* enter enchanted new kingdoms.

Díaz might have gone all the way to the Pacific had not fate intervened just after Christmas. Not far beyond the black cinder cone of Cerro Prieto, one of his dogs started harrassing the sheep and, in a fit of anger, Díaz pursued the dog on horseback, hurling his lance at it. Somehow the lance stuck upright in the ground, and before Díaz could rein in, he gored himself on it. The painful puncture penetrated his groin and tore his bladder. Díaz was mortally wounded.

The desperate soldiers reversed the march, hoping to carry Díaz by litter back to Corazones in time to be confessed by a priest there. The trip had turned into a nightmare. As they recrossed the Colorado, there were skirmishes with the Yuma Indians, stemming from an ill-fated attempt to bring one Indian back with them. They struggled on across the desert and the Pinacate lavas, but Díaz died on January 18, 1541. The soldiers recorded that they buried him on a small hill somewhere along the route. They covered the grave with a large mound of stones, and erected a cross.

Where is this remarkable conquistador's lost grave? Díaz lived 20 days after the accident, so the problem boils down to determining how far he could have been carried by the men in that time. Historical sleuth Ronald Ives attempted to solve the mystery by using data from other desert forced marches, his calculation of a full moon on January 12, 1541, and his own wide hiking experience in the area. Ives concludes that the party probably averaged between 10 and 23 miles a day, and that the lost grave lies on a hilltop in a 15-mile-wide strip of desert between Sonoita and Caborca.

The exact route is uncertain, but they probably passed Tinajas Altas and crossed the Pinacate flanks on one side or the other. An average rate slower by a few

Geothermal mud pots and sulfur springs, with Cerro Prieto cinder cone in background. This area south of Mexicali is believed to be the geothermal area described by Díaz in 1539. January 15, 1972.

miles per day, or a few days' delay in crossing the Colorado, could place the bones of Melchior Díaz in the Pinacates under a weathered cairn of rocks atop one of the lonely cinder cones that flank old trails on the north, south, east, or west periphery of the Pinacates. Díaz waits to be found.

Coronado died and was buried in a church in Mexico City in 1554. De Vaca, the wanderer who triggered the rush to the north, died in Spain in obscurity around 1556. Marcos de Niza, the friar who was cursed by Coronado's soldiers, fell into ill health after returning from Cíbola to Mexico City, perhaps of a broken spirit. He died nearby in 1558. The actors in the drama slipped away; the hoopla of opening night rapidly faded as onlookers realized that the show had fallen far short of its expectations.

Dawn in the Tule Mountains along the route later known as the Camino del Diablo, following the present Arizona-Sonora border. April 2, 1972.

For the next half century, dry Sonoran Desert winds swirled in unmapped Pinacate craters; Indians filled their water pots at the tanks and Europeans avoided the useless area.

Later, in the late 1800s, Fray Marcos was the subject of some unlikely claims by promoters of the Arizona Territory. They claimed that Fray Marcos had passed through Indian villages marking the present site of Tucson, and that other Spaniards had immediately followed him and settled there. Tucson thus had a virtually continuous Spanish presence since 1539, making it the oldest city occupied by Europeans in the United States. They even asserted that a document written by Fray Marcos had been found in the San Xavier mission and forwarded to Washington.[14]

While anonymous Spaniard adventurers could have settled in Arizona soon after Fray Marcos, Coronado, and Díaz, the stories are not very credible. Surprisingly, in an age that respected knowledge, the early geographical discoveries were being forgotten. De Vaca's and Fray Marcos' odysseys fell into legend. The discoveries by de Ulloa, Alarcón, and Díaz about the head of the Gulf and the mouth of the Colorado River were recorded on only a few maps; many Spaniards still thought Baja California was an island. The sunburned, thirsty conquistadors, like most of us, left little impression on the sands of time or the sands of the desert.

HALF A CENTURY AFTER CORONADO, around 1600, a new cycle of exploration brought northward probes leading to a reconnaissance of the Colorado's mouth. In 1596, Sebastian Viscaino left settlers in La Paz, the site of Cortés' failed colony at the south tip of the Baja California peninsula, and explored northward in the Gulf. Then, in 1598, the promoter and explorer Don Juan de Oñate led a large expedition of soldiers, settlers, and priests from Mexico into present-day New Mexico, where several colonies were started. In 1604, Oñate and thirty men struck out to the west to explore what is now Arizona. They reached the Bill Williams River, in west-central Arizona, and followed it to the Colorado, descending all the way to the Gulf. They had traveled almost all the way around the periphery of the Sonoran Desert.

Exploring the Colorado's mouth, Oñate's party met an Indian chief who told them of the strange nations of the area: the tribe with ears big enough to drag on the ground; the tribe with only one foot; the tribe that slept in trees; and of course the fabled Queen of the Island of California, a giant Amazon in whose land all the men were bald. A wide-eyed priest with Oñate recorded these tales, but prudently opined, "It appears to me doubtful that there should be so many monstrosities ... so near us." Apparently the tradition of spinning

The western border of the Pinacate lavas was a possible route for Díaz.
Lava flows of basalt are partially buried by drifting sand dunes.
West of Moon Crater. April 8, 1977.

tall tales to gullible greenhorns predated the Anglos in the Old, Old West!

If there was no Amazon Queen, why did the Indians as well as the Europeans have this legend? Records show that Indian verbal traditions of Oñate's visit to the area lasted more than a century; thus, the Amazon story was probably, in turn, a memory of questions asked by Alarcón and Díaz in the area 64 years earlier. Perhaps the Indians during that first century of contact got a chuckle out of the foolish questions asked by their eccentric, infrequent white visitors.

Journal entry. A trip along Mexico 2 from Yuma through San Luis to Sonoita. January 12, 1980. Today I am driving along the route by which the fatally wounded Díaz was carried back toward civilization during this same week of the year, 339 years ago. I expected more complete desolation—sand dunes. Instead, crossing into Sonora south of Yuma, I find parts of the route surprisingly fertile. Sparse grass softens the glare of sandy soil along the western quarter of the route. The highway runs just south of the border.

Once the highway approaches the bony-white Gila and Tinajas Altas ridges, the road gets into hillier ground. Now it winds past the pale Cabeza Prietas with their basalt caps dribbling down like chocolate sundaes. Somewhere along here I must drive across the time-blurred footprints of the soldiers carrying their dying leader. Did they cross that plain? Did they file between these hills? I pull to the side. The car grows hot. But because the country is so little changed from those days, it is not hard, on this long, lonely afternoon, to hear the metal clanking and the sheep bleating and the conquistadors

cursing and joking as they pick their way over the cinder-scattered trails amidst grass and bright soil.

Moments later, as I drive on, the Pinacates have come into view toward the southeast, dark and brooding. There are beautiful grassy alcoves here in the naked granite ridges of the Cabeza Prieta outliers. As I cross these hills, the character of the landscape changes from sandy plains and sparse grass, to scattered creosotes, palo verdes, ocotillos and saguaros. Nowadays there are half a dozen cafes and scattered ejidos, or cooperative farms, along the way; more development than I expected. The ghosts of Díaz' men are frightened and evaporate from my vision.

I pass among cinder cones on the north edge of the Pinacate lava field, and leave the looming blue Pinacate Peaks behind. As I approach Sonoita, even a shiny new billboard or two appear and a number of good new road signs. I am astonished at the new prosperity of Sonoita, which I haven't visited for a few years.

At the main intersection of Mexico 2 and 8 there is a little gathering of booths selling tacos and tamales. On the three-mile drive north to the border, numerous new houses are going up—clean, Mexico-modern construction. The imposing two-story house on the rise halfway to the border, a complex edifice that always has a new added-on twist to exhibit, has completed its years-long project of adding brick arches and a wall around itself. Mexican oil money and new Mexican government programs are bringing a new burst of prosperity to Sonoita. Civilization is setting in, "civilization" whose marks are different from the ubiquitous discarded beer cans and burnt-out buses that have previously highlighted the course of progress in the area.

3. Reopening the Frontier: The Adventures of Eusebio Kino and Friends

Has not the sign of the cross cast more men in heroic mould than ever the glitter of the crown or the flash of the sword?

J.C. Van Dyke
The Desert, 1901

Night far on the prairie is always solemn . . . our watch became one of silence and caution.

John W. Audubon, camped along Kino's route on the Gila River in 1849. *Western Journal,* 1905

IN 1638, THE OPATA TRIBE OF SONORA asked for baptism. What seemed a move toward harmony led to violence. Pioneers on the Sonoran frontier began to look north for new areas for settlement. As prospectors, priests and settlers broke new ground, friction with the Indians predictably increased.

An old story, man's interaction with man: on August 10, 1680, growing Indian resentment was culminated in violence. An Indian revolt broke out in New Mexico. An estimated 500 Spaniards were murdered, including a dozen or more friars. Unknown numbers of Indians died. As much as a fourth of the European population was dead by September, and the frontier pulled back to the south for a decade.

More consequential than this carnage was the quiet arrival in Mexico of an obscure Jesuit missionary in 1681. Fashionable historians may debate the "great man theory" of history, but whoever believes that a country cannot be influenced by the dedication of a single man must reckon with Father Eusebio Francisco Kino. Kino, during numerous journeys, single-handedly made the first maps and detailed records of the modern Arizona-Sonora border country, and promoted Spanish expansion into the area. Among his journeys were six forays directly into the heart of the Sonoran Desert, across the forbidding Pinacate lavas.

Raised in an Italian village, Kino came to the New World and began his work in Baja California. In 1687, at age 42, he moved his efforts across the Gulf to Sonora. Here, he founded a mission and small settlement, Nuestra Señora de los Dolores, a few miles east of present-day Magdalena, Sonora. Kino's mission, lying on a ridge overlooking a pleasant river valley, marked the northwestern frontier of European civilization. It would be the staging area for his probes farther north and west. Government officials showed little interest in development of the northwest, and Kino had to act on his own, promoting his results through letters and journals.

Reading these journals today, we cannot help being attracted to the man. He combined extraordinary physical stamina with great modesty. Between 1694 and 1701, while in his mid-fifties, he founded a string of new missions, traveled 7,500 miles by horseback and on foot, seeking always the new trail, the new piece of geographic information, the unvisited Indian village. Sometimes the trail took him through lazy floodplains lined with cottonwoods; more often it took him through the dusty outback. Frequently, he traveled with only one or

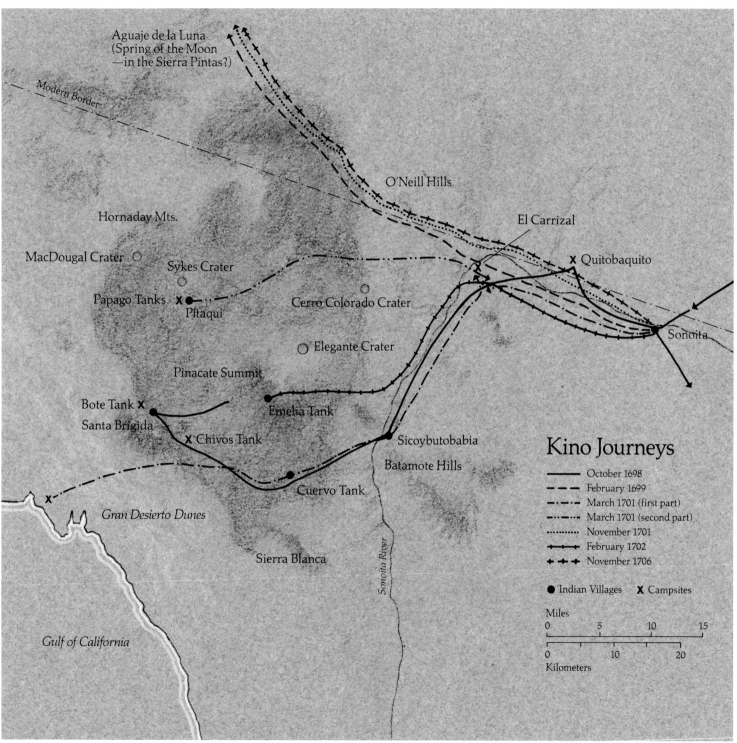

Aguaje de la Luna
(Spring of the Moon
—in the Sierra Pintas?)

Modern Border

O'Neill Hills

Hornaday Mts.

El Carrizal

MacDougal Crater ○

Sykes Crater ○

X Quitobaquito

Papago Tanks X ●
Pitaqui

Cerro Colorado Crater ○

Soñoita

○ Elegante Crater

Pinacate Summit

Bote Tank X ●
Santa Brigida
Emelia Tank

X Chivos Tank

Sicoybutobabia

Batamote Hills

Cuervo Tank

Kino Journeys

————————	October 1698
– – – – –	February 1699
–·–·–·–	March 1701 (first part)
–··–··–	March 1701 (second part)
············	November 1701
—+—+—+—	February 1702
+++++	November 1706

● Indian Villages   X Campsites

Miles
0   5   10   15

0   10   20
Kilometers

Gran Desierto Dunes

Sonoita River

Sierra Blanca

Gulf of California

Previous page: Interior tower of Tubutama Mission, Sonora, one of the missions founded by Father Kino. The present structure postdates Kino. April 3, 1976.

Map of the Pinacate region showing Kino's paths across the area.

two European companions. When he was on the road, he typically averaged around 23 miles a day. Often he endured some arduous task or life-threatening situation, only to record nothing about it in his journal; we learn of it only through the admiring reports in the journal of some companion. The most interesting companion was a military cohort, Captain Juan Mateo Manje, who provided a practical counterpoint to Kino's bursts of enthusiasm. He wrote his own book about the region.

The border lands were called the *Pimería Alta*, or upper territories of the Pima Indians. Kino saw in them a country ripe for colonization, potentially fertile and not so inhospitable as his contemporaries thought. This belief he would demonstrate by walking and riding throughout the area, which covered much of the Sonoran Desert. Its south border was the latitude of Dolores, and it stretched north into Arizona. The future site of Nogales, now a border town, lay close to its center; the Pinacates and the mouth of the Colorado dominated its northwest edge.

To see this land as Kino saw it, one must sweep away the cities and visualize the land empty and brown, with the tree-lined river valleys as the only highways. Only dusty trails along the streams and across passes connected little villages and scattered Indian rancherías. The Santa Cruz, now usually a dry wash, was a flowing stream lined by lush bosques of trees; it was Kino's green thoroughfare to the north.

Kino's main goal was encouraging his chain of missions in the pleasant valleys and hills of northern Sonora. But Kino had an additional challenge. He wanted to break out of the northwest corner of this region, to discover (once again) whether there was a land route to legendary California. The explorations of the early 1500s had been mostly forgotten. No one knew which of the old maps was best, or if Baja California was connected to the mainland. Kino's six forays into Pinacate country were designed to determine whether

this was true, and if so, whether there was a practical land route around the north end of the Gulf. He, Manje and others left independent journals of these trips. Apparently the journals were written privately, without expectation that readers could read them side by side three centuries later. They provide fascinating polyphony among strong but affectionate personalities—an unexpectedly colorful record of the opening of the Pinacate desert country.

By 1691, Kino had already made various reconnaissances. In 1692, with 50 pack animals and some aides, he first reached the Indian village of Bac (just south of present-day Tucson, Arizona), where he found the Santa Cruz River valley to be especially fertile. The next year and again in 1694, Kino and friends echoed Marcos de Niza's controversial coastward side trip: they followed Indian guides to a mountain range west of Caborca where they could see the Gulf shore and the distant blue mountains of Baja California on the far side.

In 1697, Kino's friend, Father Juan María Salvatierra began building missions in Baja. Kino wanted to discover if there was a land route to Baja, so the missions could be linked. In November, 1697, he set out with Manje and company to explore farther to the north. On November 27, he was astonished to discover a ghostly remnant of an Indian civilization that had vanished only a few centuries before—the four-story adobe ruin of Casa Grande, now a national monument north of Tucson. At that time, it was only 350 years old, half as old as it is today. It must have looked even more extraordinary than it does to us. In this land of impoverished Indians, thatched huts, and plain brown clay bowls, here was a giant adobe sentinel, surrounded by walls of a crumbling compound and piles of beautifully painted, broken pottery. Kino marvelled that it looked like a castle and was bigger than any churches yet built in Sonora.

Local Indians were superstitious about Casa Grande and avoided it, except for leaving religious

View from the Pinacate summit. High cone in middle distance is Carnegie Peak, second-highest peak in the range. Photography emphasizes and exaggerates the haze that made it difficult for Kino to see clearly whether a land bridge existed to Baja California. January 22, 1983.

offerings. (Years later, another priest destroyed these and burned some timbers from the great house to debunk the earlier myths.) Along the Gila, Kino recorded numerous other large ruined adobe buildings, which he erroneously associated with the legendary seven cities of Cíbola—testimony to the fact that Fray Marcos' actual discoveries had been forgotten.[1] On their way back to Dolores, Kino's party recorded 800 Indians at a settlement just north of present-day Tucson, 900 at Bac, and 150 at Tumacacori—an indication of the substantial villages along the river at that time.

Such ventures were not without danger. Two years earlier, on April 2, 1695, at the mission in Caborca, Father Francisco Saeta had been murdered—shot with 22 arrows—in an Indian rebellion that lasted until September. Again, in 1698, Apaches and other Indians attacked a settlement close to present-day Nogales and were finally chased to El Paso by vengeful soldiers.

Kino's courage had been demonstrated in the 1695 revolt. When the community at Dolores was warned by a friendly Indian lookout of the violence raging nearby, the few citizens fled and Manje rushed 40 miles south to get help. Like the captain of a threatened ship, Kino stayed alone in his mission. Manje returned the next day and together they hid the church valuables in a cave. At Kino's urging, they stayed in Dolores during the rest of the revolt. Kino skipped the story in his own diary; it was recorded by others.

Kino nursed his dream of finding a connecting land route around the Gulf. On September 22, 1698, he set out from Dolores to probe toward California with Captain Diego Carrasco, who replaced Manje on this particular trip. This was destined to be their first penetration into the heart of the desert and the Pinacate volcanics. With seven servants and 25 pack animals, Kino and Carrasco traversed a route now familiar to him: north along the Santa Cruz past Bac and the Casa Grande ruins, to the Gila River. That Kino and Carrasco were the only Europeans in the party testifies to Kino's love and trust of the Indians. In all the villages they were received with great festivity, even though they were the first white men many of the Indians in this region had seen.

Following the Gila to the west only briefly, they turned south across the desert in pleasant fall weather, with warm afternoons and cold nights. Soon they arrived at a little Indian village Kino named *San Marcelo del Sonoita*. This was the site of the present Mexican town of Sonoita, on the Arizona-Sonora border near Organ Pipe Cactus National Monument. Indians told them that the Gulf was only a few days to the west, and messengers brought him salt from the sea.

Like Fray Marcos, Kino wanted to observe the coastline, but the Indians warned of the hardships of any travel farther toward the coast, 65 miles to the southwest. Rugged lavas of the Pinacates had to be crossed, and beyond them, the barren sands of Sonora's Gran Desierto. There was little water or grass for the animals,

Hotspring pond of Quitobaquito. February 8, 1985.

and the autumn desert days could be hot. "No matter," replied Kino. He would take an extra mule to carry water, another to carry grass, and travel by night! Nothing stopped a Kino expedition!

On October 8, the party followed the Sonoita River west out of Sonoita four leagues (ten miles) to a place called *San Serguio* where they found water.

Part of the intrigue in reading old documents is in relocating the actual campsites and vistas described. This is much more plausible in the Sonoran Desert than in other parts of the country because the country has changed so little. In the 1930s and '40s, the historian Herbert Bolton retraced many of Kino's journeys and identified the sites visited by Kino, many of which lay just as Kino had described them. Bolton, who published an enthralling 1960 book about Kino's travels, identified San Serguio as the beautiful hotspring and pond now called *Quitobaquito,* reachable by dirt road in Organ Pipe Cactus National Monument. With its green trees and bubbling spring surrounded by brown barren hills, Quitobaquito is truly an oasis in the desert.

A few miles beyond Quitobaquito, the Sonoita River's bed turned south along the east side of the Pinacates' broad lava dome. Guided along ancient Indian trails, Kino's party followed this part of the river about 25 miles south, and then departed the riverbed to the west, across the dark flows and cinder cones of the southern Pinacates.

Here, on the volcano's southwest flank, they were led to a small Indian village they called *Santa Brigida.* Geographer Ronald Ives, a scholar who specialized in the Pinacate area, placed Santa Brigida near the water hole now called *Chivos Tanks,* while archaeologist Julian Hayden, who has more thoroughly studied the Indian trails in the area, places the village a few miles farther northwest, at a water hole named *Bote Tank.* About 20 persons lived there.

Beyond the great barrier of tan sand dunes to the southwest lay the blue Gulf. The Indians said that the Gulf's north end and the Colorado's mouth lay nearby. This implied a connection by land to Baja, but the Indians insisted that any route across the sands to the Colorado was too arid to attempt without extra pack mules. Instead, they told Kino, he could *see* the end of the Gulf if he climbed to the Pinacate summit, rising to their east.

Thus, the first European ascent of the Pinacates came on October 9, 1698. The climbers recorded that a rough trail of seven leagues (18 miles) took them up the west side of the mountain from Santa Brigida village. This distance is farther than the straight-line distance from Chivos or Bote Tanks, but the trail was probably roundabout over the rugged lavas.

What Kino actually saw in his moments on the summit is a matter of some ambiguity. He was extremely anxious to discern the northern coastline: could a land route to Baja California be confirmed? Ten years later, Kino wrote an account of his moments on the summit: ". . . from the . . . ancient volcano of Santa Clara I descried most plainly with and without a telescope the junction of these lands of New Spain with those of California, the head of this Sea of California, and the land passage . . . At that time, however, I did not recognize it as such, and I persuaded myself that farther on and more to the west the Sea of California must extend (and) make California an island."[2]

This is cryptic. Did he claim to *see* the junction or didn't he? He goes on to explain that at the time, he so strongly believed that Baja was an island, that he did not perceive the actual land connection in the distance. Only three years earlier, he had published a map showing the Gulf running another thousand miles to the north! Of course, unknown to him, the Colorado's mouth had been discovered in 1539 by Cortés' naval captain, Francisco de Ulloa. But discoveries on that desolate new frontier had a habit of being forgotten within a century.

In actual fact, the view from the Pinacate summit does not prove the case, in spite of Kino's later claims. To the south is the sea, clear enough. To the west, no sea is visible; only bright pinkish sands and jagged pale ridges of distant mountains, joining those of Baja, visible to the southwest. For all the observer can tell, a narrow channel of the sea might run north, beyond the distant sands.

Kino's claim that the California land route could be confirmed from the Pinacate summit had become a political issue by the time he wrote his later account, and Kino may have been reluctant to admit in plain words that he hadn't been sure of what he saw in 1698. The historian, Bolton, more charitably ascribes the ambiguity to a hazy day that clouded the view.

Kino named the mountain *Cerro de Santa Clara*, Hill of Santa Clara. The name came from older maps.[3] From the summit he also noted the broad bay in the Gulf's northeast corner, south of the Pinacates, and named it *Puerto de Santa Clara*. A little coastal town near the Colorado's mouth still bears the name Santa Clara, but the bay today is called *Adair Bay*.

Kino and his party descended to the village of Santa Brigida, and the next day retraced their steps back to Sonoita, whence they crossed the desert to the southeast, back to the home base of Dolores.

Kino must have sensed that the elusive land bridge to California was nearly within his grasp. Only four months later, Kino, Manje, and another Jesuit father, Adamo Gil, made an expedition to probe even farther northwest. On the winter day of February 7, 1699, they left Dolores and reached the little settlement at Sonoita in nine days. Considering the increasing aridity and desolation they had already encountered in this direction, they displayed great fortitude in planning their next step, a horseback trip, even farther from Sonoita toward what is now Yuma, at the junction of the Gila and Colorado Rivers, 125 miles away across nearly waterless desert plains.

Sonoita itself they recorded on this trip as a village of 80 "poor and naked" Indians with "very little to eat." All day and through the cold winter night, Manje writes,

Prehistoric Indian trail leading west across the south flank of the Pinacates. Kino traversed this or nearby trails in 1698 and 1701. November 29, 1985.

the priests talked to the Indians about God, while Manje himself counseled them about obedience and loyalty to the King. After this enlightenment, the local chief offered to furnish guides to the Colorado River.

The next day, February 17, 1699, they set out into the western unknown. They left 30 cows behind in Sonoita, in case the fathers from Baja California should find it possible to reach Sonoita from the west. Kino thought that Sonoita might become a major junction. They camped that night about 25 miles west of Sonoita on the Sonoita River, which they described as a stream covered with reed grass, with water that was salty and hard because of saltpeter. This campsite, called *El Carrizal*, is identified by Bolton and Ives as a site used frequently in succeeding centuries, near the river bend where the Sonoita River turns from west to south. Campsites near this spot later came to be known as *Agua Dulce* and *Agua Salada,* depending on the sweetness or

Senita cactus, with basaltic Batamote Hills in background. April 9, 1977.

saltiness of the water. These sites are near the modern highway, Mexico 2, just a few miles south of the modern border.

On this second foray into the Pinacate border country, they would cross the north side of the volcano. The second day out of Sonoita saw them traveling northwest over what they described as arid plains with no pasture. Ironically, the priest of God was now reopening a route that came to be known as the Highway of the Devil—the dreaded Camino del Diablo—a trail that Bolton called "one of the hardest in the Southwest." Two-and-a-half centuries later, as we will see, hundreds of gold rush '49ers would die along this same trail.

No Europeans had passed this way since Díaz' party 159 years earlier. Most of this country, now in the Cabeza Prieta Wildlife Refuge, looks almost exactly the same as when Kino crossed it. The weather along the Camino in February can be variable. Sometimes it is

mild and sunny; sometimes it is overcast with leaden skies subduing the colors. But always the landscape, with its dark lavas and ridge after ridge of blue mountains in the distance, seems strange, silent, dry, and deserted; the Europeans must have wondered why their God went to the trouble of creating and maintaining such a vast, empty area. No wonder they pressed on, even after midnight, in search of water. After 20 leagues (about 50 miles), including 14 leagues by moonlight, they reached water "high up between rocks and ravines."

The location of this historic Kino campsite is more controversial than the others. Some writers suggest it is present-day Tule Tank, a relatively accessible tank in low hills called the *Cabeza Prieta Mountains,* barely north of the border, northwest of the Pinacates. Bolton, however, argues it is not so far west. As we will see toward the end of this chapter, Bolton found evidence that this watering hole is the present-day Heart Tank in the crags of the *Sierra Pinta Mountains,* directly north of the Pinacates. Whichever pool it was, it must have seemed a tranquil haven that night. The moon shimmered in the black water, and Kino gave the pool the beautiful name *Aguaje de la Luna*—Spring of the Moon.

They continued to the northwest, camping at a small Indian community adjacent to tanks he called *Agua Escondida,* or Hidden Water. Manje counted 30 "naked and poverty-stricken Indians here." Bolton claims this multiple-tank site is the Tinajas Altas (High Tanks), famous in subsequent centuries as the surest water on the vicious Camino del Diablo. Others, such as historian Robert Lenon,[4] argue that these are the Cabeza Prieta Tanks, a stairstep tank arrangement of pools similar to Tinajas Altas but more hidden in the strangely black-capped Cabeza Prieta Hills, east of Tinajas Altas.

In support of the latter theory, I note that Kino's 1701 map shows a prominent diagonal range of hills leading northwest from Santa Clara; these must be the Gila-Tinajas Altas Range, which contains Tinajas Altas

Tanks. The map shows "Agua Escondida" not in this range, but east of it, north of the Pinacates and halfway between it and his Spring of the Moon. This matches the location of the Cabeza Prieta Tanks. Both Tinajas Altas and Cabeza Prieta show signs of Indian occupation in the form of bedrock mortars and petroglyphs, those at the former site being more impressive.

After leaving the Hidden Water, the party proceeded north to the Gila River, where they found 600 Pima and Yuma Indians, healthier and much better clothed than those of the more desolate village of Sonoita. Manje rode far enough west to glimpse the junction of the Gila and Colorado (present-day Yuma) from a hilltop. Practical Manje also recorded that there were no rumors of precious metals. Indians of the region remembered stories, handed down, about the Oñate expedition, which came from New Mexico along the Gila and Colorado in 1606. The Indians also gave Kino some blue shells, which were to make history later, as we will see.

AT BOTH SONOITA AND THE COLORADO-GILA junction, the Indians told a tale that raises a supernatural mystery worthy of a digression. A mysterious Woman in Blue, they said, had preached to the generation of their grandparents around 1630. The older men told these stories, and because of the large distance between two areas where they heard this strange account, Kino and Manje were inclined to believe it. The Indians said she was a beautiful woman, carrying a cross, lecturing and shouting to them in a language they did not understand. Supposedly, the tribes along the Colorado had shot her with arrows and left her for dead on two occasions, but she had returned.

This astonishing tale is one of the strangest legends of the Southwest. Did an unknown young woman in the 1620s really preach to Indian tribes from west Texas to the Colorado River, 70 years before Kino reached them?

A number of historical facts are known about the case:[5] (1) Within a few years of 1622, when the first missionaries arrived in New Mexico under Fray Alonso de Benavides, they reported being approached by Indians wanting to be converted, because, they said, they already had been preached to by a woman in blue; (2) When a second wave of missionaries arrived in 1627, they brought word that a famous nun in Spain, María de Agreda, had told her confessor that she had traveled in some supernatural manner to the New World to convert the Indians; (3) Fray Benavides concluded that the woman in blue had been Sister María, and in 1630 he returned to Spain to interview her and to discuss its miraculous implications with higher religious authorities; (4) In 1631, in Spain, Sister María told Benavides that as a girl she had developed a passionate desire to convert the lost souls among the vast numbers of Indians in the New World, especially in the Southwest, and that beginning in 1620 she had been miraculously transported hundreds of times to Indian communities, where she preached in her own language, which the Indians miraculously understood; (5) At the time of the interview, when she was about 29, Sister María was already a famous mystic in Europe, because she had published a book, *The Mystical City of God*, which recounted a detailed, apochryphal life of Mary, mother of Jesus; María's fame led to correspondence and counsel with King Philip IV of Spain and other powerful personages; (6) Although María claimed that her magical visits to the Southwest continued until at least 1631, she was never seen by Spanish missionaries there, only reported by the Indians; (7) Benavides, noting carefully that clothing of her order included a mantle of blue worn with a habit of brown and white, concluded that Sister María had indeed miraculously visited the Indians and that this was the explanation of the stories they had heard from Indians in New Mexico and Texas; Benavides wrote an extended report about the affair for Philip IV; (8) Kino and Manje similarly concluded that stories of a woman

Along the Sonoita River near the old campsite of El Carrizal.
November 29, 1987.

collection of blue shells given him by the Indians near the Colorado-Gila junction in February, 1699. On the way back to Dolores, an idea had struck him: he had seen shells like this on the Pacific coast of Baja, but never on the mainland coast of the Gulf! So they must have come by trade from Baja. There must be a trade route by land from Baja California to Sonora!

In December, 1700, Kino's old friend, Father Salvatierra, came across the Gulf by boat to join Kino in a new attack on the problem. Salvatierra expected to help find the land bridge and return to Baja "by land in latitude 31 or 32 degrees." He studied the blue shells and agreed that they were of Baja origin.

On February 27, 1701, the new expedition left Dolores on the third Kino foray across the Pinacates. Kino, Salvatierra, and Manje were the leaders. All three left diaries of the trip. If it seems strange that literary works were left by these tough Spanish pioneers (in contrast to the impoverished record left by most American pioneers), we should remember that the 1600s marked the flowering of the Spanish novel: "This was the century . . . when the king wrote comedies and the people took the same interest in literature that they took in bullfights."[6] Spanish conquistadors and settlers carted novels, paintings, bells, carved santos, and other art objects to create new homes and sanctuaries; some published best sellers about their adventures.

On March 14, Kino's party reached Sonoita, noting with pride that the 30 cattle they had left in 1699 had multiplied to 80. They waited two days for the arrival of some coastal Indians, who would be able to guide them to the watering holes along the route.

On March 16, they departed downstream, traveling westward along the river, stopping near their 1699 campsite in the field of reed grass "ten leagues" from Sonoita. Two centuries after Kino's party reached the camp spot at the bend in the river, American conservationist-writer William Hornaday viewed the indigo Pinacates from nearly the same spot:

The Cabeza Prieta (or Dark Headed) Hills, along the Camino del Diablo. During erosion of bright, granitic strata, lava eruptions formed on earlier elevated surfaces; further erosion left stranded black caps with dark lavas dribbling down their sides. This outlying peak is north of MacDougal Crater. January 12, 1980.

The twin peaks of the Pinacate Mountains loom up about west by south, shrouded in a blue haze. For three miles westward the green arboreal desert continues, then there slowly rises a wide stretch of dark ground, as if the space from the green desert up to the tip-top of Pinacate Peak were under the shadow of a thick cloud. Instinctively you look at the sun, but you see that the sky is quite cloudless everywhere, and by these tokens you know that the eastward slope of the mountain is perpetually dark![7]

The cloud-shadow illusion is very real; the Pinacate slopes look dark because they are surfaced with brown and blackish lavas that contrast with the bone-white granites of surrounding mountain ridges. Perhaps the color drew Kino: he and his companions decided not to follow their 1699 route northwest via the Camino del Diablo and Kino's "Spring of the Moon," but to retrace their 1698 route across the southern Pinacates toward the sea. Manje remarks that they were now "branching off the road and going southwest," an interesting clue that the Camino del Diablo was already regarded as the main road.

After traveling about 25 miles down the riverbed and across "rocky and stony plains," as they recorded, they camped at another settlement, called *Sicoybutobabia.* Here they noted 200 people, including an Indian woman, who, according to Manje, "appeared to be 130 years old." Kino, estimating 120, told her of his faith and baptized her. They were told a few days later that she had died.

The geographer-historian, Ronald Ives, who mapped much of the region on foot, places Sicoybutobabia near the Batamote Hills, about two miles north of the bridge where present-day Mexico 8 crosses the Sonoita River.[8]

Kino's party taxed the resources of this poor village. Both fathers participated in digging to deepen the water holes of the village, but even then there was not enough water for all their animals.

March 19, 1701, the party headed west out of the village, following trails among the crags and cones of the southern Pinacate lavas. Bolton remarks that they were embarking on "one of the hardest explorations in all North American history." The directions are important if we are to judge where they were, and if we are to solve a mystery, which we will encounter shortly, about what they saw. Manje, for instance, says they "traveled southeast and west over plains and rough country" after leaving Sicoybutobabia. It seems clear from all accounts that they traveled primarily west, swinging around the south flanks of the mountain where still-visible trails lead across mighty lava flows to the dunes between the Pinacates and the Gulf. After about 15 miles they came to an encampment of 50 "poor and naked persons," near a cluster of rocky tanks. The horses were given their first water in 24 hours. Salvatierra says the mountain was

now to the east; Manje says that they were at "a settlement, south, at the foot of the Santa Clara Mountain . . ." Thus the location of this site is not certain, but Bolton and Ives identify it as *Cuervo Tank,* a cluster of natural water catchments in the flows on the south flank of the peaks.

The next day was Palm Sunday. Now they set out across a vast plain of lava toward the sand and the sea. After about about 15 or 20 miles across spectacular lava, they reached a rocky tank of rainwater in a dry creekbed near the contact between the lavas and the sand. Manje called this tank *El Tupo.*

During these two days, March 19 and 20, 1701, Kino and his associates, in their journals, made remarkably clear descriptions of the Pinacates as an extinct volcano. Ronald Ives asserts that they made "one of the first, if not the first" identification of an extinct volcano in North America.[9] Of this two-day crossing of the southern Pinacates, Manje says:

> . . . *we set out for the sea with three Indian guides, always toward the west over rough country with very craggy spots . . . During this journey of two days, we passed hilly mounds and ravines of burnt, molten rock similar to the slag of silver ore after it is refined . . . This formation extends for many leagues all around the mountain. We judge (although this is not credible) that this, perhaps, was a volcano which was active for several years, containing sulfur, saltpeter, and other combustible materials. Because of the enormous amount of matter concentrated in the center, it erupted so violently that this excess of combustible material, the originating cause of the conflagration, was consumed, satisfying the hunger of the fire.*
>
> *It left many rivers of molten and volcanic rock, hills and mounds which we now see. Other volcanoes of Europe and those of the two Americas have lasted four or five centuries from such under-*

ground conflagrations, according to Father Atanasio Quirquerio, distinguished philosopher and mathematician. On occasion, the force and violence had been such—like Vesuvius and Etna or Montegevelo, in our time—that a large river of fire came out of the earth and flowed with such violence toward the seas as to make it ebb, filling a great part of its bed with lava rock.

The above seems to have happened at this place where we saw hills, creeks, and ravines of lava rock transformed into this mixture . . . which runs from the top of the Santa Clara Mountain. We could see a big hole of such depth that it caused terror and fear. Father Kino climbed it on another occasion to perceive the sea. It looked to him as if the waves lapped against the foot of the mountain, but he was mistaken since it is more than nine leagues [22-23 miles—W.K.H.] to the sea, and the sand dunes looked to him like waves of the sea.[10]

Salvatierra was even more struck by the unearthly prospect of this country. He wrote of ". . . horrible country, which looked more like ashes than earth, all peppered with boulders and . . . entirely black, all of which formed figures, because the lava which flows down solidifies, stops, and assumes shapes. And so in ancient times a horrible volcano must have issued from the Cerro de Santa Clara . . . Indeed I do not know that there can be any place which better represents the condition of the world in the general conflagration."[11]

Kino, who had traveled this way in October, 1698, with Carrasco, had seen much of this before and was less aghast, remarking only on their traveling "along weathered rocks like slag which long ago had been thrown out by this mountain or volcano of Santa Clara . . ."

Yet no one could fail to be impressed by the wilderness of puddled lava flows, volcanic tubes, cinder cones and craggy vents. Their journal entries are brilliant descriptions of the sea of lava now called the *Ives Flow,* which the trails cross on the southwest side of the mountain.

It would have been interesting to listen in on the party's discourses about this lava country around them as they trudged along. These were no illiterate adventurers. Although we now know that volcanism is not caused by a concentration of combustible material deep in the earth, nevertheless it may come as a surprise to see that even Manje, this soldier-adventurer, not only had a realistic conception of a volcano, but could quote the learned scholars of his day. All of them, while awestruck, knew what they were looking at. How many travelers of our day could write a better account of a newly discovered volcano? Bolton remarks dryly, "Never before nor since . . . has so learned a band of pilgrims traveled that desert trail, and I do not except a party known to me which included two college boys, a university professor, and a dean."

We now face an intriguing mystery: what is the "big hole of such depth that it caused terror and fear?" Does Manje's comment mean they discovered one of the great calderas for which the Pinacates are now famous? If so, which one? Let us defer this question a moment until we discuss the rest of the 1701 trip, which has a bearing on the answer.

The main goal was to reach the sea and determine if there was a route along its shore to the Colorado. On March 21, they left half their party and their loads at the tank of El Tupo, and struck out with the rest of the men and mules across the "very great sand dunes" of the Gran Desierto, a wasteland that looks like the popular conception of the Sahara, with rolling dunes much taller than a person. They measured their latitude as 32 degrees, accurate to within one-quarter of a degree. The distance to the sea was estimated at 8 to 10 leagues—20 to 25 miles across sliding sands.

Unfortunately, when they reached the beach, they could not see a northern end to the sea, though the Indians said the two lands did join in that direction.

*Papago Tanks, one of the largest and most reliable tanks in the Pinacate
lavas. Kino's party was first to record this complex when they camped here
in 1701. November 29, 1987.*

Manje records that the priests were already convinced, but he—like a proper skeptical scientist—waited to be convinced by his own direct observation. The priests told him to record that certain shells worn by the local Indians were found only on the opposite shore, proving that there must be an easy way to cross, because the Yumas built only reed rafts. The shells had been a lynchpin of Kino's theory all along. But skeptical Manje grumpily wrote that just "as God put the large, blue and green shells on the opposite shore of California, He could do the same at this latitude," and that, furthermore, there were ancient texts indicating a strait connecting to the Pacific, isolating Baja.

Manje wanted to launch a thrust northwest up the coast to settle it once and for all, but the Indian guides told them that this would require four days' journey through sand. The animals were already inadequately watered, and so the group retreated back around the south and east sides of the Pinacates, to their camp at the bend in the Sonoita River, El Carrizal.

Now it was time to try a new approach, to strike west from El Carrizal, directly across the northern Pinacate lavas to the northwest slopes of the mountains, to see what they could see from there. This would be their first *entrada* into the north and northwest sectors of the Pinacates. On March 31, the indefatigable party hiked 35 miles (Manje's estimate) across the lavas to a triple tank near an Indian settlement they called *Pitaqui*. Pinacate explorers Ives and Hayden independently retraced trails in this area, finding that they do lead from Carrizal to a major drainage and the most famous tank cluster of the Pinacates, now called *Papago Tanks*;[12] it seems certain that Papago Tanks was Kino's destination that night. All three of the travelers left diaries of the trip, and they all tell how they climbed a hill at dusk to see what they could see. We can imagine impetuous Kino, not even able to wait until dawn, insisting on the climb in hopes of settling the question of the land route. They were climbing, according to Salvatierra:

Sunset on the Pinacate Peaks from the southwest edge of the lavas, at Moon Crater, near Kino's 1701 route. April 8, 1977.

. . . a very difficult hill, easier to climb on all fours as a cat than on foot, but in spite of this trouble, we carried up the standard.[13]

Tougher Kino and Manje, taking things more in stride, both call it a small hill. The "standard" was a bulky painting, "Our Lady of Loretto." Kino, who had just hiked 35 miles and was now clambering up a cindery hill at dusk was, incidentally, 55 years old. From the hilltop, they watched the sun sinking over the Gulf, sang vespers and then scrambled down and pressed on to Pitaqui camp, refreshing themselves from the rocky pools, apparently after dark.

Now it was the beginning of April. They had learned as much as they could, for the guides told them it would be three days' farther march to adequate water for their animals, on the Gila River. These were the weeks when the weather turns hot, and the dominant colors of the Sonoran Desert change from tan and blue

Kino Bay, on the Gulf coast west of Hermosillo, Sonora, was named in honor of Father Kino's explorations. October, 1970.

to green and gold. The usual, stingy, grey-green of the desert vegetation becomes a more generous green, and gold spills out of the little bursts of brittle bush and poppy and in explosions of the blooming palo verde trees. The bushes puff themselves out with new growth, like a bird plumping its feathers. Winter's greyness has ended and sunny spring days frequently produce afternoon temperatures in the 80s and 90s. Kino and Salvatierra agreed that their expedition was now ended, and they must have relished their growing success in opening the frontier as they returned through the flowering desert to Sonoita and Dolores.

Now let us return to the mystery of the "big hole of such depth that it caused terror and fear." What strange formation, among the grotesqueries of the Pinacate lavas, elicited such a remarkable comment? The question has never been answered. Whatever the feature was, it must still be there. Can someone find it?

To anyone with a knowledge of the Pinacates, the answer seems obvious: the most awesome features of the region are the half dozen or so giant calderas. Three of them approach a mile in diameter and are hundreds of feet deep. Their steep walls, plummeting away to vasty, still depths, present a terrifying prospect. Surely if an early Spaniard tells us of stumbling upon a hole of such depth that it caused terror and fear, then it must have been one of these craters.

There is only one problem with this theory. There are no giant craters in the part of the Pinacates where Kino, Manje, and Salvatierra were hiking. Moon Crater is in this sector of the Pinacates, but is too shallow to inspire a strong reaction. It is so bland as seen from the ground that it was not even recorded until the 1950s.

So we are left with a paradox. In a region with the most spectacular craters in North America, a traveler records a great hole, but it was apparently not one of the craters. What was it?

I believe I have worked out a solution, but it must await a later chapter, where I will describe the diary of an obscure French scholar who traveled the same trail nearly two hundred years later.

Kino and Salvatierra had agreed to return in the fall to push back the frontier even farther. By October, 1701, however, Salvatierra had written from Baja to say that he could not make it. Nor could faithful Manje come. Disappointed but not disheartened, Kino, with one European companion and some Indians, made a journey in November, 1701, up through Sonoita, along El Camino del Diablo across the north tip of the Pinacate lavas, to the Yuma crossing. This was his fourth thrust across the Pinacate border country. For the first time he crossed the Colorado and pushed a short distance into California, where only the Europeans de Ulloa (1539), Alarcón (1540), Díaz (1540), and Oñate (1604) had preceded him. California must have looked discouraging. The empty dunes west of Yuma hardly encourage colonization!

On their way back to Sonoita along the Camino, they reached the Spring of the Moon at noon on

Lava textures on the Ives Flow, crossed by Kino in 1701.
Pinacate Peaks in distance. November 28, 1985.

November 26. Here, Kino and his companions built a ramp of loose rocks up the glassy-smooth slopes to the precious water; now their animals could clamber up to drink. Around 1930, Bolton[14] visited the modern Heart Tank, in the strange black and white mountains, Sierra Pinta. This range is a jagged ridge nearly 20 miles long, where bright granite on the south abuts dark basalt on the north, as if a sawblade were made half from black wrought iron and half from steel. Bolton asserts that the ramp, along a crevice on the north side of the slope, was still visible, and uses this as evidence to identify the Spring of the Moon. Others have questioned this identification, although it seems to fit the locations on Kino's maps of 1701 and 1705. The ramp-like feature at Heart Tank is degraded at best, as of the 1980s. Traveling on through Sonoita, the padre reached Dolores on December 8, 1701.

Kino returned on his fifth Pinacate foray only two months later. Accompanied by Father Thirso Gonzalez, who was enthused by the prospect of opening up California (Manje was detained by Indian trouble), he left Dolores February 5, 1702, passing through Sonoita and along the Camino del Diablo. They stopped at the Spring of the Moon, the tanks of Hidden Waters, and a tank called *Dripping Springs*. In camp at the last spot, the observant Kino independently discovered a naked-eye comet that passed across the constellation of Aquarius in February and March, 1702.

On they went to the Gila, the Yuma crossing and on down the Colorado to within a few miles of its mouth, affirming that the Gulf ended at this northern latitude. Now they tried a trip that sounds fantastic to anyone who has seen the country. Apparently, Kino just couldn't get it into his head that you *don't* walk directly from the mouth of the Colorado to the Pinacates. He plunged directly east into the great sand dunes of the Gran Desierto, recording "most difficult sand dunes, and with continuous, violent, and most pestiferous wind," as one translator put it.

They were heading for the village of Pitaqui (Papago Tanks), but they had no guides. After covering about half the necessary distance, but encountering not a drop of water or a blade of grass, they gave up and turned back on March 12, 1702. They went the long way around, up to the Gila and down the Camino. On the way, Father Gonzalez fell sick; he died before they could reach Dolores. This fifth trip thus ended tragically, but it added the final proof that the Gulf ended in a land bridge to California.

During the next four years, Kino sent out letters and maps affirming that the Pimería Alta extended north and west to both lower and upper California. He foresaw an era of settlement and commerce in the area. His supporters were many, but detractors—academicians, government officials, and conservative cartographers—could not accept the radical idea that California was part of the mainland. Manje, as we have seen, was dubious even as the waters of the Gulf's northeast shore lapped at his boots. Manje had now attained an influential position in the government. Recalling Kino's naive enthusiasms, Manje retained his doubts. The upshot was that Kino organized still another expedition—his sixth—to view the land route. This was to be his final reconnaissance in the Pinacates. The goal this time was to get sworn testimony of the existence of the land route, to convince the officials. To this end, two escorts and a Franciscan friar, Duran, accompanied Kino's party. One of the escorts was assigned to keep a careful diary to be signed by the others as proof for the government.

First, in Dolores, the escorts were shown the old blue shells from Baja, still treasured by Kino. On October 26, 1706, they set out for the Indian village of Sonoita, where Kino could show off a little white chapel, cattle and grain fields.

On November 5, they left Sonoita, rode four leagues, stopped for breakfast, rode ten more leagues to a tank in the Pinacates (Bolton identifies it as the one now called *Emelia Tank*), stopped for lunch, and rode four more leagues up the mountainside on the rough trail to the summit. Forty-five miles on foot and horse including the scaling of 4,200-foot Cerro Pinacate in one day—and Kino was 61 years old!

Ramirez describes the summit as consisting of three peaks, with the Kino party being on "the one which slopes to the south, whence was seen the sea."

On the next morning, November 6, 1706, having spent what must have been a cold, windy night at the top, they observed the scene again. Meanwhile, one of the escorts clambered up the highest peak, a huge cinder cone, with loose, steep, cindery slopes lying at the angle of repose, so that each step forward carries you sliding half a step back. The venturesome escort reported, "I [climbed] at the expense of very great toil because it was so high, and was a sort of rubbish heap of *tezontle* stone [basalt lava], like all this very great mountain, so that I seemed likely to end my life sooner than the undertaking." In spite of the uncertain interpretation of the view across the sand dunes to the west, all of the party concluded, just as Kino had asserted, that the land must be continuous across to Baja, whose Sierra Madre range could be seen curving toward the end of the Gulf.

They climbed down and Kino departed the Pinacates for the last time. On November 8, they left Sonoita for Dolores, arriving November 16, 1706.

Kino died in Magdalena in 1711, and was buried in a chapel there. The town grew and a new, large church was built in the 1830s. Over the years, the old chapel deteriorated and its location was forgotten. An imposing new cathedral was built. The celebration of the 250th anniversary of Kino's death in 1961, and the placing of his statue in the United States Capitol in 1965, focused new attention on the whereabouts of Kino's lost grave. By this time there were rumors that Kino's bones had been moved to an unknown location decades before. With the sponsorship of the Mexican government, a joint team of Mexican and American archaeologists and historians went to Magdalena and began a search of old

The bones of Father Kino. After the skeleton was located in 1966, it was exhibited as found for several years. More recently, the damage to the skull was repaired. A button lies on the breastbone, and one collar bone is stained by Kino's metal crucifix. December 30, 1972.

records and sketches. The records described the orientation of the original chapel and the relative positions of several other burials made after Kino's. Armed with this information, the researchers began to dig. Soon, one trench exposed the foundations of the original chapel, oriented just as described. Following the walls, they worked their way to the very bones of Kino himself on

May 19, 1966.

Today, on a sunny afternoon in the Magdalena plaza, we can stand in the little cupola designed by Mexican architect Francisco Artigas, and with no small degree of admiration, view the bones of Kino himself. On another day, climbing the Pinacate summit, we can listen for the wind's ghostly hiss among the cholla spines, and imagine Kino's spirit has returned to that very peak and stares intently northwest across lava and dunes, seeking the road to legendary California.

Journal entry. Visit to Ruins of Kino's Headquarters at Dolores Mission, Mexico. December 31, 1972. *Dolores is the mission Kino built as his headquarters and staging area for his trips to the north in search of a California route. His departures from here would take him to the Pinacate summit and across El Camino del Diablo. The ruins stand on top of a lonely hill above a ranch and a fertile valley with green fields.*

The mountains and valleys between Magdalena and Dolores are rugged and blue, and the roads are dusty. Five miles south of Dolores, at a village consisting of only five or eight buildings, the fields become green, but the hills must look much as they did when Kino came. A single electric wire loops along the road and across the hills, sometimes taking shortcuts the road can't follow, supported by crooked wooden posts that are only slightly modified parts of trees.

We pick up a fellow who had been left off a truck at a fork in the road, when the truck turned off to another village. He was walking the seven miles to his destination. He offered to guide us to the ruin. We drive through a dozen sloppy mud puddles past a couple of little ranches, to the ranch with Dolores on it. Our new friend finds the owner and discusses our visit. Approval is granted. We turn back, south of the house, northwest up the hill past the ranch buildings.

At the top on the right is a little cemetery surrounded by an old wire fence. A few yards to the left are a few suspicious-looking mounds. They bristle with plants—an indicator of high organic content, the sign of ruins. And now we catch sight of some time-battered adobe walls, standing a few feet high among the bushes thirty yards off to the left.

As we start to poke around, our guide begins to tell us treasure tales. "The local people think the padres had gold here," he says in Spanish. Believable. There were a couple of two-foot-deep pits, as if treasure seekers had been at their deluded work. We told him it was unlikely, a common myth. "Oh, but people here found some!" What? "Digging in the old corral they found a chest with money!" What kind of money? "Gold coins. They took them to the bank." Did you see them yourself? (We kept trying to pin it down—to make sure there was no translation problem.) "Yes." What did they look like? What dates did they have? "They were old gold coins." When did this happen? "Six years ago."

The desert is full of stories to keep a treasure seeker's blood running hot.

Kino's home mission was in a fine romantic setting on top of a hill with the wind whistling through the scrubby bushes, but it seemed an inconvenient spot. A nice bit of exercise was required to get to the river and back. Water for all the adobe had to be carried up the hill (no wonder Kino exclaimed at the convenience of building San Xavier on the flats where water could be diverted from the nearby Santa Cruz River to the building site).

The walls of Dolores are crumbling, though the brickwork is still plain. The ground within a few yards and farther—a circle maybe 100 yards in radius—is littered with plain pottery sherds, red and brown. I found a small flaked projectile point or knife worked on one side but left it there.

We took our new friend back to Carrizal where he had wanted to go. We had saved him a few hours walking, but we had cost him a few in guide services, so we offered a few dollars; but of course he declined with a smile.

Some 34 miles of dirt roads lead from Magdalena, Sonora, to this spot. They are so rough that by the time we return to Magdalena, a wheel on our car has shaken loose from its nuts and the exhaust manifold has come unseated, so that the car is emitting raucous noises. We spend the afternoon getting it fixed at a Mexican garage—the kind that can fix a truck with coat hangers and sheet metal if need be.

4. Revolts, New Colonies and Lost Gold

The boot mark in the dust smells of blood and iron.

J. C. Van Dyke
The Desert, 1901

. . . a lost mine ceases to inflate the adventurous sense the moment it is found . . .

Mary Austin
The Land of Journeys' Ending, 1924

IN AN ERA OF SLOW COMMUNICATION, Kino's discoveries were lost on the geographers of the day. For example, a map published as late as 1719, eight years after Kino's death, shows Baja separated from the mainland by a strait as wide as the Gulf of California, but extending twice as far north. In keeping with the ironies of history, unschooled locals knew the truth, but urbane publications and scholarly authorities (who represent History) lagged behind and spread misinformation.

For more than 20 years after Kino's death, no known Europeans reached Arizona. Finally, in 1731, two Jesuits were sent to take charge of the old missions of San Xavier del Bac, near Tucson, and Guevavi, just north of Nogales.[1] Then, in 1736, rich silver mines were discovered at Arizonac, just below the angle in the Arizona-Sonora border. A silver rush resulted. But within five years, the mines were closed by royal order, because the Spanish government was not getting its 20 percent share. These events fed rumors that there was more wealth on the frontier than had been officially reported, and that the Jesuit missionaries were operating hidden mines for themselves.

The Jesuit successor to Kino, Father Jacobo Sedelmayr, in a report based on his own observations, promoted the mineral potential of the land:

> *During the 20 years after the fathers entered the province . . . no mines were being worked. But then the Spaniards came to make their homes and they discovered many mines of silver and even some of gold . . . There comes to mind here what happened in 1736 . . . after His Catholic Majesty [may God save him] founded three missions in Pimer!a, namely Guevavi, Santa Mar!a, and San Xavier del Bac. Near these missions were discovered various mines. The last was . . . the famous Cerro de las Bolas [Hill of Nuggets, at Arizonac], in which were discovered nuggets of pure silver and many arrobas [25-pound units] of silver ore.*

Father Sedelmayr was right about mineral potential, but wrong about geography. As late as 1746, he still believed California was an island! Nonetheless, he was hoping, as had Kino, for contact and exploration with the California missions:

> *The Fathers of California from the 28th latitude, which is the mission frontier, will in short time*

Previous page: Saguaros against a lava flow, northeast of Elegante Crater. February 18, 1989.

Bleak granitic rocks frame the mouth of the canyon containing Tinajas Altas tanks. October 16, 1971.

Looking northwest along El Camino del Diablo in the Cabeza Prieta Mountains. Dark-capped Cabeza Prieta Peak in right distance. October 20, 1985.

through explorations in that island . . . come up to the 33rd parallel . . . There would thus follow what has so often been demanded [by the King], the conquest of the whole of California.

Sedelmayr knew of Kino's conclusion about the mainland connection to California, but did not accept it until seaborne expeditions re-rediscovered it in 1747.

In 1750, Sedelmayr and a party of soldiers made a little-known odyssey through the desert's heart to re-establish the knowledge that Kino had acquired. An unnamed ensign left a brief diary of this trip. An intriguing challenge is to reconstruct the route. Adding to this challenge is an inconsistency in dates that demands our interpretive skill.

On November 18, 1750, the diary records, the party left their frontier outpost and headed west toward Sonoita, which they reached on November 22.[2] Here, Indians showed them the half-century-old remnants of Kino's efforts: one substantial building and "ruins of a smaller house where Father Kino used to come and say Mass, so far as these Indians were able to remember." An entry marked November 23 describes a march eight leagues (ca. 20 miles) to a spot with pasture and salty water, corresponding to Kino's El Carrizal campground. The following entry, for November 24, speaks of traveling 10 leagues (ca. 25 miles) and camping without water or food. This would be in the barren region east of the north tip of the Pinacate lavas. There is no entry for November 25, and the next entry, for November 26, speaks of them "plodding along" in the same direction without pasture or water.

This seems clear enough so far. The only trouble is that between the November 22 entry in Sonoita and the entry for November 23, there is another entry marked November 23. *It* speaks of leaving an unnamed spot and traveling seven leagues (ca. 18 miles) and reaching "a tank of water from which only the men [but not the animals] were able to have a drink and this with the greatest difficulty. We continued on without stopping, covered another nine leagues (ca. 22 miles), and came to another spot in which there were three tanks of high elevation. To get drink from them it was necessary to take the water from the first to the second and then to the third. From this the animals were able to drink, although with great difficulty. Water had not been had for the two preceding days."

The translator of the diary[3] suggests that this entry is in correct sequence but that the ensign erroneously made the next two dates too early by one day; the translator then adds that this last tank sounds like Tinajas Altas, but that they could not have gone that far one day out of Sonoita, and that the last sentence quoted would thus be wrong, because they had just watered in Sonoita. I suggest, instead, that the entry describing the tanks is an entry for November 25, which is otherwise missing. It must have been copied out of sequence, perhaps the "25" mistaken for "23." In my interpretation the last sentence is correct; they had been without water on November 24 and most of November 25.

Where was the first poor tank and the second multiple tank 22 miles farther west? The first could have been Kino's old Spring of the Moon, with its difficult access—probably the modern Heart Tank in the Sierra Pintas, north of the Pinacates. The second tank may have been Kino's old Hidden Water. The description of a triple tank fits the multiple tanks at Cabeza Prieta Tank, in the dark-topped Cabeza Prieta Hills. The interesting thing about this interpretation is that it indicates the persistence, among Indian guides, of the same route that Kino followed 51 years before, in 1699.

Subsequent entries, starting on November 26, indicate that after leaving this second tank the party traveled 30 leagues (ca. 75 miles), encountering only one poor water hole, before reaching the Gila about seven or eight miles east of the Colorado junction, on November 28. This would fit a departure north out of Cabeza Prieta Tanks up the dry valley toward the Gila.

The traveler's adventures had hardly begun! Reaching the Colorado, they hiked downstream for five days, covering about 23 leagues (ca. 58 miles).[4] This would place them between the Arizona border and the mouth of the river and west of the Gran Desierto dunes. During the trip they were sometimes surrounded by crowds of vaguely threatening Indians, and on December 3, a skirmish ensued. Thirteen Indians were killed. Now Sedelmayr and his party fled east from the river eight leagues (ca. 20 miles) into the trackless dunes, where they camped without water. On the next morning, probably before dawn, they continued an unspecified distance east till they "came upon an abundant water hole. Here we rested for the greater part of the day."

Where was this desperate camp? They had probably stumbled on the odd brackish lake, Laguna Prieta, lost in the midst of the dunes about 23 miles east of the Colorado, halfway from the river to Tinajas Altas. The Norwegian explorer, Carl Lumholtz, visited Laguna Prieta in 1910 and found that while the main lake was saltwater, potable water could be found in springs along its margins.

Starting later on December 4, the fugitives traveled another eight leagues (ca. 20 miles) until they hit some unspecified point on the trail which they had taken west a week and a half earlier. Two leagues (ca. 5 miles) farther along the trail they came to "the water hole above referred to." Probably this was somewhere near Cabeza Prieta Tank. The diary reports on the next morning (the 5th, or possibly even the 6th?) they "continued on the trail until we reached Sonoita."

In one grueling quest, Sedelmayr's party thus not only made the difficult trip across the Camino del Diablo, but also completed the first eastward march from the lower Colorado across the Gran Desierto—a trip that had defeated even Kino half a century earlier.

IN 1750, THE SAME YEAR AS SEDELMAYR'S journey, the Seri tribe, on Mexico's west coast, revolted because of harsh treatment by the governor of Sonora and his soldiers. Troops pursued the Seris until they holed up in a mountain stronghold on the Tiburon Island in the Gulf, and the soldiers gave up the chase.

These events set the stage for a more serious revolt. At this time, a certain Don Luis Oacpicagigua, an unreconstructed Pima beyond the influence of the Church, had been appointed native Governor and Captain-General of the Pimas. Perhaps this unlikely appointment came about because Mexican civil officials fostered an antagonism against the padres whom they regarded as crafty and tyrannical in dealing with the Indians. Taking advantage of this, Don Luis stirred up the presidio captains and other officials against the missions. At the same time, he agitated among his own people against the Spaniards in general, promising them land, booty, even gold and silver if they would act against the oppressors. The motives of Don Luis may never be known. He was apparently encouraged by the handling of the 1750 Seri revolt. Did he merely want to be the most powerful chief of the area? Already, he had a title from the Spanish. Or did he want land? Or a return to the old, native ways?

In any case, he made careful plans. The Pimas would quietly withdraw their families and livestock to the desert heartland near Baboquivari, while Don Luis enlisted additional support from the Papagos living north of Sonoita.

On Saturday, November 20, 1751, the conspirators struck throughout the central Pimería. At Saric, about 30 miles southwest of Nogales, Don Luis lured about 20 settlers—men, women, and children—into his own house by warning them of a supposed Apache attack. Then he set fire to the place, killing several people. Sixteen miles to the southwest, down the Altar River, Sedelmayr was beseiged for two days in his home mission of Tubutama. He survived, but suffered a pierced arm and two gashes on the head. Another 45 miles down the valley at Caborca, Father Tello, four other adults, and

The most spectacular gold along the Camino is seen in the spring. Palo verdes in bloom. Tule Mountains. April 2, 1989.

several children were murdered. In Sonoita, Pimas and Papagos crept into the mission grounds on Saturday night. Finding the priest, Father Ruhen, sleeping by an open window, they axed him to death and killed the mayor and a servant of the priest. Today in the dusty Sonoita cemetery, a large stone monument with a metal plaque commemorates Ruhen. The monument stands near the site of the event, in lonely hills two miles east of the modern town. When I visited it in 1970, it was, following Mexican custom, bedecked with flowers, as if new.

Many other settlements saw violence, sieges and death, and many missions of the area were destroyed and looted. The rebels holed up according to plan in the vicinity of the sacred peak, Baboquivari. Not until

March, 1752, was some degree of quiet restored. Now began a six-year dispute over the causes of the revolution. Involved were the Sonora Governor, Parrilla; the priests, Fathers Keller and Nentvig; and the Indians, Don Luis and Pedro de la Cruz. There was some alignment of Parrilla and the Indians against the padres, the assertion being that the padres had treated the Indians cruelly. The curious fact is that the investigations were opened, closed, reopened, reclosed, and reached all the way to Spain, with inquiries coming even from the King. Even more curious is the fact that the hearings and gathering of testimony were shrouded in secrecy. Already by 1753 secrecy was being invoked by the superiors of the Governor. The fine for breaking the security was put at 2,000 pesos. Ultimately, by 1758, when the case was closed, the official explanation made neither side a clear winner. The Pimas had revolted, it was concluded, not because of dislike of the padres, but because of the Indians' "natural inconsistency, love of liberty, and savage passion for living unrestrained according to his appetites."

It is an ironic commentary that 20 years before the American revolution, "love of liberty" in the Southwest was regarded as evidence of barbaric tendencies. Some commentators have viewed Americans in the same light ever since.

There is a mystery here, and its existence has a scholarly blessing. Arizona historian, Russell C. Ewing, in a study of the uprising, concludes that "the impression is left that there were reasons for the civil-ecclesiastical friction which were not entirely explained by the results of the investigations. The theme . . . warrants further study."[5]

IN THE DESERT HEARTLAND, every place that *is* a place has its legend of lost gold. The Pima revolt of 1751 spawned one of the most persistent treasure-trove tales. This story says that during the Pima revolt, a mule train shipment of bullion was lost when it was caught between missions at the moment of the uprising.

This story is based on the rumor that the Jesuits had developed mines of their own, and that certain of their missions were storage places for gold en route to the Gulf, where it could be transferred by sea to European Church coffers. Modern scholars, including Jesuits, discount these tales,[6] yet they persist in lore.

The most detailed speculations about this particular legend were printed in 1965 by a California treasure buff, Paul V. Lease.[7] Lease says he bases his account partly on modern-day rumors among what he calls the wealthier classes of Mexico, stating that certain families got rich in one of the Indian revolts, which they had instigated themselves. Supposedly, the Governor and other officials learned that during the Seri revolt, a year earlier, in 1750, a treasure had been uncovered during destruction of one of the missions. This accident put the government "on" to the padres' gold scheme.

Don Luis, in this version, was actually in the employ of the officials. In turn for his exalted status, which seems curious in any other light, he fomented the sweeping 1751 attack on the treasure-trove missions. The governor's scheme was to sneak the gold out of each mission as the attacks proceeded, and haul it to a secret depository, through a countryside that would be deserted because of the bloodshed. There, the conspirators would share in the loot. The padres would say nothing because the gold was illicit in the first place. The revolt would be attributed to the padres' alleged mistreatment of the Indians, testified to by Don Luis and his followers, most of whom were ignorant of the overall plan.

Dr. Ewing's misgivings as to the real cause of the revolt lend a certain credibility to what might appear to be a wild tale. However, the rest of Lease's reconstruction appears to be pure speculation. A routine mission gold shipment, driven by priests, Indian guides, and a 100-mule train, had left Sonoita along the river to the west, he says, on the afternoon of Saturday, November 20, 1751. The party had reached the old campsite at

Lava crags east of Elegante Crater. November 27, 1986.

Quitobaquito or El Carrizal about dusk, when they noticed the fires in Sonoita on the eastern horizon, alerting them to the attack on their home mission, and probable pursuit. What to do? Their normal route to the south along the Sonoita riverbed to a coastal rendezvous point would be known. Lease assumes that the nearby Pinacate Mountains would be considered "a barren wilderness that offered poor refuge." He has the party flee not into the mountains, but in an unprecedented roundabout trek across the deserted northern Pinacate lavas for a stop at Papago Tanks, and then north across El

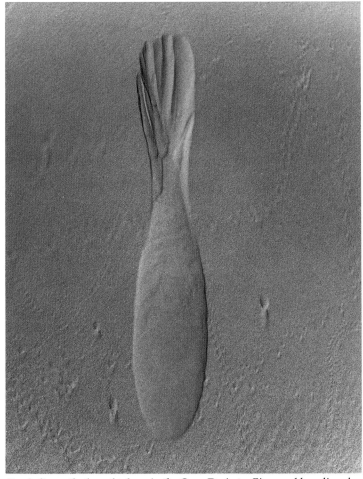

Sand-slip on the face of a dune in the Gran Desierto. Fine sand has slipped out of scalloped depressions at top, and flowed down the dune face in a smooth, liquid-like lobe. Insect tracks are also visible, along with smaller, wind-smoothed slips. February 19, 1989.

Camino del Diablo toward the Sierra Pinta range and Heart Tank, probable site of Kino's old Spring of the Moon. For some reason, Lease has them approach the east side of the Sierra Pinta, in spite of the fact that Heart Tank lies on the west side.

In all versions of this legend, the gold is hidden just before the mule train and the priest(s) are massacred by the Indians. In Lease's version, this happens in a large open canyon on the east side of the Sierra Pintas, and the gold is hidden on the slopes below a large rock. Don Luis

supposedly knew roughly where it was, but wouldn't tell. The knowledge gave him insurance in case the Governor should renege on the deal.

If one accepts the existence of such a gold shipment, one could make up many different endings. The canny priests might more likely have holed up at Papago Tanks or some other tank in the badlands of the Pinacates, instead of wandering in the hostile, exposed desert. Where better to hide than among the lava crags? If you want to believe that a fortune in gold has lain for two centuries in the desert heart, feel free to do so. In contrast to fairy stories, believing hard enough in lost-gold stories won't necessarily make them come true.

Another story of gold circulated around the border country. Seemingly, it supported the idea of lost mission gold in the Pinacates. The story was particularly strong in the area of Wellton, Arizona, the little town on I-8, about 20 miles north of the ancient water holes of Tinajas Altas. I heard the story from dune-buggy fans there in 1970. The story was that the desert heartland had yielded an ancient, golden bell.

Historian Ronald L. Ives investigated this tale and explained it. He found several bell stories.[8] Indians and Sonoita oldtimers told a consistent legend: sometime after Kino established his original outpost in the Indian village of Sonoita, a later priest arrived and insisted on installing a bell at the mission. The Indians believed that ringing the bell triggered earthquakes that plagued the region. In an effort to stop the earthquakes, the Indians stole the bell and altarstone and buried them in a cave, where they were later discovered.

Another version, told around 1932, was that white men living at Quitobaquito began a search for the gold bell, which was supposedly associated with ruins of a lost mission. A third version was that the bell had actually been found! It was on display in Wellton, in the possession of a Mr. Hugh Spain. When Ives arrived in the 1950s to investigate this version, he found that Spain had died, the building in which the bell was displayed had burned down in 1943, and the bell had been destroyed in the fire. Mrs. Spain, however, supplied a photograph of the bell and there was abundant local testimony confirming its existence. It had been made out of soft, yellowish metal and had been given to Mr. Spain by a Sonoita resident who obtained it from border Papagos.

Was it a gold bell from a lost mission? Evidently not. Ives' friend, Ygnacio Quiroz, identified the bell in the photo as one that had been owned by a colorful border resident, Cipriano Ortega, who had established a hacienda and small community called *Santa Domingo,* a few miles southeast of Quitobaquito, toward Sonoita. Ortega installed the bell in a chapel for his wife about 1875. Such bells, Quiroz said, had been cast by his grandfather and great-grandfather between 1790 and 1850 near Altar, to the southeast. Ives concluded that the Wellton bell was one owned by Ortega until about 1895 when his hacienda was abandoned, and that it was then carried off by Papagos, and changed hands in Sonoita about 1920.

Despite the violence on the mission frontier and the "gold" bell burned in Wellton, there is no tangible evidence of lost mission treasure. The real treasure is the trove of intriguing border stories. Each year it slips further into the past.

AN AMAZING DISASTER struck the missions throughout the Arizona-Sonora area on the night of June 24, 1767. By royal order, all the Jesuits were unceremoniously kicked out of all Spanish colonies! Mystery still surrounds the Jesuit expulsion, an operation of magnitude unprecedented in all history. Some scholars say Charles III of Spain was convinced by his advisors that the Jesuits, highly prosperous and developing an international outlook, challenged the throne of Spain. Charles III sent sealed edicts throughout the empire in the late spring, with orders that they be opened by the highest authorities June 24. To the astonishment of everyone on the frontier, the edicts commanded that all Jesuits be arrested within 24 hours. They were allowed to collect only their personal effects and clothes before being shipped back to Spain. All their church records were to be seized for evidence. This astonishing action fed rumors that the Jesuits had been operating covert gold mines. Historians have been unable to clarify the real reasons for the expulsion because the royal records of this event were destroyed some years later; no firm evidence ever surfaced to tie the events to secret Jesuit gold.[9] In any case, all the padres in the Pimería were arrested on hours' notice, herded together under miserable conditions, and eventually most were shipped back to Spain. Many died en route.

Franciscans were now sent to replace the Jesuits, but the missions were never the same. Some had deteriorated before and during the interregnum. San Xavier del Bac had been plundered.

The most intriguing personality among the new Franciscans was 30-year-old Father Francisco Garcés, who arrived at San Xavier in the spring of 1768. This was the northernmost frontier mission, subject to Apache attack. But Garcés set to work and soon, "all those of Pimería Alta venerated him as an oracle, and his fame reached the neighboring gentiles, called Papagos, . . . to whom he sent many loving messages . . ."[10] Garcés' reconstruction of San Xavier del Bac resulted in the beautiful two-towered cathedral completed in 1797 and still visited by tourists and worshippers alike.

Garcés must have come off the same assembly line as Kino and Sedelmayr. Within a few months of his arrival, he set out on a series of treks, without military escort, to reconnoiter the country and search for a route to California. In September, 1768, and again in 1770, he reached the Indian villages along the Gila, where he was feted. On such a trip, he says in his diary, "Only one awkward thing happened to me . . . In all places, and not only once, [the Indians] offered me women, etc.; but I, fixing my eyes on the crucifix . . . and raising it up towards heaven, gave them to understand that in that particular I did not live as they did. On this account they showed me much affection, and obtained a higher idea about a matter which to them appeared strange."[11]

On a journey across the desert heartland, he left San Xavier on August 8, 1771, determined to reach the Yuma Indians around the lower Colorado River. He packed a horse with the paraphernalia needed to say mass, and set out with a respected local Papago. To attempt a hike into the Sonoran Desert heartland in the 110F heat of August seems madness to us today—something attempted only by crazed Tucson outdoorsmen who undertake such adventures on occasion. But in the ante-auto era, August journeys were favored because the nights were pleasant and the rocky tanks were likely to be filled by the late summer "monsoon" storms, which, if one was lucky enough to get caught in one, would cool the traveler's afternoon.

Eight days later Garcés arrived in Sonoita. When he announced that he wanted to reach the Colorado River, the locals insisted it was too hard a trip; there was likely to be little water. Nonetheless, he set out the next morning with reluctant guides and reached a ranchería (Quitobaquito?), where the guides refused to continue. Garcés insisted, and set out to the west with the guides in tow.

Passing farm fields that had been abandoned for lack of water (El Carrizal?), they proceeded west until they were stopped by lack of water, and then they "turned by way of the volcano of Santa Clara toward the Gila."[12] A path into the Pinacate (*Santa Clara*) lavas would have been an unusual detour for a party trying to reach the Gila. Perhaps they sought a reliable water hole, such as Papago Tanks, or perhaps this phrase merely means that they crossed the northern tip of the lavas on the usual Camino del Diablo route. Five days after leaving Sonoita, after crossing "wide sand plains," they arrived at an unknown point on the Gila. After the

desert, the Gila must have looked fine; the stream was shaded by leafy green cottonwoods.

Now Garcés commenced an incredible, confused journey, pushing down the Gila and eventually down the Colorado, often alone, losing and recovering his horse, and wandering among salt marshes, barren plains, jungle-like riverbank undergrowth, stretches of "very fine country," and warring Indians of different tribes, whom he tried to council in ways of peace. At one point a disgusted Indian guide broke their only container of water and departed, hoping to force the foolish padre to turn back, but Garcés traveled on two days alone before finding another Indian group. Often he traveled through the night. Floundering in grassy marshes, he apparently approached the Colorado's mouth around September 8. Eventually he returned to the Gila on about October 7, and thence back through Sonoita in late October. He remarked in his diary that he had been in poor health at the beginning of the trip, but was flourishing at the end.

Next year, in 1772, Garcés recommended to the viceroy further explorations of a land route to California. South of Garcés' Tucson mission, the garrison at Tubac was now commanded by Captain Juan Bautista de Anza, another extraordinary personality. De Anza would now lead two major expeditions to the west, not only entering California, but pushing on to the north, where he founded San Francisco. Several participants of these adventures left diaries.[13] Those of de Anza himself rank with the best.

On a preliminary junket to reconnoiter the route, de Anza, Garcés, 28 soldiers and aides, 35 mules and 65 cattle set out from Tubac, south of Tucson, on January 8, 1774. They started north through Tucson, but were threatened by Apaches. To find a new route free of this menace, they reversed direction and traveled southwest down the Altar Valley through Caborca. By January 28, they reached Sonoita. Here they found six Indian families in residence; others were out on food-gathering

"The voiceless river." J. C. Van Dyke The Desert, 1901.

Sunrise over the Colorado River near its junction with the Gila River. This major crossing point was the scene of many early struggles. June 1, 1986.

expeditions. De Anza noted potential for gold ore in the rock types here, though his tests netted no actual samples of the precious metal.

The next day, they set out down the Sonoita River. After a few miles, their guide pointed out "a round peak, conspicuous for this shape, for it is the only one among several in whose midst it stands, and it is composed of salt, or veins of salt." The Indians described how they dug salt out during the rainy season, "when it softens somewhat." Apparently, this was between Sonoita and El Carrizal. The historian Bolton visited the area in 1928 to confirm the route, but was unable to find any trace of the salt dome. Nor have I found it mentioned in other travel accounts, though the water in the area is sometimes described as salty, and the hills just west of the river's southward bend are mapped as Sierra de la Salada, the Salt Hills. Perhaps an adventurous sleuth will locate this ancient salt mine.

After camping at El Carrizal, they departed on the 30th to the northwest, toward Heart Tank in the Sierra Pintas. Once again they were affirming that this was the main route, and supporting the theory that Heart Tank matched Kino's Spring of the Moon. Here, de Anza decided there was not enough water for all the animals, who were following behind, and he rode ahead to the Cabeza Prieta Tanks, northwest of the Pinacates. He arrived February 1. The mules and their drivers, exhausted, eventually caught up two days later. De Anza wrote a clear description of these tanks, and the piles of associated mountain sheep horns, left by Indians in some rite designed "to prevent the air from leaving the place . . . to molest everybody and cause them . . . troubles." Here we are encountering the same Tohono O'odham myth, about havoc wrought by winds escaping from magical abodes in the earth, that Kino and Manje encountered so dramatically at the "House of the Wind" near Tucson.

On February 4, de Anza's party reached water holes near Tinajas Altas. They crossed the stark white Tinajas Altas range through the pass north of the tanks, pioneering a route up the west side to the Gila River. Near the modern site of Yuma, they met the Yuma Indians. The chief of the Yumas was an interesting man, with the Indian name of Olleyquotequiebe, but known to the Spaniards as Salvador Palma. Historian-geographer Ronald Ives[14] describes him as left-handed and probably asthmatic. He befriended the Spaniards, helped them ford the river, and took care of some of their animals while they pressed on to the Pacific coast. The Yuma crossing, at the junction of the Camino del Diablo and the route along the Gila River, was a key site in the future history of Sonora-Arizona-California traffic. Palma was destined to play an ill-fated role in its history.

Having established a possible route through the desert to California, de Anza's party returned through Yuma and along the Gila, demonstrating that it, too, was a possible route. At last it was time for the dreams of Kino to come to fruition. The land route to California was now firmly established.

De Anza organized a mammoth expedition with no less a goal than to establish a colony on the California coast at San Francisco. Just as a new nation was being born on the east coast of the continent, de Anza set out from Tubac on October 23, 1775 with 240 people, 355 cattle and 695 horses and mules. For this trip, de Anza prudently chose the route along the Gila, rather than the Devil's Highway. The huge party traveled north along the Santa Cruz past San Xavier del Bac and across the future site of Tucson, arriving October 31 at the imposing ruin of Casa Grande, near the south bank of the Gila River.

Here they marvelled at the crumbling four-story ruin that Kino had discovered years before. Garcés and a fellow priest, Pedro Font, measured the building. Font recorded an interesting Indian legend that, through the peculiar upper-story windows of various shapes, the "Prince" of the community "looked out . . . upon the sun when it rose and set, to salute it."[15] Modern scientific studies support this legend in an unexpected way. Since the 1960s, archaeo-astronomers have found that certain ancient structures, such as the famous Stonehenge in England, were designed to facilitate determining the date of summer or winter solstice. Such astronomical observations assisted in monitoring the calendar, and determining dates for planting and other annual events. Similarly, studies of Casa Grande indicated that the peculiar-shaped upper windows had been carefully designed for astronomical use. The diagonal view through one window marked the position of the sun at summer solstice sunset. At first, archaeologists scoffed at the idea of Casa Grande as a calendar observatory. Nonetheless, anthropologists' records showed that as late as the 1800s, Indians in New Mexico pueblos were using window alignments to measure dates. In the great cultures of prehistoric Mexico, priests made even more sophisticated astronomical observations from multistory stone observatory-temples. To test the idea of solstice observations at Casa Grande, I was allowed to take photographs at the date of solstice while perched on a ladder at the Casa Grande "solstice window." These show that the diagonal view does impressively frame the summer solstice sunset. My guess is that the structure did see use as a calendric observatory.

By the legends told to dusty Garcés and Font at Casa Grande in 1775, we are reminded that the Sonoran Desert only a few centuries earlier had been the northern provincial frontier of a lost but cultured civilization of Mexico. Here, "country" priests in their adobe buildings echoed the grander ceremonies and urbane sciences of the great stone temples to the south.

De Anza's expedition pushed on down the Gila to Yuma, where the Yuma chief, Salvador Palma, helped them across the Colorado and was rewarded with a dazzling uniform. They plodded on through California and successfully founded San Francisco. In today's bustling America, few people remember that mighty San Francisco is the child of dusty Tubac and Tucson. As a result of de Anza's success, the Gila became the major California route. The austere desert heart to the south languished. Even today, Interstate 8 follows the Gila and carries more traffic than two-lane Mexico 2, which follows parts of El Camino del Diablo, just south of the border.

Once San Francisco was established, a party of 29, including de Anza and Father Pedro Font, made a return trip, this time retracing de Anza's 1774 steps along the Camino. Again, de Anza and Font kept diaries. By Friday, May 17, 1776, they were at one of de Anza's old camps, south of the Gila on the west side of the Tinajas Altas range, still some miles north of the tanks. While other parts of the country basked in spring, the desert near the Tinajas Altas range was already blazing by day; at this time of year, rain is virtually unknown. Due to the heat, Font says, "the burning of my mouth became worse. The road was level . . . but over sandy country, dry and most difficult, with no trees except some scrubby mesquites. . . ."[16] De Anza recorded discomfort by 11 A.M., "when the sun overcomes men and animals . . ."

At 5 A.M. on May 18, they left camp to make a push for the Sonoita River, some 60 desolate miles away. By about 9 A.M., they reached their first water at a spot where Font describes ". . . some wild and naked sierras or very high cliffs in which there are some concavities called *tinajas*, in which there is usually water. At this place, there are nine tinajas formed in the rocks, one above the other . . ." This sounds exactly like the Tinajas Altas with its nine-tiered tanks, some 12 miles and four dawn hours from their camp. Nonetheless, Bolton questions the directions and identifies them as the Cabeza Prieta Tanks. In any case, they watered their animals and took siestas from late morning until 5:45 P.M., when they left on a march toward the old campsite of El Carrizal. They crossed the north tip of the Pinacate lavas, traveling "three leagues northeast over malpais," Font says, and then nine southeastward, finally making camp in

Windblown sand has partially buried this volcanic range in the Gran Desierto northwest of the Pinacates. ca. 1963.

front of the Agua Dulce Hills. De Anza and the pack train followed Font's lead party, making an all-night march, and catching up to Font at four in the morning. At once, the group continued to El Carrizal, arriving at 11:30 A.M. on Sunday, May 19. They had covered about 60 miles in 18-1/2 hours. At El Carrizal, Font says, "the heat left us exhausted, although by nightfall it became so cool that a blanket and the doubled *capote* did not suffice to keep out the cold." Ah, yes, Sonoran Desert hiking.

The next day they passed through Sonoita, where Font noted that a cross had been set up on the little hill where the Indians had killed Father Ruhen a quarter century earlier "at the foot of a saguaro, from which they hung his holy crucifix."

The trip back from Yuma was all the more interesting because Chief Palma accompanied the group. Palma was on odyssey to Mexico City. Here, the aboriginal diplomat from the Colorado River gazed upon the vanquished capitol of the Aztecs, met the viceroy, dictated to de Anza an account of his own life (still in the Mexican archives in de Anza's hand),[17] and was baptized.

He returned to Yuma in 1777 with a book full of promises about the improvements his people would experience as the Spanish developed the road through Yuma to California.

Unfortunately, in their zeal to expand, the Spanish had made more promises than they could keep, and more settlements than they could supply. For instance, Father Garcés decided to expand the chain of Sonoran missions along the route, and in 1779 he and an escort of two soldiers traversed the Camino to the Yuma area. Garcés established a mission here on the California side of the river. In 1780, soldiers and families of colonists founded two settlements on the Colorado, one at Yuma and one eight miles downstream, appropriating some of the Yuma Indians' best land.

When supplies ran short, settlers and their animals found the Indians' crops too inviting to resist. While Chief Palma counseled cooperation, his villagers now began to realize what the colonization of California augured for them. It was no longer a case of annual visits from padres with smiles and gifts. Now it was a stream of colonists, governors, and rough men with a gold glint in their eyes. On July 17, 1781, the Yumas rose up and massacred the men in the settlements, taking the women and children captive. Confessing some of the wounded in the midst of the slaughter, Garcés and his assistant were taken prisoner by the bloodthirsty revolutionaries. On the next day, Palma argued in their behalf, noting the priests had always been the Indians' greatest helpers. Other Indians reviled them as "the worst of all," and over Palma's objections, 43-year-old Father Garcés and his assistant were beaten to death.

By October, 100 troops were dispatched north from Altar to retaliate against the 3,000 Yumas and recover the hostages. They traveled an old Kino route north across the desert to Gila Bend, then west down the Gila. A message came from Palma asking for peace and in ensuing negotiations, 62 hostages were ransomed. But in a few days, a coalition of Spanish troops and Indians who were enemies of the Yumas made a devastating attack on the Yumas, and then retreated back down El Camino del Diablo to Sonoita.

Next month, on the morning of November 23, 1781, the troops trekked west from Sonoita for another blitzkrieg on the Yumas, covering about 75 miles across the Camino by the evening of the second day. After skirmishes, they rescued a few more captives, including a newborn baby, and recovered the bodies of Garcés and three other missionaries. During this encounter, Palma was almost cornered, but escaped death when a soldier's pistol misfired three times in a row. Palma, the peacemaker and diplomat, disappeared from history as

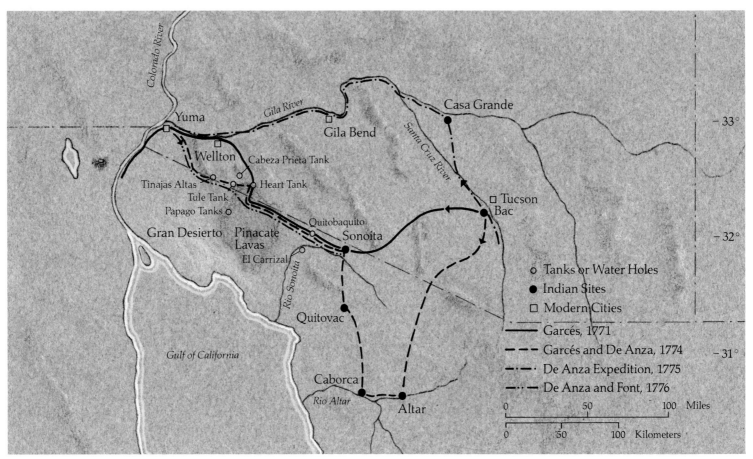

Travels of Garcés, De Anza and Font. 1771-1776.

a hunted fugitive. Some church valuables were recovered, but the Indians had taken the baptismal font "to cook squash" according to a report. The priests' bodies were returned to Mexico, and according to Ives[18] still are preserved at the Colegio de Santa Cruz de Queretaro in the very case in which the soldiers packed them in 1781.

During the same campaign, three mission bells were recovered, but one additional bell disappeared. In a biography of one of the soldiers on this campaign, Ives gives a fascinating but frustrating footnote about this bell:

> A bell, inscribed San Luis Gonzaga, Anno 1719, was offered for sale by 'desert rat' in the early 1960s with a story of its finding that suggested that it might be the missing Yuma bell. After lengthy travels and several changes of ownership, the bell was determined to have been illegally acquired and imported, and it was returned to Mexico by U.S. authorities. [It] may be the missing great bell of Yuma.[19]

The current whereabouts of the bell is unspecified. This bell may have added to the legends persisting in the area more than a century later about missing missions and missing bells lost in the desert.

A final additional attack on the Yumas was deemed appropriate, this time to be launched simultaneously from the California missions on the west and Sonora on the east. On February 27, 1782, troops set out from near Altar with 39 soldiers, reaching Sonoita March 2, crossing El Camino del Diablo, and reaching the Colorado on March 11. They crossed the river without resistance and proceeded to the California coastal missions. Here, the joint attack was set (after some false starts), for August. By the time it was carried out, it seems to have been anticlimactic. Nearly 60 troops from California and some 100 from Sonora converged on the site of modern Yuma and some skirmishing occurred, Salvador Palma's

brother and several dozen other Yumas were killed (out of a population of about 3,000). The Spanish lost four soldiers and 49 horses and mules. Palma himself remained secluded in the mountains.[20]

The violence at Yuma closed the desert routes for years, causing California to develop from the coast inward, instead of from Arizona as it had started. El Camino del Diablo and the Pinacate lavas were left deserted, drowsed in sunlight and starlight.

Journal entry. A trip on El Camino del Diablo. October 18, 1985. 2 P.M. We are about to make a car-camping trip along the route that Díaz, Kino, Garcés, de Anza and Font traveled.

All the way along the road from Tucson to Three Points, these days, every mile or so, are little torn-up patches, little enterprises. Once we pass Kitt Peak the land looks better. Cultivated fields and undisturbed masses of gold-green creosote rising to eye level, taller mesquites here and there with their black bark, and low clumps of yellow-flowering bushes. Rising beyond, the basalt and granite hills, russet and tan at close range, purple in the distance.

A warm, sunny, pleasant afternoon. A few puffs of cumulus in the distance around the horizon. About 75F. Our group, mostly from a major environmentalist organization in Tucson, projects a devil-may-care cheeriness, having been freed for the weekend from the jobs that environmentalists need to support their habit. (The developmentalists' lawyers, who argue for tearing up the desert, never need basic support jobs; they get paid for sitting through citizens' hearings . . .)

We stop at Quijotoa trading post. Busier than usual, with six or eight cars and trucks out front, and an Indian couple drinking root beer on the porch, their arms resting on their whole case of root beers. The wonderful contents of Indian trading posts: candy bars, sturdy socks, Cokes and Pepsis and Seven Ups, rifles, and the ancient style of enameled-metal plates and coffee pots that I used to see at my Grandma's farm.

7:30 P.M. We stopped at the Wildlife Refuge headquarters, the most modern building in Ajo, surmounted by solar panels, and now we are headed down the Camino as darkness sets in. A few days ago it rained, and we are concerned about the state of the playa just beyond O'Neill's grave: will it be a sea of mud? Instead of camping to enjoy the scenery at dusk, and proceeding by daylight, this incautious group, with four vehicles, barrels on down the road in the dark, hoping to reach a preselected target spot for the night. The dreaded playa is 20 miles ahead when the road turns slightly damp. Then, there is light mud. One rule in such a situation is: don't stop! Barrel on through! The lead driver tries to gun it. Now, it is turning into heavy mud; now, a trickling stream with mud gushing and spraying on the sides. Vehicle 1 bogs down, mud up to the axle. Do other drivers follow at a prudent distance, detect the problem and wait at the start of the mud? Of course not. These are not cautious types. The next three drivers, following only a few car lengths apart, try to accelerate to keep from getting stuck, and bunch up tighter behind number 1. Keystone-cops fashion, they all zoom into the bog and mire down in the mud. In truck number 2, we are on a high spot on the seafloor under the mud; number 3 has slipped into a hole; number 4 discovers he has a little traction and eventually backs out.

We now recall that our leader, an ardent lady environmentalist, had decreed back in Ajo that to reduce "vehicle impact," we would leave our fifth vehicle there, 26 miles back. That was the vehicle with a winch. Our leader still manifests a "Gosh-aren't-we-having-fun" approach. I am having uncharitable thoughts about the way this trip is going.

8:10 P.M. With our free vehicle, we attach cables to number 2, spin it around 90 degrees, and then watch it sink into the mud, tailpipe spluttering. But at last it is pushed and pulled loose. At the same time, headlights appear on the dark Camino, coming from behind us. We are joined by a new carload of companions who had left Tucson late. Now we are five.

8:45 P.M. With tow ropes from our two free trucks pulling number 1, we pull it backwards. It starts to budge. But the two tow ropes leading to the two trucks straddle a hapless 7-foot creosote bush. I say "The team that pulls the truck on their side of the bush wins." Others, more practical, bring an ax and shovel and begin to dismantle the unfortunate bush, incidentally dislodging an ancient, 6-inch horned toad who crawls off indignantly into the slimy night. Truck number 1 is free.

9:00 P.M. At last, all vehicles are free. We decide to camp and assess the road in the morning. We search in the dark for relatively dry ground.

October 19, dawn. It has been cold during the night and the tent is soaked with condensation. Someone rouses the party to come and see "Lake Okefenokee," where we were stranded last night. The creosote bushes around the tent have glistening fat droplets of water hanging off their black, wet branches. I study the droplets closely—little universes. They make inverted images and turn into gleaming stars as the sun rises.

I think of the two magic moments in the desert day— dawn and dusk—when there is a half hour of change and promise: it is getting dark, it will be cool and pleasant; or, it is getting light, it will be warm and dry. Two moments of reward are all the desert grants in its day of testing. At night, it grows cold when you are outside; and in the midday it grows hot, parched. We must survive through ten hours of day, to reach the magic moment of dusk. Dawn and dusk are moments we ignore in ordinary life. We brush our teeth, stare at a groggy apparition in the mirror during the magic morning; at dusk, we are driving home, jockeying with strangers for position in the middle lane. Simplify, simplify, Thoreau said. The desert simplifies things for you and tells you what's important.

1:10 P.M. Having survived the playa, we approach the low, craggy, north-reaching tongue of Pinacate lava. We climb up ten feet or so onto it, bumping over lava cobbles. Broken ground and brooding, dark cinder cones stretch before us. We stop to discuss looking for Díaz Crater, a shallow crater I helped identify in the '60s from Gemini astronauts' photos. We named it after Melchior Díaz, figuring that he must have passed very near here. We promptly discover our truck's tire is going flat due to a puncture sustained as we climbed up the sharp lava rocks onto the flow. Ours turns out to be the only 5-lug-wheel design among the five vehicles, so now we are without an additional spare for this vehicle. But we are halfway across the Camino to the nearest exit, so might as well press on.

As this is being discussed, several of our hikers make a macabre find. Human bones lie near a tree about 100 yards north of the Camino. Among tattered fabric, cans, and skull fragments are five Mexican coins. The most recent coin is 1979. Once again, the Pinacate country has claimed a victim. We leave a partial ring of basalt boulders to mark the remains: the newest grave along El Camino del Diablo.

4:10 P.M. We have crossed the lava, and proceeded on the dusty desert floor along the Camino through a profusion of desert plants. We've reached Tule Well, in the hills at the west end of a long flat stretch of the Camino. These hills, the Tule Mountains, are chocolate-brown basalts protruding above a sea of green ocotillos. The granites of the Sierra Pintas, in the distance, glow with soft pink light. On the brown-painted metal water tank that has replaced the older structure, another traveler, doubtless trying to reach a U.S. city from Mexico, has lettered a poem during his rest at Tule Well:

> Yo no tengo
> Pasado el tiempo
> Se lo llevo
>
> La mejor creacion
> An sido mis hijos

The wording is a bit odd, but later at a dinner with some Mexican friends we render it as:

I have no past.
Time took it away.

The best creation
Has been my children.

October 20, 7:30 A.M. Camping near Tule Tank in the Cabeza Prieta Mountains. Sun has risen on the desert. In spite of the white, bone-like dryness of the mountains and desert here, they have their life. If I sit still on my rock, I hear numerous bird songs out in the flats that wind among these broken hills. And there were the bugs that produced numerous welts on my head in the night. And at about seven, songs of the first noisy silver birds: the roar of flashing jets arcing through the sky. A complete five-inch cannon shell, with bullet and casing, lying on the ground at Tule Well, was a reminder that the jets from Luke Air Force Base pursue their maneuvers here throughout the seasons.

Last night, around the fire, the environmentalists' campfire conversation began with a critique of the narrow-mindedness of a certain Southwestern religious zealot, and then turned to a lament against development. They work themselves to righteous wrath, bailing in the darkness with their word buckets against the tidal wave sweeping across the Southwest. Instead of being recreated by the desert, they have brought their city tensions with them. Long into the night, they talk their we-they language, planning like zealots themselves how to manipulate events before the developers manipulate the landscape. Even the owners of mountain cabins near Tucson are condemned. Because the mountains are beautiful, they should be left alone and road removed.

I am reminded of Pasternak's partisans in Doctor Zhivago, planning their neighbors' grim destinies in ill-lit back rooms, all in the name of good. We-they. Gone is the innocent grace of seeing humanity as a oneness, cast up on our desert isle in space.

5. Tales from the Old, Real West

Like dead scales, the superficialities, the falsities, the habits that had once meant all of life dropped off, useless things in this stern waste of rock and sand.

Zane Grey
Desert Gold, 1913

It is in the great wildernesses, on lofty heights and on desolate deserts, that one feels the greatness of Nature's mysteries. In the starlit heavens mind outruns vision . . .

Raphael Pumpelly
My Reminiscences, 1915

THE EARLY 1800s SAW THE BIRTH of modern Mexico, independent from Spain. In the 1820s were a series of revolutions and abortive governments; and in the 1830s, the breakoff of Texas. The future of a Mexican California was particularly in doubt because of American and Russian trading along the coast, and the fledgling Mexican government began prudent efforts to develop the land route from Sonora to California. These developments meant renewed attention to the old Camino del Diablo and the Colorado River crossings.

In 1819, Father Felix Caballero and two Indian guides traveled much of the circumference of the Sonoran Desert in a clockwise direction. They left their mission in Baja California, crossed the Colorado River and traveled up the Gila River then south through the Mexican village of Tucson and on to Arizpe.

With this success a reverse expedition was sent out from Tucson toward Baja in 1823 to consolidate the route and look for sites of potential missions and presidios. This ended in a disaster, pivotal for the subsequent history of the whole region. Under the command of Captain José Romero, commandant of the Tucson Presidio, Father Caballero and ten soldiers set out from Tucson in blazing June weather, reaching the Gila River in

two days. Pima Indians welcomed them and their promise to bring instruction in new agricultural and religious arts. Romero's party then traveled west down the Gila, but cut to the south across the desert east of the Colorado, probably somewhere near present-day Wellton or Tacna. Here they crossed over the Tinajas Altas range through the pass that de Anza had pioneered during his 1774 reconnaissance, prior to the colonization of San Francisco. Led by Indian guides, Romero's party then made what must have been a miserable crossing of the formidable sand dunes and reached the Colorado.

Here the Indians again seemed friendly, showing the Mexican party possible mission sites and offering to help build the rafts needed to cross the river. Romero noted that the Indians were so enthusiastic, "it seemed as though they had been raised among us."[1] The Mexicans placed their gear on the best rafts, and began the crossing. Suddenly, at midstream, the Indians guided the best rafts and horses back to the eastern shore, leaving the Mexicans drifting down the swollen river. They were saved when members of their group jumped into the water and pushed them to the western bank, from where they could see the Indians making off with their horses and supplies. Romero's party, starting

Previous page: A moment of gold. Cholla at dawn, Organ Pipe Cactus National Monument. November 26, 1986.

A storm in the desert was the only hope for filling the water tanks along El Camino del Diablo. Organ Pipe Cactus National Monument. May 14, 1987.

with virtually no clothes or supplies, made a desperate trek across the torrid summer deserts of northern Baja California, reaching missions there by July 6, 1823.

Because of the Indian hostilities, the whole region now became an obstacle instead of an avenue. In spite of several forays in the following years, the turmoil seems to have deflated Mexican efforts to establish missions, presidios and mail routes across the desert heartland.

EUROPEAN EXPLORERS of a new nationality came from a different direction in 1826. In the summer of that year, an English ex-naval officer, R. W. H. Hardy, out of employment after the Napoleonic wars, accepted a position with a venturesome company reconnoitering the commercial pearl and coral possibilities of the Gulf of California. After travels throughout Mexico, Hardy got a boat whose crew was

> the most wretched set of people . . . that ever set foot on the deck of a vessel . . . I never in my life was disposed to play the tyrant until I joined this vessel, and here the apathy of the whole crew rendered harsh measures necessary . . . I have therefore been in almost one uninterrupted rage since we left . . .[2]

Armed with scanty records of Kino's explorations of the Colorado's mouth, Hardy's crew became the first since Alarcón's in 1540 to explore the same region by boat. Moving north along the coast, he named Rocky Point, site of the present-day Mexican fishing and resort town of the same name. It is ironic to learn that Rocky Point was named in English, because sensitive Americans take pains to call it by its "proper" Spanish name, Puerto Peñasco. As he sailed by, Hardy noted Kino's Santa Clara Volcano in the distance. Stopping on the beach east of Rocky Point, he described it as a deserted coast "visited only by the elements." Sitting on that beach, not far from the sandy mouth of the Sonoita River, Hardy ruminated:

> A traveler sees many things which give rise to a multitude of feelings . . . some of them pleasing, some painful, and yet others productive of wonder and surprise. My own sensations were of this latter kind . . . [This country] is probably in the same state that it was ages ago . . . Those who love the total absence of sound, and of the 'busy hum of men . . .' would here find a solitude so absolutely melancholy, that they would never willingly again quit the society of their fellow creatures.

Commemorating a friend, Hardy then named Adair Bay, the broad bay south of the Pinacates. He left other names imprinted on lower Colorado maps, including Hardy's Channel, which he named, he said, for his family.

Hardy's expedition was neither cheerful nor successful. Two nights before entering the Colorado, his boat endured such a severe Gulf storm that Hardy had to tether himself to the deck to maintain his position. Soon after entering the river the boat broke its rudder by crashing into the bank. Then, as the Colorado delta's notoriously strong tide went out, they found themselves stranded in sand about 200 yards from the bank. They had to wait eight days for a new moon, which (because it is acting in a line with the sun) produced high enough tides to float their boat. At various times, they were surrounded by Indians, who, while not violent, seemed vaguely threatening. Eventually, they ended their "26 days' difficulties in the Rio Colorado" without finding the pearls, corals, gold or other valuables they had hoped for. Hardy celebrated the departure from the Colorado's mouth by firing off a salute of two guns and small arms, and then distributing brandy.

Civilization was now circling around the Sonoran

Desert heartland like a moth around a flame. While Hardy's boat probed from the south, Yankee mountain men and trappers began probing the Gila River from the north and east. The fad for stylish beaver hats led to a lucrative trade in beaver pelts, and the Gila and Colorado were swarming with beaver, as amazing as that might seem to a modern reader. Word of this got out in 1825 and 1826, bringing hordes of Americans from the Midwest through New Mexico and along the Gila River.

All these lands were still Mexican territory. American incursions were a headache for the Mexican officials of the region. In theory, permits were supposed to be issued, and in some years American trapping was outlawed altogether. But undermanned Mexican garrisons in Tucson and elsewhere could hardly stop small parties of intruders.

Because many of the expeditions were covert and the trappers uneducated, there are few records of these trips. One exception is a reminiscence by James Ohio Pattie, who trapped on the Gila in 1826 and 1827.[3] On the latter trip, Pattie and a party of trappers went the length of what Pattie erroneously called the "Helay, a river never before explored by white people." Reaching the Colorado, they built eight dugout canoes and floated down the Colorado looking for (nonexistent) Spanish settlements in which to sell their pelts. Exercising the restraint so typical of Anglo civilization's advance, they continued decimating the beavers, "almost as fast as we could wish. We sometimes brought in 60 in a morning." Camping somewhere in the delta, they were surprised to have their camp flooded by the curious tidal bore of the Colorado—the frothy wave of water that funnels into the Colorado's mouth as the tide rises, and rushes chaotically *upstream*. Eventually, they had to abandon their canoes, stash their hundreds of furs, and strike out in an arduous journey on foot toward the Pacific coastal settlements.

In 1829, young Kit Carson traveled with another party on a similar journey down the Gila to Yuma. Based on this experience, he later became a guide to the region. All such journeys served to reinforce the Gila route more and more firmly in preference to El Camino del Diablo as the overland route to California from Texas and New Mexico. Throughout most of this period, the Pimas and other Indians living in villages along the Gila were great friends of all travelers. However, the Apaches and a few other tribes who roamed throughout the area terrorized travelers who strayed too far into the wilds.

The next decades brought more unrest and the spice of another story of lost gold. This straightforward tale of a lost mine has much less historical background than the tale of the missing gold shipment from Sonoita. Some time in the 1840s, two or three travelers on the Devil's Road reportedly reached the first fork in the road west of the old watering spot of Quitobaquito, and nearby discovered rich gold ore, which they brought to Sonoita. A second trip was organized to make good on the discovery, but this time, after they had made camp at the spot, "wild Papagos" fell on them, stealing the mules and supplies, killing all but one who was left for dead. The survivor, who struggled into Sonoita to tell the tale, was a soapmaker who went by the name of *El Jabonero*. Years later, after growing blind from the wounds inflicted by the Indians, El Jabonero passed on a description of the site.

The gold supposedly lay on the far side of the central hill in a cluster of three low hills that were noticeable only from the fork of the road—to the right as you go west from Sonoita. The question is: where was the first fork in the 1840s? Searchers in the early 1900s concentrated on forks near or just *west* of the Pinacate lavas, for example the fork that goes north into the Sierra Pintas and Heart Tank. But the travelers of the story were supposed to be only half a day out of Sonoita, which could hardly bring them past the playa just east of the lavas, perhaps near the fork noted by Manje, near where the Sonoita River turns south.

This story, of course, has the classic touches of

legions of unreliable lost-mine stories: the discovery, the loss—often by violence—and the old prospector who passes the story on in a cryptic way. The genre of the lost-mine story remains popular in spite of the lack of variety in the plot. There is no guarantee of reliability to the story and indeed, Harold Weight, who tells the story in his little book on lost mines, mentions several different versions he gathered from various old-timers.[4]

Nonetheless, like the lost-gold-shipment story, this one has some tantalizing bits of support. For one thing, marauding bands of "Sand Papagos" (another name for the roving Papagos of the western deserts near the Pinacates) did live in the vicinity of Quitobaquito. Second, researcher W. J. McGee, who camped at Tinajas Altas in 1905, told of prospectors passing through his camp hoping to reclaim a mine they had found in ridges a few miles northwest of MacDougal Crater, on the west side of the Pinacates. In recounting this story, naturalist Bill Broyles (who retraced the prospectors' route), notes skeptically that the region immediately around the Pinacates is a land "richer in legends than actual ore . . . this gold is at best flirtatious, luring prospectors and then breaking their hearts." He notes that flecks of gold are not unusual in rocks of the area, but more than a century and a half of gold prospecting has produced only "bread money, not riches."[5]

At Quijotoa, on the other hand, only some 80 miles northeast of the Pinacates, turn-of-the-century explorer Carl Lumholtz was able to recount how Papago Indians of his day were finding thousands of dollars worth of gold nuggets. When he was camped at Tinajas Altas in 1910, miners "on a prospecting tour to Pinacate" came by. Lumholtz had already heard of gold-bearing lava "picked up in the region north of Pinacate," but he remarked that lava fields were generally not good places to find gold. In response, the prospectors showed him "a most unusual sample of free gold that literally studded a dark brown piece of . . . old lava," apparently from the Pinacate region. Lumholtz brings up the issue of the region's gold even in his preface:

> *The mineral prospects of the region, especially as regards gold, are great. There are numerous large veins south of Sonoita which should be examined and the mountains of the western desert explored. Free gold which undoubtedly has been encountered in the malpais in the northern part of Pinacate should also be followed up.*[6]

Lumholtz also cites a Mexican official who reported around 1850 that in this border region "there is not a town or a ranch that has not at least one vein of gold, silver, lead, or copper," and that surface deposits were known where "gold was gathered in the same way that fowls pick up corn."[7]

Lumholtz also recorded that the colorful border character, Cipriano Ortega—the man who installed the "Wellton bell" in his wife's chapel—had mined silver in a little range called the *Sierra del Viejo* about 20 miles northwest of MacDougal Crater, in the area where McGee's prospectors were looking in 1905. Lumholtz recorded that the Ortega silver mine had been lost and "never found again."[8]

Thus, while this land may be richer in legends than in ore, the many stories of lost treasures and lost mines—rampant from the 1840s to about 1910—cannot be completely dismissed. Who knows what discoveries may have been made and lost among these harsh hills?

DURING THE 1840s, DRAMATIC EVENTS affected the Sonoran Desert. After the breakoff of Texas from Mexico and continued skirmishes along the Texas border, the United States declared war on Mexico and invaded New Mexico and California. When the war ended in 1848, the region north of the Gila, as well as California and most of New Mexico, became United States' territory. The Pinacates, El Camino del Diablo, Tucson, and the rest of

The original, fertile appearance of rivers in southern Arizona is still shown by the headwaters of the Santa Cruz River, where the water table remains high. Sonora; eight miles south of the border. September, 1987.

The frank, confident manner in which [a Maricopa Indian] approached us was in strange contrast with that of the suspicious Apache. [The Pimos'] mode of approach . . . was perfectly frank and unsuspicious. Many would leave their packs in our camp and be absent for hours, theft seeming to be unknown among them.

We were at once impressed with the beauty, order, and disposition of the arrangements for irrigating and draining the land. Corn, wheat, and cotton are the crops of this peaceful and intelligent race of people . . .

To us it was a rare sight to be thrown in the midst of a large nation of what is termed wild Indians, surpassing many of the Christian nations in agriculture, little behind them in the useful arts, and immeasurably before them in honesty and virtue. During the whole of yesterday, our camp was full of men, women, and children who sauntered amongst our packs, unwatched, and not a single instance of theft was reported . . .[9]

southern Arizona south of the Gila were still part of Mexico.

Down the Gila River from New Mexico in November, 1846, after wresting Santa Fe from the Mexicans, came General Stephan Kearny and his "advance guard from the Army of the West." Guided by Kit Carson, they made a military reconnaissance of the lands the United States was about to inherit. An official report by Lt. William Emory gives a good description of the northern edge of the Sonoran Desert heartland at that time. Two days after he visited Casa Grande ruin, Emory marvelled at the character of the "Pimo" and Maricopa Indians and their beautiful lands along the Gila River at the site of present-day Phoenix:

Twelve days later, when they were crossing the Colorado River near the present site of Yuma, Emory's notes record in very different terms the hearsay they received about the southern route along El Camino del Diablo:

Departing from the ford . . . in the direction of Sonora, there is a fearful desert to encounter . . . All accounts concur in representing the journey as one of extreme hardship, and even peril. The distance is not exactly known, but it is variously represented at from four to seven days' journey.

Based on this evidence, Emory recommended the Gila route over El Camino del Diablo. Kearny's army passed on across the Colorado through even drier country, eventually reaching San Diego to take California.

The Treaty of Guadalupe Hidalgo in 1848 made the Gila the border between the United States and Mexico.

In 1849 everything changed. The California gold rush led to the migrations of the '49ers. In the Southwest, travelers had to choose between the Gila route and the Mexican route. Although it was the best route, the Gila was plagued by Apache raiding parties. Many travelers thus attempted the Mexican route, which was relatively free of Indian raiders, especially in the summer. The Mexican route took travelers south and west from Tucson, down Sonora's Altar River valley, and then north from the rough frontier towns of Caborca or Altar toward tiny Sonoita and a dash across El Camino del Diablo. Broiling August continued to be a favored season for travel, not only because of the lack of Indians, but also because of the sporadic summer afternoon rains that, with luck, filled the tanks. Sonoita and the rock-bound tinajas on El Camino del Diablo were suddenly the focus of life-and-death interest. Travelers who embarked without clear knowledge of the tinajas faced likely death. There were many ill-informed souls; an estimated 400 gold-seekers died along El Camino del Diablo during the 1849-50 gold rush and the following decade!

There are few records of '49ers' trips across the region—perhaps because most of them would have preferred to forget the experience. One record tells of a trip by John Woodhouse Audubon, son of the famous bird painter. Encouraged by his father, John also became a naturalist and painter. By the time of the gold rush, he was 36 and had joined one of the California-bound parties. Interpersonal strife, early bouts with cholera, and the prompt defection of the leader, left Audubon in charge of the remaining group of 48 men. One morning in September, 1849, at 4 A.M., they left the Altar River and headed northward across the central Sonoran Desert. Audubon's journal lacks geographic specificity, but they traveled more or less north all the way to the Gila River before turning west downstream to the Colorado.

Along the beach where Hardy sat in 1826, near mouth of Sonoita River. November 28, 1986.

Audubon gives a striking description of the Indians east of the Pinacates in the fall of 1849:

> *The people live on turtles, and what game they can get . . . We came to some of their burial mounds, and saw the kettles and culinary articles of this poor people left for the dead . . . They are happy in their faith, and with no dissenting voices about this method of salvation or that . . .*
>
> *Why it is that these Indians settle in such a country, I cannot conceive, for even the lizards, in most places innumerable, are scarce here.*[10]

Audubon pressed on across the desert, and down the Gila—"such travel, as please God, I trust none of us ever see again . . ." Audubon's party reached California, but some curse of the desert dogged Audubon years later. During the trip, he had made nearly 200 watercolors and sketches—an invaluable frontier record that we might yearn to discover. But when he had them sent from California, they were lost in a shipwreck, along with the life of a close friend who was transporting them.

At the end of his life, Audubon reminisced about "the Gila desert of awful memories." He dwelled on it even in a delirium on his deathbed 13 years later.

A second record of a '49er trip recounts a journey of a less famous but no less courageous party, who traveled directly along El Camino del Diablo. In the spring of 1850, Don Francisco Salazar, at age 17, joined about 20 Sonorans who left to get rich in California.[11] Though the gold rush was only months old, Salazar already observed signs of the horrifying toll El Camino del Diablo would exact in the coming years. This unique record is worth quoting in some detail.

> For food, we carried large quantities of carne seca [sun-dried beef], pinole [parched corn or wheat meal], and panocha [a sweet product made from sugar cane]. Our water bags—absolute necessities on such a trip—were made of 'vaqueta' [leather], well smeared on the outside with tallow and then covered with a woven mat of grass . . . These water bags were then [and yet are] made by the Indians of Mexico.
>
> Not all of us had horses . . . Each member of the party carried 'dos pistolas' [two pistols] and a 'carabina' [rifle] . . . We had to travel at night for fear of the Apache, and concealed ourselves and stock during the day . . .
>
> Between Sonoita and Tinajas Altas [water could be obtained only at] Las Tinajas del Tule . . . and between the Tinajas Altas and the Colorado, there was absolutely no water of any kind.

> When nearing Tinajas Altas, we camped in a secluded spot some distance from the tanks, fearing an Indian ambush. We then drew lots for the purpose of selecting three men who were to go after water; it fell to my lot to be one of that group. Water was not plentiful at the Tinajas and we had a great deal of difficulty in getting sufficient for our needs . . . All these activities had to be performed after nightfall under the supervision of our guide.
>
> At Tinajas Altas—in the old days—Apache were always skulking in the nearby hills and arroyos ready to pounce upon weary or weakened parties or some careless and unwary traveler. The Indians—sneaking from place to place—would signal each other by imitating the cry or call of various wild birds and animals, such as the owl, crow, coyote, etc. At times—around the tanks—these calls could be heard continually, giving to the surroundings a weird and unearthly setting, as if the evil spirits of countless generations were hovering about the place.
>
> The immediate area around the Tinajas was a vast graveyard of unknown dead and the road from there to the Colorado was marked the whole way by the dried carcasses of mules, horses, and cattle and the scattered bones of human beings, slowly turning into dust. In such a region but little time can be given to conventional things and the dead were left where they fell to be sepulchered (if at all) by the fearful sand storms that sweep at times over the desolate waste.

The reason for the "vast graveyard" at Tinajas Altas was that these fabled many-tiered tanks were the destination of most travelers, and many of them found the lowest tank emptied by previous visitors. Water might exist in the second tank or the third, but the upper tanks required a hard climb up smooth, steep rock faces. Having dragged the last dozen miles across the featureless, flat approach to Tinajas Altas, many travelers arrived too exhausted to make the climb and perished at the foot of the steep slope, only 50 feet from lifesaving water. Others climbed partway to higher tanks, only to slip to their deaths.

IN 1854, THE MAP CHANGED AGAIN with the Gadsden Purchase, which acquired lands south of the Gila River. The new border between Arizona and Sonora had to be surveyed. An early proposal placed the diagonal line south of the Pinacates, terminating at the Colorado's mouth. But for the stroke of a pen, the Pinacates and their craters might have become an American national park, and there might have been a booming American shipping port on the Colorado delta. Instead, the Arizona-Sonora border eventually took its present form, running west-northwest from the bend just north of Arizonac, where silver had been found in 1736. It passed just a few miles north of Kino's old stopover at Sonoita, and only a few hundred yards south of the history-rich springs at Quitobaquito. Continuing in a straight line, it crossed the north tip of the Pinacate lavas along the old Camino del Diablo, a mile or so south of Tinajas Altas, and on to the Colorado about 19 miles south of Yuma.

The readjustment prompted new Yankee exploration. Our tales so far have been of travelers passing across the Sonoran Desert without penetrating into the black heart of the Pinacate lava fields, where Kino and friends had found wonder, knowledge, and terror. At last a new generation of rough explorers began to rediscover and rerecord the Pinacates' natural wonders. In his monograph on the area, geographer Ronald Ives[12] asserts that shortly after 1850, local folklore already told of holes that "went clear down to Hell," echoing the terror experienced by Manje, Kino, and Salvatierra.

In 1854, Col. Andrew B. Gray led a survey across the Sonoran Desert to find a route for the Southern Pacific Railroad. Gray published a detailed but dry report, which was reprinted in 1963, with a more vivid personal memoir by Gray's assistant, Peter R. Brady. Brady called his leader "one of the most amiable and even tempered men . . . He was an optimist of the first order and everything was rosy hued to him." Gray's expedition yielded the first "modern" description of the volcanic features of the Pinacates. Gray wrote:

> *Fifteen miles from Adair Bay is an immense bed of lava and volcanic stones, burnt and twisted into every conceivable shape; also a large and distinct crater. In some of the cavities of these rocks, we came across vast natural tanks of delicious water, and discovered an extensive field of obsidian . . .*[13]

Gray's assistant, Brady, described more vividly their journey across the Pinacates from their camp on the Sonoita River close to Kino's old El Carrizal:

> *We made a very early start and about nine o'clock we arrived at a very large tank of clear water up in the mountains, in what appeared to us to be the crater of an extinct volcano, which it really was and was known as the Pinacate Mountain. There was said to be five or six of these extinct craters in other parts of the mountain. We did not see them, but from the enormous quantity of lava, comparatively of recent formation, we could readily believe it. However, the one we camped at was the largest and contained thousands of tons of water. It was evidently a favorite camping ground for the Indians at certain seasons of the year. There were signs of old huts, fish bones, turtle and marine shells, which showed us that we were not very far from the gulf.*
>
> *We left in the afternoon, made another dry camp, and next day after wading through a chain of sand dunes, we came in sight of the waters of Adair Bay, that had not been visited by white man since Lt. Hardy of the Royal Navy, in 1827. I did remember the name of his blasted little brig but*

have forgotten it and sincerely wished that he had never sailed . . .

The last outburst was occasioned by the fact that Gray insisted on the uncomfortable trip across the dunes only because he had read Hardy's account and wanted to claim his own visit to the coast, dragging Brady along on what Brady considered a foolish trek.

What Gray and Brady mean by "crater" is unclear. No tank lies *in* a major crater. The standard route to Adair Bay from El Carrizal was down the southeast side of the mountains and across the south flank to the large tank cluster and Indian campground at Cuervo Tanks, south of the peaks. This is the route Kino followed in 1701, and the route documented by a subsequent French traveler in 1878. The persistence of this route over nearly two centuries is remarkable, and lends credence to the identification of Cuervo Tanks as the spot where Gray's party stopped. The guide who referred to five or six extinct craters may have been thinking of the handful of spectacular giant pits, such as Elegante, Sykes, and MacDougal craters, but Gray and Brady probably never saw them.

Next year, in 1855, Lieutenant N. Michler charted the new border for the Office of the United States and Mexican Boundary Survey. Like Audubon, he was fundamentally an Easterner: he loved leafy vistas and was aghast at the barren desert. His report is a dry account, but he could not help inserting a vivid personal recollection of El Camino del Diablo:

Well do I recollect the ride from Sonoita to Fort Yuma and back, in the middle of August, 1855. It was the most dreary and tiresome I have ever experienced. Imagination cannot picture a more dreary, sterile country, and we named it the 'malpais.' The burnt lime-like appearance of the soil is ever before you; the very stones look like the scoriae of a furnace; there is no grass, and but a sickly vegetation, *more unpleasant to the sight than the barren earth itself; scarce an animal to be seen . . . naught to give life and animation to this region . . . All traces of the road are sometimes erased by the high winds sweeping the unstable soil before them, but death has strewn a continuous line of bleached bones and withered carcasses of horses and cattle, as monuments to mark the way.*

On our way to the post from Sonoita we met many emigrants returning from California, men and animals suffering from scarcity of water. Some men had died from thirst, and others were nearly exhausted. Among those we passed between the Colorado and the 'Tinajas Altas' was a party composed of one woman and three men, on foot, a packhorse in wretched condition carrying their all. The men had given up from pure exhaustion and laid down to die; but the woman, animated by love and sympathy, had plodded on over the long road until she reached water, then clambering up the side of the mountain to the highest tinaja, she filled her bota, (a sort of leather flask) and scarcely stopping to take rest, started back to resuscitate her dying companions. When we met them, she was striding along in advance of the men, animating them by her example.[14]

Michler was not impressed with the village of Sonoita, which he described as "a resort for smugglers, and a den for a number of low, abandoned Americans, who have been compelled to fly from justice . . . It is a miserable poverty-stricken place, and contrasts strangely with the comparative comfort of an Indian village of Papagos within sight."

Michler did not actually enter the Pinacates, and seems curiously unaware of the volcanic nature of the Pinacate Mountains. Apparently relying on hearsay, he reports that their main features of interest are masses of rock salt!

[South of Quitobaquito and the nearby Cerros de la Salada, or Salty Hills] the country is open, presenting to the view a bold and isolated mountain group at some distance, known as Sierra Pinacate. Its name, signifying beetle, does not seem to have reference to any peculiarity in appearance or formation. In consequence of the entire absence of water, the Sierra Pinacate is almost inaccessible; it is, however, celebrated throughout Sonora for wonderful and inexhaustible layers of rocksalt, which is said to be stored up in immense masses, arranged in diversified strata and of a variety of colors.

The Pinacates are *not* known for salt deposits; probably Michler was confused by local stories of the salt deposits near Quitobaquito, described by Garcés and de Anza in 1774, or by accounts of Indian journeys through the Pinacates to reach colorful salt deposits some twenty miles beyond them, on the shore of the Gulf.

After months in the desert heart, Michler headed back east along the Gila from Yuma. Here, desert-weary Michler waxed ecstatic over the fertility of "old Arizona"—the Arizona lost to us forever, due to the consumption and lowering of the underground water table. It is ironic to read these reports of the green valleys where barren Phoenix and Tucson now stand, and realize that we are converting the modern environment of most urban Arizonans into the very sort of desert that horrified Audubon and Michler! Between Gila Bend and Phoenix, an area noteworthy today for its visual sterility, Michler remarked,

As we journeyed along this portion of the valley of the Gila we found lands fenced in, and irrigated by many miles of acequias, and our eyes were gladdened with the sight of rich fields of wheat ripening for the harvest—a view differing from anything we had seen since leaving the Atlantic States. They grow cotton, sugar, peas, wheat, and corn . . .

Not everyone accepted the sanctity of the new boundary line being charted by Michler. Through Sonoita in 1857 came Captain H. A. Crabbe and his "filibuster" expedition (the word is derived from Dutch for freebooter, or pirate), bent on conquering a piece of Mexico. They got as far as Caborca where they beseiged the embattled population in the town church. A Papago Indian shot a flaming arrow onto the roof of the building the filibusters occupied. The filibusters were driven out and killed. The American bullet holes in the Caborca church were visible for years.[15]

THE FIRST REALLY PERSONAL ACCOUNT of travels through the area describes travels in 1860-62 by Raphael Pumpelly.[16] Pumpelly had come west at that time as a mining engineer for a mine near Tucson, but ended his career as a world-ranging travel writer and mining consultant. Pumpelly's was a journal of sensations and feelings. Even Kino's diary, by comparison, becomes that of a theologian whose mythic constructs and optimistic goals were more important to him than what he *saw* or *felt*. Pumpelly rivals Zane Grey for thrills and sensations, yet wrote not as a novelist romanticizing the West decades later, but as an eyewitness. Once he described riding into his camp near Tucson to discover that everyone had been massacred by Apaches only hours before. Pumpelly's were the kind of observations from which Hollywood created the mythos of The Old West (in that bygone era when Hollywood drew on original source material instead of copying itself). Pumpelly portrayed life among both the Anglos and the natives:

There was hardly a pretense at a civil organization; law was unknown, and the nearest court was several hundred miles distant in New Mexico. Indeed, every man took the law into his own hands, and the life of a neighbor was valued in the inverse ratio of the impunity with which it could be taken. Thus

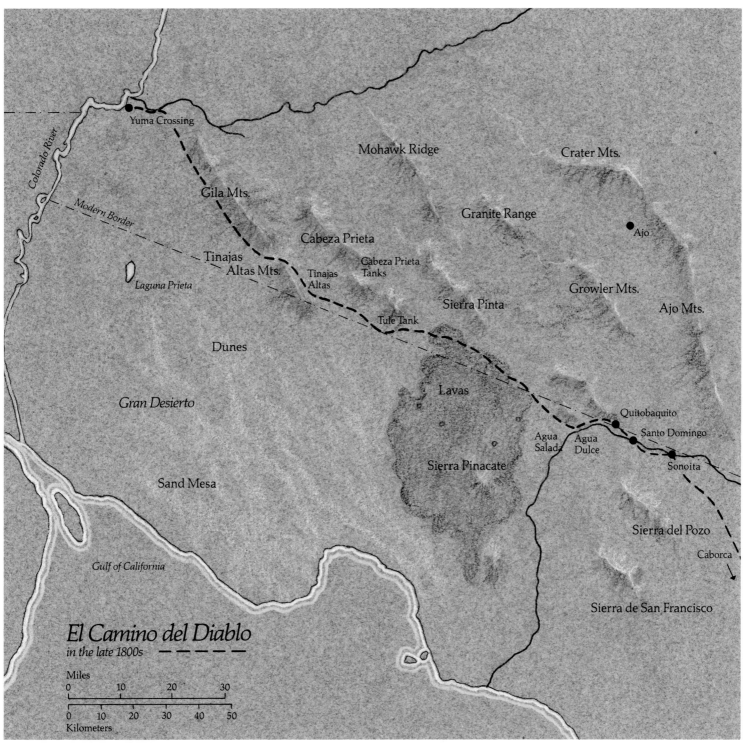

Map of El Camino del Diablo route.

Lower tank at Tinajas Alta. In some years, water from this tank was used up. Several tanks tens of feet higher on the cliff usually contained water, but many exhausted travelers died attempting to climb the sheer rock walls to reach them. Photo, Gayle Hartmann, April 1, 1989.

public opinion became the only code of laws, and a citizen's popularity the measure of his safety . . .

With the influx of a mining population, the Indians . . . are gradually driven to the most barren parts of the mountains . . . Whether they oppose bravely at first the inroads of the whites, or submit peacefully to every outrage until forced by famine to seek the means of life among the herds of the intruder, the result is the same. Sometimes hunted from place to place in open war; sometimes their warriors enticed away under peaceful promises by one party, while a confederate band descends on the native settlements, massacring women and children, old and young; . . . No treaty or flag of truce is too sacred to be disregarded, no weapons too cruel or cowardly to be used or recommended by the Americans.

In the towns and camps of Pumpelly's Old West, violence flares and women nurse the survivors. Setting out on one occasion, he reflects on "leaving a country where the men are mostly cutthroats and the women angels . . ."

One day, Pumpelly and an early Arizona explorer, Colonel C. D. Poston, found themselves in Caborca. Seeking a way back to California, they decided on the dangerous route northwest to Sonoita and across El Camino del Diablo, in spite of being warned that Fort Yuma, at the Colorado River crossing, had been abandoned and the sparse water holes were nearly dry due to two rainless seasons. As if that weren't enough, a local priest had recently been murdered, and 12 desperados in Caborca were openly organizing a band to follow and waylay Pumpelly's party "for the sake of the large quantity of silver we were supposed to have in our baggage. Our friends . . . advised us to increase our force before continuing the journey."

Pumpelly and Poston recruited a Mexican guide and an American named Williams, who had lately ap-

peared in Caborca "dying from hunger and thirst," and had been nursed back to health by the kindly old sister of the recently murdered priest. The party now consisted of four well-armed men, who set out northwest toward Sonoita. By the third day, they found that the 12 brigands were already on the trail ahead of them, planning an ambush, and heading for Sonoita. Pumpelly's band prudently took a shortcut around Sonoita, toward Cipriano Ortega's tiny settlement, Santo Domingo, between Sonoita and Quitobaquito. Here a messenger informed them they had pulled ahead of the desperados.

As Pumpelly's party headed west across the desert the next morning, they were joined on the trail by two more armed Americans. Now they felt safe from their pursuers, but as they pressed on, one moonlit night among the dark lavas and snowy-light granite hills, Pumpelly and Williams fell behind in conversation. Williams, induced by his brandy to share his thoughts, pointed out along the trail a grave of someone he had shot on an earlier trip.

"He's rotten now, I reckon," Williams said. "I told him I'd spit more than once on his grave, and by God I've done it." As Williams' violent conversation rambled on, the truth dawned on Pumpelly: Williams had been one of the party that had murdered the priest back in Caborca; ironically, it was the victim's unwitting sister who had nursed him back to health a short while later. Pumpelly now confronted Williams with the accusation:

"Who kept the priest's robes?" I asked, looking him full in the face.

At these words, Williams started and made a motion toward his pistol; but seeing that I had the advantage, inasmuch as my hand rested on my revolver, he simply exclaimed: "What the devil do you know about the priest's robes?"

But Pumpelly had gained Williams' confidence with the sharing of brandy, and Williams readily confessed the tale, adding as a good joke that the sister had given him a letter to deliver to her daughters in California.

This exchange in the moonlight occurred, appropriately, along El Camino del Diablo. Now Pumpelly and Poston began keeping a wary eye on their murderous colleague. At the same time, Pumpelly described the country through which they were passing, west of Quitobaquito, during that late summer of 1861. Around them lay the relics of the '49ers:

> *In the distance, on either side, arise high granite mountains, to which the eye turns in vain for relief; they are barren and dazzling masses of rock. Night brought only parching winds, while during the day we sought in vain for shelter from the fierce sun-rays. The thermometer ranged by day between 118 and 126 degrees in the shade . . . The routes over these wastes are marked by countless skeletons of cattle, horses, and sheep, and the traveler passes thousands of the carcasses of these animals wholly preserved in the intensely dry air. Many . . . had been placed upright on their feet by previous travelers. As we wound, in places, through groups of these mummies, they seemed sentinels guarding the valley of death . . .*
>
> *. . . Before us lay a continuous ride of nearly thirty hours, before we could hope to find the nearest water . . .*
>
> *But during the night the sky was overcast with black clouds, and there came the first rain that had fallen on this desert for more than two years. Never was storm more welcome; . . . with the rising sun began the heat of another day. A broad sheet of water, only a few inches deep, covered the playa for miles . . . and banished . . . all fear of suffering.*

Years later, in 1918, Pumpelly wrote that this storm saved their lives. As they rode across the plain,

Pumpelly commented also on the Pinacate lavas:

> *Across the center of this great plain there stretches, from north to south, a mass of lava about one mile wide, and extending southward as far as the eye can reach. On this lava wall there stand two parallel rows of extinct volcanic cones, 100 to 300 feet high, with craters. In crossing this remarkable remnant of recent volcanic action, I could look down the long and perfect vista of regular cones, till they faded away in the perspective and behind the curvature of the earth.*

Pumpelly noted that one of the cones here seemed hollow to him. This curious remark demands further exploration; but perhaps there is nothing extraordinary here, since many lava flows sound hollow due to underground lava tubes, or drained conduits, buried under lava crusts less than a foot thick.

At Tinajas Altas, he noted that for dehydrated travelers who arrived too weak to climb to the pools above, "the tanks, in which they seek for life, become their graves." From Tinajas Altas they rode on to the Gila and thence to the Colorado. And what of Williams? By the time they reached the Colorado, Williams was obviously laying a trap to attack the party. Poston, gun drawn, confronted Williams, at a moment when they had him alone, and ordered him to disappear. "With a hearty laugh, Williams held out his hand. '. . . You're sharper by a damned sight than I had thought you was; . . . bully for you!'" He rode off and that was the last they saw of him. Pumpelly concludes, soberly, "I have given this scene in full, as an illustration of the character of a representative of one type of the frontiersman."

As for the bandits that had tried to waylay them at the start of their journey, Poston later heard in Sonora that 12 of them had tracked Pumpelly's party for more than 200 miles along the Camino del Diablo into California, but "finding us always on the watch, had not dared attack . . ."

Cipriano Ortega's hacienda, Santo Domingo, west of Sonoita. Photo from MacDougal expedition, November, 1907. (Courtesy Arizona Historical Society.)

A MICROCOSM OF BORDER LIFE in the later 1800s was the little oasis of Quitobaquito. Here, water percolates to the surface through underground faults caused by the ancient seismic turmoil of the area. The water's warmth testifies to the latent geothermal power of the region. Water at 80F bubbles from the ground in springs scattered over several acres at the base of some brown, barren hills about 15 miles west of Sonoita and 20 miles east of the Pinacate lavas. The site is now reached by a picturesque 18-mile dirt road in Organ Pipe Cactus National Monument. In contrast to the sun-blasted hills and sparse desert growth around it, Quitobaquito offers tall, shady cottonwoods and green havens for birds, small game, and human travelers.

At Quitobaquito, Kino had found a small Indian settlement that he called *San Serguio.* Indians frequented the place because of its sure supply of water. On the dirt road near the springs, one can still see an Indian trail shrine—a cairn where travelers used to leave good-luck offerings.

Michler's Boundary Commission party in 1855 set the U.S. border about a hundred yards south of the springs. Already the local Indians were grouped under the term Wild Papagos, because some of them had the disturbing habit of assaulting Anglo and Spanish travelers. Within a few years, an American, Adolf Dorsey, displaced the Indians and began to make Quitobaquito his own. Dorsey began his improvements in 1862. By clearing alluvium and plants from the fissures, he increased the water's flow rate. The National Park Service estimates that the total flow of all the springs reached 40 gallons per minute. The present rate is less, but an idyllic pond remains. Dorsey built a dike and irrigation ditches. Quitobaquito prospered.

In its heyday, the oasis boasted a store, an ore-grinding mill, and a small cattle ranch. Alphonse Pinart, a French explorer who came through in 1879, described Quitobaquito as a rancho of a few *casas,* some on the Mexican side and some on the American side. Among the desert characters who frequented the area was Cipriano Ortega, the man who, around 1875, installed the Wellton bell in a chapel built at his nearby hacienda, Santo Domingo, and worked a silver mine in the Sierra del Viejo, about 20 miles northwest of the Pinacate lavas.[17] Wild burros were common in the area and one of Ortega's exploits, reported by Lumholtz, was to shoot 100 of them to sell their fat to soap manufacturers. A Park Service sign at Quitobaquito identifies Ortega, somewhat misleadingly, as a "colorful . . . Mexican bandit."

Three Americans, Tom Childs, Rube Daniels and John Merrill, married three Papago sisters and settled at Quitobaquito. Ives[18] records that according to local gossip in 1932, Childs, born in 1870, had married a Papago to learn the secret location of gold that had supposedly been stolen by Indians from the old Sonoita mission many years before. Childs eventually left to take a job in the copper mine at nearby Ajo, Arizona, and helped later researchers develop a history of the area.[19]

Among the few signs of Quitobaquito's short-lived status as an outpost of civilization are overgrown irrigation ditches and the prominent grave of a little-known resident, José Lorenzo Sestier, whose inscription testifies to an unusual life: "Born Brest France . . . Died Quitobaquito Ariz . . . Feb 3 1900 . . . Age 74."

Indians remained important at Quitobaquito until well into this century. The Papago chief medicine man of the area from the 1860s to the early 1900s was named Juan José. He was followed by José Juan Orosco, who maintained grazing rights in the area until about 1945.

Today the pond and its dirt access road are part of Organ Pipe Cactus National Monument. A few hundred

The circle monument along El Camino del Diablo, west of Cabeza Prieta Hills. Looking east, showing pebbles in disarray, right. Photo, Vincent Roth, January 1, 1959.

yards south, on the other side of a low barbed-wire fence, cars whiz by on Mexico Highway 2, bound between Sonoita and San Luis, Mexicali, or Tijuana. On the American side, a few cars stop in the parking lot and travelers picnic under the cottonwoods by the pond or watch the birds who know the oasis as a welcome stop-over.

In the late 1800s, the dirt path from Quitobaquito west into the desert still led to death for many. In 1871, a mysterious visitor named Nameer traveled the old road. Perhaps he died there. No one knows. But beside the Camino, on the black, gravelly lavas of the northernmost Pinacate flows, boulders have been left undisturbed for a hundred years spelling out in neat but strangely out-of-place ciphers:

1871
NAMEER

Looking northeast, showing one of the dark-topped Cabeza Prieta Hills and the "restored" figure 8. April 1, 1989.

The site is called *Nameer's grave.* Or is it merely a 19th-century "Kilroy was here?"

Farther west along the Camino is a prominent stone circle with a bar of stones across it, and a cryptic figure next to the bar. This site is usually associated with a party of eight who died and were buried on the Camino, and the figure was said to be a figure 8. In 1949, writer Harold Weight described the figure as looking like "a crude figure of a man running," providing a photo. In a 1959 photo the figure looks too amorphous to be a clear 8; the stones are more like a cluster. But in later photos, it shows up again as an 8; apparently someone has "restored" the figure.

There is mystery about this site. As early as 1896, an account was published by D. D. Gaillard, who had traveled through the region around 1893 as a member of an International Boundary Commission.[20] He remarks that no vehicle had traveled El Camino del Diablo since

1877. A keen observer of the morbid trail, he counted 50 graves at Tinajas Altas. He describes the story of the circle as one of the "best known and most pathetic cases of death from thirst" along El Camino.

> *. . . an entire Mexican family of six or eight persons, . . . were pushing on toward Las Tinajas Altas, their total supply of water contained in a wicker-covered glass demijohn. When about eight miles from the tanks, their horses gave out, and in unloading the wagon, by some unfortunate accident, their demijohn was broken. . . . the husband set out to find [the tanks, but failed and] returned from his unsuccessful search and joined his dying family under a neighboring palo verde tree where their bodies were all found by the next traveler, and buried in a single grave beside the road. Pious hands had piled stones on the grave in the form of a cross, and had encircled the whole by a ring, about thirty feet in diameter . . . The wagon tracks made when the poor Mexican drove his exhausted team to one side of the road, were plainly visible thirty years afterward, and at the very spot still remained pieces of glass and wickerwork from the broken demijohn, and the skulls of two horses.*

Gaillard's account implies that the event happened in the 1860s. He apparently observed the rocks carefully in 1893, and says they were in the form of a cross, rather than the figure 8 observed later. He gives a photo of the site from the 1890s, showing a central cross and no bar across the circle. National Geographic Society vice-president W. J. McGee also described a "great pebble cross" in 1900.[21] Weight, in 1949, says that the caliche stains on the rocks in the center showed they had been arranged more recently than the rocks in the ring, consistent with the idea that the original cross had been dismantled and rearranged.

Weight said he had been told on an earlier visit that

the structure was an old Indian sign, with the bar pointing toward Tinajas Altas, about 10-1/2 miles to the west. But Weight cited Gaillard as the more authoritative source. The matter might have ended there, but a month after Weight's article was published, a letter appeared in the same magazine from Thomas Childs, the well-known old-timer of the area.[22] Childs said he was writing "to correct your information as to the death of the Mexican family where the rock circle and the crosses (sic) were erected along the road near Tinajas Altas." Childs claimed that it was a murder site. He said he had traveled on El Camino in about 1884 with two old Papagos. When he asked them "about the crosses" they said they had killed some travelers in the area. Having no use for the gold they were carrying, the Papagos had thrown it among the creosote bushes, but kept the leather bags, which they could use. Childs later married the daughter of one of these men, and said "she recalled her father had told her about it, and that it was just about as I have stated above." He also claims that Mexicans in those days would not carry their water in glass, but in goatskin bags, "so the version of the tragedy could not have been as written in your magazine."

There are three problems with Childs' version. First, Gaillard specifically mentions seeing the glass fragments in 1893, supporting his version. Childs had probably not read Gaillard's original version, and hence does not respond to the glass fragments actually there. Second, Gaillard mentions that the story he recounted was one of the "best known" tragedies of El Camino. Third, Childs refers to "crosses" when apparently only one stone cross existed at the site. There were, however, many graves and probably many crosses at Tinajas Altas by 1884. I am inclined to accept the Gaillard record. Possibly, Childs is speaking of a different site with a circle and several crosses. Alternatively, perhaps his Indian friends had constructed their own tall tale.

In 1887, the region displayed its tectonic energy.[23] Sonoita was shaken by an earthquake of considerable

Barren country along El Camino del Diablo. View northeast in the Tule Mountains, with basaltic ridges in mid-distance and pale, granitic Sierra Pinta ridge in distance. October 19, 1985.

violence. Known locally as a *temblor grande*, the earthquake caused some interesting results. Most striking was a reported shift in the course of the Sonoita River channel where it wound through the little village. As the river moved, so moved the town. By about 1890 to 1900 the town shifted a couple of miles to the west, leaving the ancient Indian village site and the ruins of Kino's and Ruhen's mission to the remorseless desert.

Journal entry. Music of the Desert Heart. June 14, 1988.
Many places have their own music. If you have never been to the lava country, you can understand its somber beauty if you listen to English composer Ralph Vaughn Williams' Symphony No. 7, Sinfonia Antarctica. We are in the first generation who can put the Sinfonia Antarctica on a cassette in our Walkmans and amble across the torrents and cataracts of

rock—a unique confluence of two universes. Words convey certain facets of a landscape; pictures, others; but music conveys still other essences.

Vaughn Williams composed the music in 1947-48 for a film about Scott's explorations, and recast it into a symphony by 1952. It dates from the same period when Ives was making the first systematic explorations of the Pinacate region. Vaughn Williams created this aural universe when he was 80.

How can a symphony about antarctic ice evoke the Sonoran Desert, someone will say. The essence of a desert is not heat, but lack of liquid water. The essence of lava is that rock matter has melted and spewed forth as liquid, and then frozen, as if in a moment of surprise at finding itself in the surface. In both Antarctica and the Pinacates, there is lack of water. In the Pinacates, the rocks are made of silicon; in Antarctica, the "rocks" are made of ice. Both places manifest contorted masses of fluid "rock" matter, frozen in place. Vaughn Williams quoted poetic passages at the beginning of each movement of his symphony. Each of them could apply to the explorations of the Pinacate country: ". . . To defy power which seems omnipotent . . ., This is alone life, joy, empire, and victory." (Shelley); "I do not regret this journey; we took risks . . . things came out against us . . ." (Scott,

from his journal as he perished in the ice). And by amazing confluence he prefaced the ghostly and godly third movement, Landscape, with these lines in which Coleridge describes ice flows at dawn, but, as well the lava crags: "Torrents, methinks, that heard a mighty voice, and stopped at once amidst their maddest plunge! Motionless torrents: Silent cataracts."

You need one more piece of music on your tape to experience the Pinacate landscape. That is a second film score, the Academy Award-winning music by French composer Maurice Jarre for the 1962 film, Lawrence of Arabia. Through its own musical content and through the screen images of David Lean, this becomes music for El Camino del Diablo, the cinder flats, the majestic dunes of the Gran Desierto—geologically and climatically the same kind of country T. E. Lawrence rode through in Arabia. This music, with its combination of otherworldly mystery and jaunty innocence, seemed personal to me in my early trips to the Pinacates: I was entering this desert from leafy Pennsylvania at about the same age that Lawrence was entering his desert from leafy England. The experience left some of the same effects. The desert became a presence in one's life, like an old love affair or a brush with death. And the music crystallized a sense of the desert heart, beauty haunted by tragedy, with Manje's fear and terror lurking around every pastel corner.

6. Explorer-Writers: The Great Expeditions

On a whizzing cold night in January, 1907, Dr. Daniel Trembly MacDougal said to me: "Look here! I wish you to go with me on a fine desert trip, in the near future; and I also wish you to know there are mighty few men whom I ever invite to go with me into the deserts."

William Hornaday
Camp-Fires on Desert and Lava, 1908

. . . an expedition of this kind directs one's thoughts into other channels than those of the ordinary humdrum of life. The starlit sky, under which one sleeps with impunity, invites imagination to take flight into the infinite universe, and one has time to reflect on the beauty of existence and the grandeur of nature, a pleasure . . . denied to most dwellers in cities.

Carl Lumholtz
New Trails in Mexico, 1912

JUST AS A PROPHET IS WITHOUT HONOR in his or her own country, a landscape is without honor among its own residents. Thus, few Southwesterners have written books about the desert's heart. But with the beginning of the 20th century, naturalists and travel writers from distant climes began to savor the Sonoran Desert for its own sake. They followed in the great tradition of English writers who traveled to darkest Africa, Arabia, and the South Seas to seek adventure, gain wisdom and write a book. With their enthusiasm and erudition, these new travelers created a genre of American travel-adventure book, which flowered in the early decades of this century but has faded in an age of intrusive television and closing frontiers.

These expeditions launched a new century of exploration. The first and strangest commenced in 1898 when John C. Van Dyke, a 42-year-old Rutgers University art historian and critic, rode alone, eastward into the desert near what is now Palm Springs, California. With a fox terrier, a pistol, a rifle, minimal supplies and usually with his Indian pony, this asthmatic aesthete wandered for nearly three years across the deserts of California, Arizona, Mexico and even farther afield. Un-

fortunately, his exact route is not known, and even he did not always know where he was. In an early part of the trip, he traversed the Salton Sea Basin, crossed the Colorado below Yuma on a raft he built himself, followed the railroad line just south of the Gila River to Tucson, and then set out west into the desert near Baboquivari and on into Sonora where he wandered for months, sometimes without seeing another soul for six weeks. We may guess that he passed near the Pinacates, but he also visited Hermosillo, Guaymas and other sites. He was motivated to seek both health and beauty in the dry lands. He says that the desert "never had a sacred poet; it has in me only a lover."

He produced an amazing, unique book, *The Desert*, published in 1901. It is not a book of personal adventure, but a description of ruminations about civilization and descriptions of extraordinary effects of light and color in the empty air. "Pure sunlight requires pure air," he said—a lesson we have barely begun to learn in our hazy cities. An apostle of his own concept of "sensuous seeing," he analyzed with scientific precision and poetic prose the causes of various phenomena, from erosion to sky colors, from evolution to the causes of our aesthetic

Previous page: Elephant tree near Emilia Tank. May 24, 1978.   *Grass and basalt at Papago Tanks. April 6, 1977.*

responses to different landscapes. He wrote very little about his personal day-to-day adventures. Later he said that most of the book was written during his first desert summer "at odd intervals when I lay with my back against a rock or propped up in the sand." He mailed the manuscript to Scribner's from Del Rio, Texas, in May of 1901. The legacy he leaves the reader is that

> *The aesthetic sense—the power to enjoy through the eye, the ear and the imagination—is just as important a factor in the scheme of human happiness as the corporeal sense of eating and drinking; but there has never been a time when the world would admit it.*[1]

The second expedition was a party headed by W. J. McGee, vice-president of the National Geographic Society. McGee's party passed through Phoenix, Gila Bend, and Ajo, then south through Sonoita to Caborca; they visited the coast and then returned north to Santo Domingo, Cipriano Ortega's tiny village a few miles southeast of Quitobaquito. In November, 1900, a six-mule wagon and McGee's party departed Santo Domingo to explore the "Old Yuma Trail," as McGee called El Camino del Diablo. Eight travelers included McGee, artist De Lancey Gill, Tucson professor R. H. Forbes, and five stockmen and interpreters. McGee ultimately recounted the adventure in a two-part illustrated article in National Geographic published the same year as Van Dyke's book about the same general region.[2]

McGee noted that west of Quitobaquito, the old Camino near the Sonoita River had been cut so deeply by wheelmarks that the river had diverted from its old channel to flow in the old road, and a new trail had been started. They recorded "the first graves of the Old Yuma Trail" as early as the Agua Salada campsite at the southward bend of the Sonoita River.

The party now crossed the northern tongue of Pinacate lavas, where they noted the volcanic forms.

Claiming to "rectify the reports of the pioneers," he ironically garbled the volcanic geology, misreporting that the "Sierra Pinecate" (sic) was "a range [that] rises from the Red Desert quite like the other ranges" and that the lava "malpais stops miles short of its nearer base."

As they reached the far side of the lavas and approached the hills of the Tule range, McGee described one of the most vivid desert storms in Southwestern nonfiction. The storm mass was 3,000 feet high and six miles wide, as seen in the distance over the hills, and it approached them at an estimated eight mph. Light sprinkles grew to a downpour so quickly that prompt action was required to protect the wagon. Ten minutes later, a 35-mile-an-hour gale was driving the drops in a nearly horizontal sheet above the dune tops, while the temperature fell from some 70F to about 35F, and small hailstones formed apparently within a dozen feet of the ground. Ten minutes more and the gale was down to a breeze.

That night they made their second consecutive "dry camp," though McGee noted ruefully that their drenched blankets and fitful showers belied this term for a desert camp between water holes.

The third day they passed the mysterious circular trailside memorial mentioned in the last chapter. A few miles beyond they made a third dry camp, still with damp blankets, and the animals ate the last of their hay and drank the last of the water. Arriving at Tinajas Altas at noon the next day, McGee remarked on "threescore cross-marked graves—and how many unmarked no man can tell." He counted 11 tanks, perhaps more than usually reported because of the storm and lack of recent travelers. He also counted "hundreds if not thousands" of old Indian bedrock mortars in the surrounding rocks, as high as the highest tank.

The party continued north to Yuma, explored the Colorado's mouth, and then returned to Phoenix via the Gila. Summing up his experiences on both sides of the border, McGee glumly considered what his own eyes had told him as early as 1900:

> *In legion ways the adjustment of American settlers to new environments has been destructive, yet no new contacts have been more disastrous than those between the pioneers from humid fatherlands and the finely balanced vital solidarities of desert regions.*
>
> *The natural potentiality of the country traversed . . . is proved by the condition of the neighboring plains on the southern side of the Sonoran boundary which have never been overstocked—plains still mantled with herbage and grazed by herds of deer . . .*

BY 1907, THE OLD PIMERÍA was beginning to assume its modern guise. Tucson was turning from village into city. There were scientists in the city, interested in the curiosities of the incompletely charted Sonoran Desert to the west. In the Desert Botanical Laboratory, sitting on the ancient Indians' walled citadel of Tumamoc Hill, financed by the Carnegie Institution, and directed by Dr. Daniel Trembly MacDougal,[3] imaginations were fired by the lack of knowledge about northwestern Sonora in general and the Pinacate Mountains in particular. MacDougal invited the widely known zoologist, conservationist and travel writer Dr. William T. Hornaday to join local explorer Godfrey Sykes and photographer John Phillips in an expedition to study the region. Hornaday's recently reprinted book,[4] still entertaining today, conveys the bumptious enthusiasm and innocence of the last of the 19th-century Americans:

> *Pinacate, the mysterious! On two or three maps it appears as a small blotch in the midst of a great blank. On two of those maps it is far out of its proper place. For 200 years of historic times the country surrounding Pinacate has been totally un-explored and wholly unknown save to a few Papago Indians, and possibly one or two local Mexicans who are unknown beyond the Sonoita Oasis . . .*
>
> *Why, we asked each other, is the Pinacate region unknown? Why is it that no American traveler, no explorer, geographer, sportsman, or naturalist ever has set foot in that area, nor mapped its mysteries?*

As we can now see, Hornaday exaggerated the ignorance of the area. He might more accurately have said that no one had made thorough explorations or published a book about the Pinacates.

So Hornaday came out by train from New York to Tucson, where "the brave little Santa Cruz River . . . attempts to run through [town], but is held up and robbed at every turn." On November 2, 1907, the outfit left Tucson: seven men, a number of horses, a dog, and two mules "one size larger than jack-rabbits." Their journey would be a proto-Hemingwayesque festival of hunting, mapping, photographing and adventuring.

In Sonoita, they rendezvoused with Jefferson Davis Milton, the colorful local lawman, who was an agent of the Immigration Service and patrolled the border from Sonoita to Yuma. Milton had arranged that the MacDougal expedition be considered part of his patrol work. He had arranged with MacDougal to join up as a guide and local expert, having absorbed some of the knowledge of the still-earlier local explorer and mining engineer, Ygnacio S. Bonillas, who had reportedly made several forays into the Pinacates. Bonillas, an unsung hero of desert heart exploration, had apparently discovered some of the giant craters, but left no known notes. Hornaday, this time without exaggeration, called Milton "the most interesting man in Sonoita, or for that matter a hundred miles around." On November 10, the jaunty group departed Sonoita to the west, down the river bed toward Quitobaquito. A few others joined the group. Near Quitobaquito they chanced upon two peculiar

Sonoita lawman Jefferson Davis Milton contemplates a rattlesnake in his bedroll. Photo by John M. Phillips, 1907. All 1907 photos in this chapter are from the MacDougal expedition files. (Courtesy Arizona Historical Society.)

The MacDougal-Hornaday expedition approaches MacDougal Crater, November 1907.

Japanese who were evidently not long out of Japan, poorly equipped, and very closemouthed. The MacDougal party concluded that they were making a reconnaissance of the Camino as a route into the United States and Hornaday remarked that "a full report . . . is at this moment in the hands of the Japanese bureau of intelligence . . ."

Historian Bernard L. Fontana has remarked that the Japanese are a mystery, but he reports that Gilbert Sykes, son of expedition member Godfrey, said his father had told him that the Japanese carried a plane table with them. Hornaday had not mentioned this fact, which, according to Fontana, "lends credence to the possibility that they were indeed 'spies' of some kind."[5]

Quitobaquito, Hornaday described as "one of the spots in which I would not like to die, and would hate to live." He asked one of their new companions why he chose to live there. "'Oh, I'm not staying down here because I'm stuck on the country. Like everybody else, I'm looking for an opening, somewhere. But after all, there are much worse places for a man to live than little Quito and Sonoita.'"

From Agua Dulce, the watering spot on the Sonoita River, they headed west toward the Pinacates. Here they beheld their first crater, Cerro Colorado, or Red Hill, the pink cone enclosing a shallow floor, a beautiful hidden amphitheater dotted with shrubs. ". . . We rode across the zone of ashes and straight up the side of the volcano. When we drew rein upon the rim, a gorgeous scene lay before us and the adjectives began to fly like hail.

Aerial view of MacDougal Crater and Hornaday Mountains (top), looking north. Hornaday Pass, where MacDougal expedition entered the area, is at right tip of Hornaday Mountains. November 28, 1985.

called the *Hornaday Mountains.* You can't begrudge them the names. After all, these features had lain unmapped, not far from routes being traveled for two centuries! Virtually all of the names they assigned stuck.

As they emerged from the pass, they had unknowingly entered the Pinacates' main concentration of extinct volcanic calderas. Suddenly Godfrey Sykes came running with news of a giant crater he had just discovered as he climbed what looked like an innocent ridge.

We quickly turned and followed the Geographer up a brown slope covered with small pieces of lava, toward the crest of what seemed to be a ridge. On reaching its summit, like a picture thrown upon a screen an immense crater suddenly yawned at our feet! . . .

Far below, a floor almost as level as a lake spread across the abyss. Its surface was of clean yellow sand, but a dark area in the centre looked like moisture that had settled there during a recent rain . . .

The crater floor was most strangely planted . . . In places the things were growing in rows, radiating from the centre . . .

They named the phenomenal depression "MacDougal." Hornaday portrays the discoverers standing awestruck on the rim, "admiring the crater at the rate of twenty interjections per minute." The discovery date was (judging from the annotated map) November 13, 1907. The 3/4-mile diameter they derived by walking the circumference is within a percent of the value listed in a 1981 geological study.[6] Phillips' photo shows the central dark splotch; each Pinacate crater has a year-round garden of green in its central, low "drainage patch."

Hornaday comments insightfully on the frustrations of crater photography. The pit subtends 180° as you stand on the rim, necessitating a three- or four-section

'Magnificent!' 'Grand!' 'Vesuvius in the desert!'" Milton, who told them the crater's name, had apparently heard of Cerro Colorado from Bonillas or visited it himself, for (to Hornaday's credit) Hornaday does not class it as a "discovery."

Soon they had flushed out six pronghorn antelope on the ashy outer erosion blanket of Cerro Colorado, and shortly thereafter a coyote came by and lay down 21 paces from Hornaday, oblivious to his gun and his shouts for his friends to come and have a look.

From Cerro Colorado they swung north around the lavas into the U.S. and back down the northwest side of the Pinacates. Heading south along the lava edge, they traversed what they called *MacDougal Pass.* It runs to the southwest between the lava and the end of what they

Exploring Sykes Crater. April 26, 1964.

mural, or a modern fisheye wide-angle lens. "But when an effort is made to reduce all that down to the length of a book illustration, the grandeur of it goes all to pieces, and the reduction is a tame spectacle." How true! Giant craters are a gift of nature not transferable onto film. The angular scale of a panorama printed in a book is all wrong; it doesn't *surround* you. And even David Lean, panning with a 70mm camera, could not capture the sense of space and silence that comes when you stand alone on the rim of such a vast, hollow structure. In an age of media fantasy, we can be thankful that some such phenomena are left!

On November 15, they set out from their camp at Papago Tanks to hunt both game and geology. ". . . Mr. Phillips and Mr. Sykes . . . scored heaviest on that day . . . Mr. Sykes had two splendid new craters to his credit . . ." The first crater they aptly nicknamed *the cloverleaf*. It comprises three pits, round, sand-filled and divided by low, sloping ridges. In honor of Señor Olegario Molina, Mexican Secretary of Development,

they eventually named that discovery Molina Crater.

The second crater is one of America's grandest sights. Hornaday was enraptured:

> . . . *in craters, the Wonder of wonders was reserved for the last. You seem to stand at the Gateway to the Hereafter. The hole in the earth is so vast, and its bottom is so far away, it looks as if it might go down to the center of the earth. The walls go down so straight and so smooth that at one point only can man or mountain sheep descend or climb out. There the roughness of the rocks renders it possible for a bold and nerveless mountaineer—as much as possible unlike the present incumbent—to make the trip . . .*
>
> *The Washington Monument is 555 feet high. Imagine a round hole wider than the length of Battery Park, New York, going down so far that with the monument standing on its floor you would have to look down two hundred feet farther in order to see the aluminum cap on the apex.*

Irrepressible Sykes climbed down into the crater to observe the plant life and measure the depth. The value he derived with his barometer was only four percent above the modern estimate of 722 feet. The new crater was named for him. In Mexico another name, also fitting, is sometimes used: *Grande*. Which name is older is unclear, because Sykes/Grande might have been locally discovered by earlier wanderers. Some spectacular cinder cones next to Sykes Crater were named for another member of the party: Phillips Buttes. These offer some of the most impressive vistas in the Pinacates.

The final challenge was the ascent of the Pinacate Peaks. Looking for a suitable route that avoided the roughest lavas, they headed south to a campsite at Tule Tanks, on the southwest flank of the mountains, closer to the main peaks. During the stay at Tule Tanks, Godfrey Sykes made a fantastic side trip. The blue gulf

Papago Tanks with Hornaday (kneeling) and Phillips getting a drink.
Today the water is polluted by cattle. November, 1907.

waters across the bright sands had attracted the group, but the thought of a harrowing trek across miles of lava and loose sand made them give up the idea of a trip to the beach. As wry Hornaday put it, "Gulf Coast stock dropped eighty points, with a hard thud."

But Sykes argued that they should extend their expedition to the sea, and that he needed to reach the beach in order to calibrate his barometer at sea level. He set off without a word to anyone the next afternoon at 1 P.M. Never worried about finding his way back to camp, in spite of the fact that neither the camp nor the tanks could be seen "until we were almost ready to fall over it," he crossed the lavas and trackless dunes, and then grassy flats to the beach. There was a bright moon that rose about dusk, when he had gotten nearly across the flats. Steering by stars and moonlight, and with "a latch-key to my own particular sleeping-rock at Tule Tanks," he arrived back at camp about 1:30 A.M.

"I thought I would go down to sea level with my aneroid," he explained calmly. His pedometer indicated a 43-mile round trip, in 12-1/2 hours! Bill Broyles, a Tucson scholar, retraced the route of the MacDougal expedition on foot, 77 years later to the day. He has written a fascinating behind-the-scenes account of the expedition based partly on letters and interviews with Sykes' son Glenton, and he unearthed a different opinion about Sykes' motivation.[7] He notes that Godfrey Sykes loved the sea as much as the desert. "I don't think he really needed to calibrate it," Glenton Sykes said. "That was just an excuse to walk down to the Gulf . . . I think he just wanted . . . to look around." This fits the Sykes' family trait of ceaseless curiosity; Broyles remarks that Sykes emerges as the most interesting character of the group.

November 20, 1907, marked the first *recorded* ascent of Cerro Pinacate in more than two centuries. The morning temperature at Tule Tank was a brisk 43F. The gradual ascent was long and arduous. The final climb, up the steep, 40° incline of loose lava and cinders on the actual

Hornaday Mountains with flowering brittle bushes in foreground, on the approach to MacDougal Crater and Papago Tanks, northwest Pinacates. November 16, 1969.

summit cone, was all the more exciting for the party— MacDougal, Hornaday, Sykes, Phillips and Milton—because they maintained the delusion (despite whatever Milton might or might not have said) that they were the first explorers to do it.

> *Each climber was generously determined that some other man should have the honor of being the first white man to set foot on the summit of Pinacate, so in order to get there we actually had to form in line and march up simultaneously, five abreast! . . . Then a riot began . . . "Pinacate's busted!"*

Of the insanity at the top of the Pinacates that day, perhaps the most graphic was that Sykes decided to stand on his head, and did so, his size-11 hiking boots waving in the wind. Phillips photographed the spectacle

—a photo that the Sykes family retains in Tucson to this day. In Sykes' judgment, it was only fitting for him to imitate the Pinacate beetle.[8]

Of course, Hornaday was wrong about any of them being the first white man to set foot on the Pinacate summit. Kino, for example, had been there, but Kino's diaries were not yet published; Hornaday wouldn't have known. The more serious charge against Hornaday is a flat conflict between his claim and the evidence that their own guide, Jeff Milton, had been there before. Milton's biography,[9] based on direct interviews with Milton as well as with his friends, says Milton and his friends had been on the summit earlier, and claims that the MacDougal party actually "tore up a little cairn of stones that Jeff, Rube [Daniels], and Joe Meeks had built long before, to build another and encase a can with a notation of their pioneer mastery of Pinacate Peak . . . in commemoration of 'The Hornaday Expedition.'" Broyles agrees that Milton had been to the summit and quotes a recollection of Godfrey Sykes' son Glenton that "'Milton had built a cairn on the peak. I think MacDougal and Hornaday demolished it to build their own.'" If this were true, we might expect Milton to have been outraged. Photos of the festivities on the summit add spice to the mystery, because they show Milton peacefully participating. One of Phillips' summit photos shows the cairn, and is labeled ". . . planting the first tin can . . ." Is this a careful wording to avoid saying "the first cairn?" Amazingly, the photo shows Milton adding or removing a large boulder as Hornaday himself works on the cairn. We may never resolve whether Hornaday knowingly misrepresented the case.

The whole relationship between Milton and the MacDougal party was evidently strained. MacDougal apparently irritated Milton at the outset by treating him as a local hired hand, an attitude projected by Hornaday as well. The situation was aggravated when the expedition dismissed Milton's friend, Rube Daniels, for blasting away at every target along the trail.[10]

Certainly it was clear to the party that Jeff Milton knew the country, and Milton's biographer legitimately regards Hornaday's volume as making "some extravagant claims about the country's being unknown." In Hornaday's favor, he did credit Milton with knowing the name and location of Cerro Colorado. But MacDougal, Sykes, and Hornaday were the first to make scientific measures and publish an account of the area, while Milton had only ridden through and told yarns about it. Thus, according to the genteel but aristocratic Eastern academic tradition, members of "The Expedition" could regard themselves rightfully as discoverers. MacDougal's and Hornaday's letters, cited by Broyles in his behind-the-scenes article, ring with sincere enthusiasm over their discoveries. They show no sign of cunning self-aggrandizement. In the enthusiastic minds of Hornaday and MacDougal, the *real* expedition was *their* group from Tucson. That local rubes might have roamed the Pinacates ahead of them was incidental. Typical of overly enthused intellectuals, they may have been capable of adjusting the facts to fit their self-delusions. Milton, meanwhile, was not above pulling Eastern greenhorns' legs; perhaps it was in disgruntled silence that he let them have their fun on the Pinacate summit. It is interesting to try to read his thoughts as he stands smiling in the background of the photo in which Godfrey Sykes celebrates upside down.

As their excitement on the summit cooled, they made geographical observations about the surrounding area. To the northeast, they sighted a new crater (later named Elegante) lying on a line between them and the distant, pink, dimly visible Cerro Colorado. The distance of this new feature they put at about six or seven miles, about two miles too far.

Now the great expedition was nearing its end. On November 22, 1907, they broke their camp at Tule Tanks and headed out of and around the lavas on their way back to Sonoita and Tucson. Broyles' account describes wide reports of the successful expedition by papers in

Godfrey Sykes emulates the Pinacate beetle on the Pinacate summit, with Hornaday (left) and Milton looking on. Photo, John M. Phillips, 1907.

Milton (standing) and Hornaday working on the controversial rock cairn, Pinacate summit, November 20, 1907.

Washington, D.C., London, and elsewhere, and reveals a letter from MacDougal to Hornaday a year later, calling the expedition "certainly the finest episode of our lives." Even Teddy Roosevelt expressed interest in seeing the Pinacates, and MacDougal and Hornaday hatched a plan to guide him surreptitiously into the area as soon as his term in office expired. The plan fizzled when Teddy went to Africa instead.

The Pinacate Pirates, as they dubbed themselves, were remarkable men. Hornaday went on to campaign for wildlife refuges and protection laws, both in Mexico and the United States. Of his many books, more than half a dozen were in print as reissues during the 1980s. MacDougal published more than a hundred botanical research papers. And he helped introduce writer Mary

Austin to the Sonoran Desert. She dedicated her book, *The Land of Journeys' Ending*, to him. Photographer John Phillips served on Pennsylvania's Board of Game Commissioners, the board of the Boy Scouts, and was awarded a 1923 medal as the leading American conservationist. Colorful Godfrey Sykes built one of the telescope domes at Lowell Observatory in Flagstaff and became a renowned Sonoran Desert authority; we will encounter him again. When Hornaday, MacDougal, Phillips and Sykes died at midcentury, their ages were, respectively, 82, 92, 92 and 87. Something of their hardy desert life must have agreed with them.

Some modern writers have criticized the hunting orientation of the MacDougal-Hornaday expedition, yet they championed the cause of preservation and made photography a goal of greater import than the kill. Sykes never even carried a gun. Hornaday lamented that "the sheep of Pinacate could easily be exterminated in three years or less, by the Mexicans of the Sonoita Valley for meat, or by the scores of American sportsmen who are willing to go to the farthest corner of Hades itself for mountain sheep." This prophecy was nearly fulfilled. Today mountain sheep and other big game are only occasionally spotted in the Pinacates.

Taking a still larger view, Hornaday predicted from the rate of destruction of wildlife at the time, 1907, that "fifty years hence there will be no large game left in the United States or in Canada outside of rigidly protected game preserves. It is therefore the duty of every good citizen to promote the protection of forests and game preserves." He was right.

IN 1907, THE SAME YEAR as the MacDougal expedition, another bit of history was taking place in Sonoita. The site of the old mission, begun two centuries before by Kino, was marked only by "two low, rather insignificant, mounds." The local Papagos had an oral tradition that their ancestors had attacked and burned the mission and killed the priest or priests. This was true, of course; it happened in 1751, during the Pima revolt. In 1907, M. G. Levy, of Ajo, speculated that gold might have been hidden in the old church foundations during the revolt. He obtained permission to excavate the ruins, which lie east of the modern town. Thick adobe walls and a hard, whitish floor were found. There were a few skeletons, one with "an abundance of blond hair, and a colored stone disk of unknown use"—but no gold. Charcoal throughout the ruined walls testified to the mission's violent fate. The skeleton with blond hair is thought to be that of Father Ruhen, who was murdered November 21, 1751.

This incident is one of many recorded by Carl Lumholtz, a Norwegian author and naturalist, who

The dunes crossed by Godfrey Sykes, west of Moon Crater, with Pinacate Peaks in rear. April 8, 1977.

explored the Sonoran Desert in 1909-10. He published a classic book about the region, *New Trails in Mexico*.[11]

Curiously, Lumholtz found that nobody in Sonoita in 1909 knew El Camino del Diablo by that name. He speculated (incorrectly?) that contemporary use of that name resulted from confusion with a small canyon near Tule Well, known as Cajon (sic) del Diablo. Not knowing of Díaz' odyssey, Lumholtz credited the Jesuits of Kino's time with being the first Europeans to traverse the Camino, but erroneously believed that "there is no evidence to show that they ever traversed the country south of it"—that is, the Pinacate region. He says that to postulate that the early explorers traveled such a "supposed route is absurd to one who knows the region in question." The detailed diaries of Kino, Manje, and others came to light only in the following decades due to historian Herbert Bolton's archival sleuthing in Spain, Mexico, and elsewhere—"nosing into musty bundles," as Bolton put it. With such records available today, we realize that the first European trailblazers, with the help of Indian guides, actually did accomplish "absurd" deeds! In spite of limitations in the background data available, Lumholtz' records of the Sonoran Desert are a remarkable product of adventurous spirit multiplied by intellectual curiosity.

Lumholtz became *simpático* with various old Indians around Sonoita and Quitobaquito. Instead of bulling into the Pinacates with the Anglo enthusiasm of MacDougal and Hornaday, he quietly learned more of the ancient Indian trails and traditions in the Pinacates. There was a sacred cave, the Indians said, at the top of the mountains. It was called *I'itoi's* (Ee'-ee-toy) *Cave*, named after the chief god and "Elder Brother" of the Tohono O'odham, or Papagos, as they were still known. (Elder brother—a pleasant concept for a god!) An old Papago medicine man named Quelele, so old that he could not ride on horseback and had to be drawn in a wagon, offered to guide Lumholtz to the cave.

There were certain duties required of visitors to the sacred cave. You had to spend a night there singing the old songs, and you had to bring sacrificial offerings: beads, feathers, etc. Quelele was worried, too, about the Mexicans who were going to assist Lumholtz on the journey; they might reveal the location of the cave and give away the ancient secret, jealously guarded by the Papagos. After all, the cave was believed to run westward under the lava and the desert and the sea to the island home of the wife of I'itoi. Lumholtz reassured old Quelele, and they set out for the first stop—a visit to Quitobaquito where there was another old medicine man who knew the rituals and would provide them with the proper sacrifices.

Discussions at Quitobaquito established that four small eagle feathers would suffice as an offering; these

Sonoita in 1907.

were purchased for a dollar (no small sacrifice, since the four big feathers initially demanded were priced at 16 dollars, the price of a horse).

Back across the border to the Sonoita streambed, down past the old campgrounds at the bend in the river. Ahead, to the southwest, loomed the dark-blue Picos del Pinacate, the twin cinder-cone peaks that form the summit—Pinacate Peak and Carnegie Peak, as MacDougal's party had named them.

The detailed lore of the Pinacate summit, related by solemn Quelele, showed that in spite of any arguments about who were the first Anglos on the summit, the Tohono O'odham had been making treks there for centuries. While they had not recorded their knowledge in western-style maps and books, they had passed accurate

I'itoi's cave, with summit cinder cones in background. April 14, 1963.

geographic information from generation to generation.

Four days after Christmas, 1909, Lumholtz' party passed the pinkish rim of Cerro Colorado Crater, with its "deep furrows from the top down, and with an air of recent formation about it." The old medicine man, who had last been on the lavas 40 years before (about 1870), pointed out the ancient trail up the Pinacate slopes. Follow the trail, he said, to where you can see an abrupt descending ridge halfway up the mountain. At its base would be water and a campsite. This they did, and on the next day they sighted small birds that led them to pools in the rocks. Remembering a friend in Boston, Miss Emily Beebe, Lumholtz named the spot *Las Tinajas de Emilia* (Emilia Tanks) and so it is known today. Lumholtz seems to have had no shortage of feminine friends back

on the east coast. During his peregrinations in the area, he named not only Emilia Tanks, but Sierra Niña and Paso de Juana for acquaintances in Boston and New York. One wonders if the ladies were all shown the same map.

The small party, consisting of Lumholtz, old Quelele, and several Mexican and Papago hunters and guides, camped at Emilia Tanks for several days. This rough and beautiful country, with lava flows, brittle bush, and cinder cones all about, was an area unexplored by MacDougal's group, which had climbed the other side of the mountain.

Quelele helped arrange the sacrificial objects and felt he should spend a night singing at the cave. The rest of the party talked him out of this, with the excuse that no one knew any of the old Pinacate songs. He decided that there were so many offerings that they alone would suffice.

Monday, January 3, 1910, saw their assault on the summit. An hour's uphill hike took them to the vicinity of the sacred cave, which lay at the base of the large cinder cone, Carnegie Peak. Old Quelele, poking around among the rocks, couldn't find the cave for a half-hour because he hadn't been there for four decades. When he did find it, he was dismayed to discover that the roof he had known years before had collapsed along a ten-yard stretch around the old entrance. Perhaps it was the earthquake two decades earlier that did the evil deed.

Lumholtz recognized that the cave was an ancient lava tunnel. As the molten lava oozed down the mountain, its surface cooled and hardened, while inside the red-hot fluid streamed along in a tunnel of its own making. Somewhere farther down, the fluid lava broke out of the tunnel and drained it. As the eruption stopped, a hollow tube was left a few feet below the surface. Such tunnels are common in many lava flows and appear in other parts of the Pinacates.

This tunnel was about 20 feet deep, more than big enough for a man to stand in, and about 10 to 20 feet across. The entrance, enlarged by the collapse between 1870 and 1910, is a yawning elliptical hole about 40 by 15 feet wide. Two of Lumholtz' Papago guides clambered down the jagged, steep walls into the tunnel and left the sacred objects they had collected for this important moment near their god: an arrow, a prayer-stick, a bunch of yucca fiber, feathers, a blue glass bead necklace, and (demonstrating the uplifting influence of 20th-century western culture) some cigarettes, "for the god's personal use."

At 2:40 P.M., January 3, 1910, Lumholtz and his friends (except for Quelele, who was too old to climb the steep and cindery cone) reached the top of Carnegie Peak. Temperature: 41F. Surprisingly, Lumholtz does not comment on the impressive, funnel-shaped crater that occupies the summit of Carnegie cinder cone. He does describe "the other peak" (Cerro Pinacate), "west . . . scarcely a mile off, and visibly higher."

Just as had Kino, Manje, Salvatierra and others down through history, Lumholtz and his companions surveyed the mighty vista of sea, sand, and cinders, noting that the Pinacate volcanic complex "seemed to be composed of several hundred volcanoes." Lumholtz took photographs until a strong northwest wind knocked over his tripod, breaking one of its legs. Then the temperature dropped to 32F. After building a little fire from a few scarce sticks, the shivering party departed for their camp, arriving after dark.

Next day, Quelele, suffering from the cold, departed on his buckboard for home with one of Lumholtz' guides, Alberto Celaya. Years later, Celaya told a story about the ensuing journey. The weather turned worse and frail Quelele nearly froze. Celaya built a fire and set Quelele on the ground in front of it. Finally, Quelele, who was about 80 years old, recovered. The old Indian looked Celaya in the eye and said, although in a much cruder Spanish vernacular, "Oh *compadre,* I was afraid I'd never have another chance to make love to a woman!"[12]

On the way to the summit, Lumholtz had spotted the same crater that MacDougal's group had seen to the northeast on a line toward Cerro Colorado. Lumholtz notes that it was "little known among the very few Mexicans who visit the Pinacate region." On the other hand it must have been visited earlier (at least by Bonillas), because Lumholtz says "it had been mentioned to me as the largest and the most beautiful of all the craters here."

After a few days around Emilia Tanks, with miserable weather and ice forming on the pools, they set out for the new crater. They approached from the south, up the "long, low slanting ridge which is its rim, rising only . . . about one hundred and fifty feet above the surrounding country." Then Lumholtz experienced that stunning phenomenon of large craters: walking the last few steps up the rim of what might be a butte, only to discover that it falls away into a vast pit, an enclosed world. In front of them was a panoramic view: "the magnitude and beautiful regularity of the circular opening which yawns impressively before one is surprising." He did not climb down into it but again implies that earlier visitors did: "a descent . . . is said to be feasible to very difficult, and it looks difficult, too . . . It is probably the deepest of all the craters there, and is by far the most beautiful, so the name Crater Elegante would be appropriate for it." The name stuck.

They rode around the rim on the old Indian trail, which, he says, the Indians used in their pursuit of sheep that occasionally went into the pit. He judged the crater to be three miles around and 800 feet deep; modern measures[13] give about 2.3 miles and 820 feet, respectively. Lumholtz was way off on circumference, but within three percent on depth.

Lumholtz aimed to explore the lower Colorado River, and unknowingly followed exactly in Kino's 1698 footsteps on a trip around the south end of the mountains. First they camped at the Cuervo Tanks cluster of tanks south of the peaks. A large shell still lay at Cuervo

Tank itself, used by the Indians to drink from the pool. Moving west and north across the relatively fresh lava flows, they came to Chivos Tank, one of the Pinacates' largest, and its sister, Tule Tank. Then, on to Papago Tanks by a circuitous trail that led out to the western sand dunes and then back across the rocks. These trails led past sites of intense prehistoric activity.

Here was the site of Kino's little village of Santa Brigida, where 20 natives had shared food with the Jesuit. At the edge of the dunes, they discovered old Indian camps with "rude corrals of stones" and various pits. Lumholtz remarks that on a nearby plain, great ceremonies had been performed, which had more recently been moved about 45 miles to the southeast to the village of Quitovac.

Camping at Papago Tanks, they trekked to nearby MacDougal Crater, which they easily descended. Lumholtz regarded MacDougal as "second only to Crater Elegante" in beauty. Whether he had seen other large craters is not clear. He says, "there are several large craters in the Pinacate region, but none as perfect in shape as these two, which present very clearly the phenomena connected with their structure and origin and must be of unusual interest to geology."

On the following day, Lumholtz departed the Pinacates for the Colorado River. He passed northwest across the scrubby sands toward the Cabeza Prieta Mountains, pale pinkish-grey with their peculiar dark volcanic caps. Soon he arrived at the tanks of Tinajas Altas:

> Tinajas Altas is a landmark in the local and recent history of that desolate region. It is a dismal looking place and, after having been accustomed to the absolute cleanliness of nature, the experience of again meeting with pieces of cast-off clothing, rusty tin cans, and other cheerless marks of human occupancy which were apparent here was not a pleasing one.

Litter already in 1910!

Lumholtz counted 60 graves at Tinajas Altas. At these stairstep tanks, Lumholtz repeated a story of three exhausted prospectors who wore their fingers to the bone in futile efforts to scratch their way to one of the upper tanks. Their bodies were found near a dry lower tank, below a water-filled upper tank. On another occasion shortly thereafter, however, Lumholtz found Tinajas Altas less morbid when he arrived after a strenuous trek. We may leave him ruminating in the shade of a *palo fierro*:

> To me the desert is radiant with good cheer; superb air there certainly is, and generous sunshine, and the hardy, healthy looking plants and trees with their abundant flowers inspire courage. One feels in communion with nature and the great silence is beneficial. Could I select the place where I should like best to die, my choice would be one such as this. I hope at least it may not fall to my lot to pass away in New York, where I might be embalmed before I was dead and where it costs so much to die that I might not leave enough wherewithal to defray the expenses of a funeral.

Lumholtz was 58 years old when he made his Pinacate trek. He had already published several books of exploration, and a few years later he gathered material in Borneo for another two-volume work. He died (in New York State, but not in dreaded New York City), in 1922 at age 71. In the preface to his book on the Sonoran Desert, he had followed the code of the West, understating his achievements:

> When I, in the easy surroundings of civilized life, read my notes from the field, it sometimes occurs to me that what this or that which I went through was well done; but what appears as hardship, privation, or risk amounts to little when actually happening . . .

SOON, VISITS TO THE PINACATE COUNTRY were becoming too frequent to describe in detail. In early 1915, naturalist Charles Sheldon spent a month in the area, taking notes and shooting bighorns and other game for taxonomic collections. His journal, published in 1979, includes interesting observations and Sheldon's remarkable photograph of the gorge at Papago Tanks in flood after a severe rainstorm on February 11. Rapids and waterfalls of white, frothing water swirl and splash across perhaps 100 yards of black rocks. "The volume of water which soon began to pour through Papago Tanks was tremendous," he wrote, "and one can realize how the tanks were made after seeing this." Sheldon hiked the jagged three-mile crestline of the Hornaday Mountains; "I do not think any other mountain here is situated so that the panorama is as beautiful from the crest." From there, he noted the Tuseral Mountains rising "mysteriously across the sand," and "MacDougal Crater appearing like a vast hole in the earth. Beyond is the lava." A descent into Elegante he described concisely as "cragwork." Near the Pinacate summit, in one of his typical Spartan journal entries, he noted "three Indian arrowheads of obsidian in a pile of rocks and saw three varieties of butterflies."

In the Pinacates, he found two records of earlier visits. On the summit was a "monument and in it a tin box with a card bearing the names of Rube Daniels (who had been excommunicated from Hornaday's party), Dr. L. D. Ricketts (a well-known mining engineer), and C. Veanway of Warren, Arizona, dated March 22–23, 1914." At Emilia Tanks he found a can with a note from a party including Ricketts and John Greenway, who had been a Rough Rider with Teddy Roosevelt, and was now a mining executive in Ajo. It noted that they had camped on the summit on November 24, 1914.

A poignant journey through the desert heart occurred in early March, 1915. Raphael Pumpelly, the traveler whose 1861 Camino del Diablo escapade was recounted in the previous chapter, returned to the

O'Neill's Grave. October 19, 1985.

Southwest after the death of his wife. Now he was an old man of 77 and a well-known travel writer. He decided to take his grown children on a tour of the sites of his 1861 adventures as a young man. They were a creative brood. One daughter and a son wrote poems of the occasion; one daughter made watercolor paintings along the way; and one daughter kept a journal.[14] Reaching Tucson, ". . . we decided to strike out boldly to a point about 100 miles distant on the Mexican border where we should reach the 'Old Yuma Trail' [El Camino del Diablo] on which Poston and I had escaped . . . It seemed a simple thing to do with three Ford cars and three drivers. With the chauffeurs we made a party of eight."

After a few days they were heading south out of Ajo, with an attitude that now seems characteristic of the era—more foolhardiness than sense. At age 77, Pumpelly had hired Tomaso, an 85-year-old Indian, "the only Indian who had seen the Tinajas Altas." Their canvas water bags were designed to hold water only after two days' soaking; lacking this treatment, they began leaking during the first day, at the end of which the water hole they reached turned out to have bad water. The next day, near a site that would soon become known as O'Neill's Grave, they passed a returning sheephunters' party (Sheldon?), who warned them not to try to reach Yuma on the Camino; it had never been done by car. Later they learned that the hunters had wired from Ajo to Yuma to send out a rescue party for them. In the same region, Pumpelly reports falling on a "devil's pincushion" cactus, and "it took the party a half-hour to pluck me."

In washes east of the lavas, their cars kept bogging down, and they found both their radiators and their canvas sacks were running dangerously low on water. "There was clearly an element of real danger in our situation. Unless we could find some way to avoid this stalling we should die of thirst, for on the dry desert one cannot live two days without water, nor could the automobiles."

Eventually they gained the firm playa and the northward Pinacate lava tongue beyond, where Pumpelly had ridden with the desperado Williams, 54 years before. "Eastward beyond the lava field and its cones, and far away over the desert plain, crumbling mountains shone red in the sunset glow. [Night] . . . closed over the wonderful scene . . . The mood of the desert is never sad."

The next day they tried to refresh themselves with the "brackish and offensive" water at Tule Well (only to be told a few months later that two years before, a dead man had been found and left in it). Pumpelly notes his belief that "it is a matter of history that more than 2,000 persons have died of thirst and exhaustion" in this region. This figure seems exaggerated.

Reaching Tinajas Altas, Pumpelly reported significant changes in half a century. The dried carcasses of cattle and horses, which he had seen before, were gone, "buried [he speculated] under debris washed by cloud-bursts down from the ever-crumbling mountains." The temperature was 100F—a balmy spring day at Tinajas Altas. One car gave out as they headed north to the Gila River, but eventually they reached that stream and Yuma beyond—apparently the first successful crossing of El Camino del Diablo by car. Pumpelly added that, "shortly after our experience," three men tried another automobile crossing and two of them died, probably just east of the playa.

IN 1916, ANOTHER GRIM PAGE was written in the history of El Camino del Diablo. An old prospector named David O'Neill had been out in the desolate mountains on the American side of the border northeast of the Pinacates. According to geographer Kirk Bryan, who surveyed water resources, gave a road log, and chronicled the area in 1925, O'Neill's "burros wandered away from camp in a storm, and after searching for them at least a day he died with his head in a mud hole . . ."[15]

When the burros wandered into a nearby community, searchers went out and found O'Neill and buried him on the spot, where his grave is still prominent, a rock-filled plot surmounted by a cross, a few feet from the Camino in a pass in what are now called the *O'Neill Hills*. A 1925 photo by Godfrey Sykes, who traveled widely in the Sonoran Desert after his participation in the Hornaday expedition, shows a wooden cross; it has been replaced by a metal one which, though rusty, is in good condition. A hundred yards away, the small wash often contains scattered damp spots. Boulder-strewn hills rise nearby. It is a beautiful, peaceful place, but a lonely spot to die.

Desert explorer Bill Broyles[16] reports that the grave was desecrated a few years ago, a sad and perhaps inevitable incident that will be repeated by future ignorant vandals who think that they are the first graverobbers. Passing the grave, which is restored to its original dramatic state, one can't deny morbid curiosity about the circumstances of O'Neill's lonely fate, nor can one escape the feeling that O'Neill still lends his presence to this quiet desert site.

AN ASTONISHING BOOK, published in Mexico in 1928, tells of a Mexican expedition out of Sonoita to explore the Pinacates in 1926. Written in Spanish by Sonoita school teacher Gumersindo Esquer, this little-known book carries the title "Campos de Fuego" or "Camps of Fire" (echoing Hornaday's title, "Camp-Fires on Desert and Lava").[17]

The book affirms a feminist's nightmares about the life of men on their own: the travelers hatch their expedition plan with rowdy good humor in a bar in Sonoita, and begin their month-long trip by blasting away at most animals in sight. In the first days they report shooting two mountain lions, 14 antelope, several javelinas, and a bighorn sheep, whose head they kept as a trophy. But the expedition was primarily one of exploration and discovery; it was a horseback journey planned for a month and supported by three wagons and a dozen mules. Three engineers made a number of measurements, including barometric elevations. Esquer complains that the three wanted to measure every rock that was passed.

Soon they pass through Quitobaquito and arrive at Cerro Colorado, which they greet: "Three times hail, Watch Tower of the Desert! Hail, silent witness of dreadful cataclysms." The next day, they are off to explore the lava flows, crossing two kilometers of desert and several kilometers of lava. Here, they discover a sunken region a kilometer in radius, at the center of which is a lava cave. Suddenly, they make a tremendous discovery: Indian offerings and religious artifacts including bronze Christ figures and oil paintings, and a burial that they interpreted as that of a priest of the early Spanish era. The materials appeared very old and partly encrusted with accumulated bat guano.

Breathlessly, we read on to discover the details of this mystery grave; we are only in Chapter 3 of a 12-chapter book. But now the story becomes more unbelievable with every page! Soon, they have found mastodon bones in the cave, and eventually, ruins of a city which had been buried when the lavas erupted!

The whole book turns out to be merely a lighthearted fabrication! While Esquer tells his story with a straight face, it is a fantasy adventure. The father of Pinacate archaeologist Julian Hayden, Irwin Hayden, translated the book around 1969 and reports in his preface the same experience I had upon first encountering the work:

> (At first) I accepted "Campos de Fuego" at its face value . . . I became more and more interested in it, not only because of its literary worth but the apparent truth of it. There came, however, a time when I could not believe what I read. It was then that I perceived the significance of the statement on the title page of Esquer's book: 'a brief histórico-fantástico account,' or, in plain English, a narration compounded of fact and fiction . . . a hoax, no less. It was, however, entirely good-natured, as the author gently 'spoofed' his host of friends and cronies . . .

As recounted by Irwin Hayden in his preface, and later by Julian (1987, personal communication), the two Haydens discussed the book with one of the purported members of the expedition, Don Regino Celaya. This confirmed the playful hoax. There had been one actual trip into the Pinacates by Celaya and a handful of others, including a Mexican friend from Phoenix, "who wanted to inspect a cave in which a deposit of guano was burning," according to Irwin Hayden's preface. This trip, on which Esquer was not present, bagged one mountain sheep, and brought back a harvest of stories. Esquer, having heard additional wild rumors and legends of the unknown Pinacate in smokey Sonoita *cantinas*, decided to add it all together into a grand parody of his friends.

From its title and its wagonloads of supplies, to its barometer readings and devil-may-care camaraderie, "Campos de Fuego" reads like a transmogrified mixture of Jules Verne and William Hornaday. By Chapter 8, the explorers have used their tent fabric to parachute into a deep crater, discovered buried treasures of gold and silver coins, and found a lost mission of Father Kino, complete with bells, buried in the dunes. In true Vernesian style, the characters give lectures on lava formation and interior conditions in the Earth. The book deserves publication in English (but perhaps the edition would have to be sent back through time to an era when more Americans enjoyed reading).

Of Esquer himself, the Haydens learned that he was a gentle man, probably of Indian descent, and given to long journeys on foot in preference to automobile travel. On one of these journeys, in August 1940, he died from thirst under a tree about a mile from the home of his friend, Señor Celaya. He had failed, this time, to carry enough water. Realizing this, he wrote on the rim of his hat "I died of thirst through my own fault." The hat was later preserved in a museum in Caborca.

During the same period, the inimitable Godfrey Sykes was maintaining a set of rain gauges along the Camino del Diablo to measure climate conditions for MacDougal's Desert Laboratory in Tucson. On July 22, 1925, he set out in a "heavy touring car" to check his gauges. Crossing the playa just before encountering the northern tongue of Pinacate lavas, he found windblown sand had virtually obscured the road. He got stuck, and found that he would have to do a lot of digging to free his vehicle. The day was even hotter than usual; he measured midday temperatures between 112F and 115F. In his laconic words,

> . . . I realized . . . I was in for a strenuous after-
> noon. Having been accustomed to observing facts

and incidents from a scientific angle . . . I considered this would be an excellent opportunity for observing the combined effects of exceptionally high temperature, heavy physical exertion and absence of cooling drinks, upon the human organism.

> *. . . I noted my pulse, which stood at 72 when I began shovelling . . . ranged upward to 145 after a particularly strenuous half hour. My age at that time was 64 . . . I approached the recognized danger point of a dry skin and labored breathing twice . . . but was able to avert collapse on both occasions by taking short rests in the shade of the car. The water in my canteen was quite hot—about 95—and I used it very sparingly, principally for rinsing out my mouth in the Mexican manner. [The next morning in Yuma] I . . . found I had lost 14 pounds . . .*[18]

Such were the men who kept alive the history of El Camino del Diablo! Godfrey Sykes is a forgotten hero of early Arizona—a man of action and a man of intellect. Besides participating in the Hornaday expedition and studying his rain gauges on the Camino, he wrote a book on the Colorado Delta,[19] designed the main dome for Percival Lowell at Lowell's famous astronomical observatory in Flagstaff, and built a boat that he sailed down the Colorado and the Baja coast. The house he designed for himself stands at the foot of Tumamoc Hill in Tucson, and includes an early application of reinforced concrete. His autobiography[20] is a classic.

Journal entry. Pinacate Explorations. April 6, 1977. A party from the Southern Arizona Hiking Club has come to the Pinacates for a general tour. Glenton and Gilbert Sykes are with us, white-haired, aged, squinty-eyed, and enthusiastic— the sons of Godfrey Sykes in body and spirit. We reach MacDougal Crater through Hornaday Pass, just as their father did, almost exactly 70 years before.

Our group has individuals representing a wide range of desert experience. As we stand on the rim of MacDougal, surveying the great volcanic saucer, I overhear a woman: "You mean there was no machinery here? This whole thing formed without machinery?" Is this woman serious? She seems to be.

April 7, 1977. *An expedition to Sykes Crater, where both Glenton and Gilbert (ages exceeding 75!) made the arduous climb up the rim. Others of our group climbed to the bottom and back out, clambering up the final slopes on all fours. Sykes is like a huge cavern, laid open on its side. It has a presence, unlike a random piece of ordinary landscape, as if it has a life of its own. What does it do the rest of the time, when there are no visitors climbing around on holiday, laughing and hollering?*

The smooth ash slopes angle upward, toward the sun high in the afternoon sky. The sun casts long, tapering shadows of the bushes across them. Evening shadows in mid-afternoon.

April 8, 1977. *Today a search for tanks around Moon Crater, in the vicinity of early Indian settlements in the southwest corner of the Pinacates. Temperature is 40F before dawn, 90F by noon and 92F by 2 P.M. Pebbles near here have parallel windrows on the leeward side, showing the strong prevailing wind from the southwest.*

Bote Tank is a 60-foot-wide depression in the wash about a mile uphill from Moon Crater. It is dry; coyotes have been digging for water. Coyote droppings, coyote bones, bedrock mortars, and plainware pottery sherds are scattered around. Here we are in the general vicinity of Kino's Santa Brigida village.

Crossing rolling lava and vegetation about 5 miles east-northeast of Moon Crater, we come to a ravine perhaps 50 feet wide and 30 feet deep, cut through coarsely layered basalt. In a narrow, shaded chasm, at the foot of sheer rock walls, is a pond some 20 feet across. This is Tule Tank, five or six feet deep, with dark-green water. White bands on the rocks show old water levels. Modern-looking petroglyphs upstream about 300 feet from the tank include arrows (one pointing toward the tank) and initials.

An old Indian trail passes parallel to the top of the ravine on the west side. Broken shells and sherds are scattered about. Grinding tools and bedrock mortars also mark the area.

Lumholtz camped near these tanks, and Sykes left his party near here, when he made his 43-mile junket to the sea. The lava flats and distant dunes look like they are just waiting for some other fool to try it.

Later we head south toward Moon Crater. I get to ride with the crater's discoverer, Glenton Sykes, son of Godfrey. I sit next to him in his pickup. He drives with grand reckless joy, his unruly shock of white hair, which he referred to as "randomized," rippling in the breeze.

Moon Crater is a shallow saucer with a fine dark cinder cone set off dramatically by the flat, bright-dusty crater floor. We explore the dunes abutting its west side. They consist of powdery material, coarser than flour but finer than sand. Abundant animal life is evidenced by tiny criss-crossing tracks all over the dunes. Tracks of lizards. Tracks of rodents and insects. Perfect-circle tracks of drooping, pivoting branches, blowing in the wind. The occasional bushes and trees give habitats to bugs; but we also see little holes where tiny creatures have disappeared into the dust. The dunes have sensual, female forms; graceful curves seen against still more distant graceful curves. Curves the eye can trace from a hard edge to a fade-out. Big dunes covered with small dunes. The steep sides of the dunes display slips where sand, magically transformed for a moment into fluid, flows down in little, overlapping trickles, and then freezes back into dry powder.

April 9, 1977. *Admiring the landscape, we pass north past the wash leading to Papago Tanks. Near this wash we pass through a broad Indian site, scattered with shells, flakes and potsherds.*

The vegetation around us is iron-green, with straw-colored grasses. There is an interesting foreshortening effect in the desert: anything standing even a few inches higher than the surrounding surface gives its color to the tops of ridges and to distant plains.

We cross the north side of the lavas, going east on Mexico 2, and turn south down the road toward Lumholtz' Elegante Crater. Glenton tells how, a few years back, he encountered a geology class on a field trip on the rim of Elegante. He decided to enlighten them on the local rock types. "They say there're no fossils here in the Pinacates, because it's volcanic rock," he wheezed. "But I'm living proof that they're wrong."

Here on the Elegante's lower rim slope, we are surprised to find a parking lot outlined by whitewashed rocks and little barriers. The "improvements" installed in connection with the new Mexican park, or Federal Reserve, as it is called. The parking lot is cinder-covered, with the turnoff from the road well-marked. I count at least 20 Mexicans, apparently on picnic from Rocky Point, and ranging from about three to 40 years in age. The family seems to be strewing a trail of garbage: cans, plastic diapers, food wrappers. Friends tell me I should not report this in my manuscript. What can I do but report here what I see?

"Lying down there in the sands of the desert, alone and at night . . . your eyes staring upward at the stars . . . we keep sending a hope, a doubt, a query up through the realms of air to Saturn's throne."
J.C. Van Dyke, The Desert, 1901.

Time-exposed star trails over the barren Cabeza Prieta Mountains. October 19, 1985.

7. Volcanoes and Indians

Alien, ponderous [the dormant volcanic] mountains seemed to emit a deep purring sound, too deep for the ear to hear, and yet audible on the blood, a sound of dread. There was no soaring or uplift or exaltation, as there is in the snowy mountains of Europe. Rather a ponderous . . . weight, pressing terribly on the earth, and murmuring like two watchful lions.

D.H. Lawrence
The Plumed Serpent, 1926

. . . this vast, savage, howling mother of ours, Nature . . .

H. D. Thoreau
In the essay "Walking," 1862

LONG AGO, THE TOHONO O'ODHAM'S elder brother, the god I'itoi, learned that the world would be destroyed in a great flood. He fashioned a boat and warned the coyote and the Pinacate beetle to save themselves from the coming deluge. When the floodwaters gushed forth from the tops of the mountains, I'itoi floated around the world four times. As the flood was subsiding, his craft came to rest on the Pinacate summit, giving the Pinacates a sacred status. Soon he and the coyote and the beetle got together again. They could not find a dry place to sit, so they dug a tremendous hole. Then I'itoi created the red ants, who went down still farther into the earth and brought up dry soil for them to sit upon. Thus were I'itoi, the coyote and the Pinacate beetle saved from the flood, according to the legend told to Lumholtz in 1909 by the Tohono O'odham.

Is there a fantastic coincidence here, between Indian legend and the Biblical story of Noah's flood? In the 1800s, such parallels fueled a faddish belief in mysterious links between New World and Old World peoples. From such similarities, Ignatius Donnelly in 1882 popularized mythical Atlantis, the Atlantic mother-culture that supposedly spawned civilization in Europe and Middle America, thus explaining the common leg-

ends. Even today, ideas play a unique role in the Southwest, where Mormon church leaders assert that lost tribes of Hebrews colonized the New World and spawned prehistoric Indian civilizations.

The saga of Sonoran Desert exploration suggests a more realistic, but no less fascinating, explanation for the I'itoi-Noah parallel. I'itoi's boat may be a corrupted version of the story of Noah's ark, preached to the Indians by Spanish priests, and grafted onto native mythology, as long as 300 years before Lumholtz heard it. Indeed, Kino found the shape of one nearby peak reminiscent of Noah's ark, and he so named it. Thus, Kino himself probably introduced the flood-and-ark myth! Ethnologists who recorded "native" legends in the 1800s, sometimes neglected the lingering effects of the almost-forgotten Spanish missionaries. We know from records of other events, such as Esteban's death in Cíbola, that the Indians were very effective at preserving stories about some of these early incidents.

Why does the legend have I'itoi create ants as a means of bringing up dry soil? There is keen observation here. A desert rain may soak only the upper inch of soil, and burrowing ants then bring up dry soil from a zone beneath the mud. But more specific observations may be

Previous page: Prehistoric pictograph on underside of rock ledge, Tinajas Altas. October 17, 1971.

Tohono O'odham shrine at Santa Rosa. February 22, 1981.

involved—a connection with the volcanism of the region. I'itoi's boat was supposed to have come to rest on the Pinacate Mountains' summit, capped by two large cinder cones, one with an impressive funnel-shaped crater. The hole that I'itoi started to dig may be a mythic explanation of this pit. There is a still more subtle observation: well-developed cinder cones mimic the shape of desert anthills; loose material is thrown out around a central "vent" and piles up at the angle of repose. Centuries ago, some unsung Leonardo of the desert noticed this similarity between two landforms, 10,000 times different in scale, and built it into his mythic epic of creation. Perhaps the I'itoi-Noah myth is a metaphor for volcanism in the ancient past, with I'itoi and his ant friends spewing material out of the ground to build the vast cinder-cone anthills of the Pinacates.

Tohono O'odham legends show a curious fascination with erupting vents. This common thread has gone little noticed. One instance was the encounter between Manje and the "House of the Wind" at San Xavier del Bac in 1699. Manje's book also mentions a similar wind-emitting hole near the Indian village of Imuris. Another, more modern, example can be seen on the Tohono O'odham reservation near Santa Rosa, where a rock-slab shrine covers a hole from which, according to legend, a flood of water issued and threatened a village "long before the white man came."[1] Four children were sacrificed in the vent, stopping the flood. Reportedly, around 1910, some Indians disturbed the rocks, evoking a "sudden wind that roared from the hole and would not stop until they put the stone back over the hole." I visited the shrine in February, 1981, and found, within a 40-yard fenced area, several piles of rock slabs and piles of creosote-branch offerings. A cactus-rib enclosure, about four feet wide and as much as nine feet tall, surrounded a rough cairn of rock slabs. A 1963 account notes that only offerings of shells and beads were appreciated, not metal or coins; but by 1981, I noted that times had changed: combs, sunglasses, and a few quarters, dimes, and nickels lay with prayer-sticks and sheaves of grass.

Another reference to air-emitting vents comes from the Pinacate region, where bighorn sheep horns were piled near the *tinajas* to "prevent the 'Air' from leaving the place." Visitors were cautioned against removing them, "because that element would come out to molest everybody."[2] Pima Indians in this century told researchers that bighorn sheep horns must always be treated with repect and placed at designated sites, lest they interfere with wind and rain.

Still another story of wind-emitting vents makes an amazing connection between a second category of Sonoran Desert legend that we discussed earlier—that of missing mission bells. In 1969, University of Arizona archaeologist Bernard L. Fontana[3] undertook to locate the ruins of a mission, "Santa Ana de Cuiquiburitac," built in the Tohono O'odham country north of Sells. Inquiries among Indian friends revealed that the site was well known, bearing not the name Santa Ana, but the vestigial name Santan. Fontana and colleagues found the foundations and a hole that once had been a well. In 1970, further inquiries revealed that some of the Indians used to go there and dig because, as one Indian told Fontana,

> . . . *they were digging a well there in the old days. While they were digging the well, the wind came out of the ground, and to stop it, they threw the church bell into the hole and covered it up. Once in awhile someone digs there to try to find the bell.*

Fontana said he was "flabbergasted" at this news. His Spanish records indicated that the well had been dug to about 72 feet but not finished. Two years later, by chance, more pieces of the puzzle fell into place and the "bell" was identified. Fontana was visiting the Smithsonian Institution in Washington when he saw a Spanish mission-period baptismal font, handmade from copper, in their collections. It was a two-foot-diameter

Aerial view of Moon Crater and Pinacate lavas (foreground), Gran Desierto dunes, and Gulf of California (horizon). September 14, 1972.

None of this settles the question of when the *very last* eruptions occurred. The youngest of Lynch's dated rocks, a 150,000-year-old basalt, came from the walls of Elegante Crater. But it is not necessarily a piece of the last lava flow. Statistically, Lynch was unlikely to have chanced on the very youngest flow in his first dozen or so samples, even if he were seeking the last eruption site.

Lynch actually collected two samples that seemed to have too little radiogenic gas to give well-determined dates. This could mean that they are less than some 40,000 years old. One was from the central peak of Moon Crater and the other, from a cone near Mexican Route 2, west of the roadside tavern at Los Vidrios.

Interestingly, Ives[7] also focussed on Moon Crater as possibly a young feature. At Cholla Bay, on the Gulf shore southwest of the Pinacates, Ives studied a stratum of ash he thought came from Moon Crater. From stratigraphic relations, he concluded Moon Crater had produced this ash eruption only 2,000 to 40,000 years ago. Lynch was able to show that Moon Crater punched through a 340,000-year-old lava flow from a neighboring cone. It must be younger than that, but it does not *look* particularly fresh. Lynch believes that the cone, flow and crater are not unusually young, but formed within a few years or centuries of each other, as part of one eruptive sequence 340,000 years ago. Lynch concluded that both of his seemingly young rock samples had given spurious results—a circumstance not uncommon in the rock-dating business.

Still another candidate for a young site is Cerro Colorado Crater, on the northeast edge of the lavas. Unique in the Pinacates, it has a high rim of soft, eroded, pinkish ash, giving it its name of "Red Hill," Cerro Colorado. Its salmon-gold walls make it one of the Pinacates' most beautiful spots. Tramping around this area, Ronald Ives convinced himself that the "most recent major activity at Pinacate was almost certainly the last ash eruption at Cerro Colorado."[8] He also thought he had found a stratigraphic layer that contained both volcanic ash and Hohokam Indian pottery. From this he concluded that the last eruption occurred after 700 A.D., and possibly even more recently than Kino's visits around 1700! He also felt that the rapid erosion rates on the adobe-like gullied flank of Cerro Colorado supported a young age. But Ives' claim for centuries-old activity at Cerro Colorado was demolished by the clever sleuthing of University of Arizona geology graduate students, including Douglas Shakel,[9] who camped in 1969 on the northwest rim of Cerro Colorado and collected pottery fragments later identified as Hohokam Indian ware from about 900-1100 A.D. The sherds were not embedded *in* the crater deposits, but dropped *on* the crater, and Shakel and co-author Karen Harris concluded that Cerro Colorado must thus be *older* than 1100 A.D. Tucson archaeologist and Pinacate explorer Julian Hayden mentioned to me in 1988 that he has found still much older stone tools on Cerro Colorado. Cerro Colorado was unsampled in Lynch's work, and no firm date has been established. The crater's erosional state, and the ages of lavas elsewhere in the Pinacates, suggest (but do not prove) Cerro Colorado is thousands, not hundreds, of years old.

My candidates for the youngest major flows lie west and north of Elegante. These flows show up as extremely dark and well-defined in aerial photos, as if too young to have been weathered and veneered by light, windblown dust. Lynch concurs that some lava in these areas may be too young to date by the radioisotope techniques—i.e., less than 40,000 years—although at this writing he has not attempted dating in these areas.

Still more extreme are allegations of activity as recent as a few decades ago! A large earthquake shook the area on December 31, 1934, and a veil of dust and smoke was reported lingering over the Pinacates. In 1935, Ives made the startling suggestion that an eruption might have occurred at this time. In Ives' photo albums,[10] I located one of his sources, a *Denver Post* article dated January 10, 1935. Datelined Yuma, the brief article was headlined DORMANT VOLCANO SHOWS SIGNS OF LIFE. It makes explicit reference to the Pinacates and reports:

Accompanied by deep rumblings and eruption of smoke, a long-dormant volcano . . . is showing signs of activity . . .

The entire southwest was shaken by earthquakes which centered near the volcanic formations below the border on Dec. 31. The shocks were felt as far north as Phoenix Ariz., and to the west in Southern California.

The headline was overly enthusiastic: the earthquake proves geologic unrest, but it did not prove that an eruption had occurred. Because of the conventional wisdom that the Pinacates are inactive, the experts were more cautious. Ives himself allowed that the pall of smoke might simply have been dust thrown up by an earthquake-triggered avalanche. Hayden has speculated that smoke cited in this period also may have been from the burning of brush during the drought of that decade. He particularly mentions a "dry jungle" at the west end of Papago Wash; he observed in the late '50s that it had been burned over some time earlier.[11]

Ives also cited older stories of smoke plumes from the Pinacates as evidence of eruptions in historic times. But Julian Hayden suggested that those were ordinary fires.[12] (See next chapter.)

In summary, there is no proof of fume venting or lava eruptions within the last few thousand years, and the conventional wisdom is that the Pinacates have long been dormant. Probably there have been no major eruptions for a thousand years or more, though a minor vent may have been active here and there more recently. Lynch concluded that, on the average, eruptions during the million-year Pinacate heyday occurred roughly 3,000 years apart and lasted less than a year. Eruptions in active volcanic complexes can be as brief as a few hours. Thus, it is still plausible that somewhere in this dark labyrinth of winding flows and sprawling cones is an undiscovered young vent, perhaps only centuries or decades old. Julian Hayden has noted that such features might be identified by the absence of caliche layers that build up on rock and soil surfaces exposed to intermittent moisture. Glassy textures and mineral deposits such as sulfur crystals would also be clues to a recent eruptive site. Hayden remarked to me in the 1970s that much of the summit region (apparently singled out in the Papago legend) remains to be explored from these points of view. On the other hand, Lynch's studies suggest most summit flows are older than the youthful outlying flows and craters. Another fertile hunting ground is the relatively unexplored southwest sector, with its relatively young "Ives Flow." In Chapter 9 I will recount an eyewitness claim of volcanic venting in this flow!

The whole Pinacate region of the desert heart offers clues to the possibility of future activity. Earthquakes still shake the region. Even the springs at Quitobaquito still emit 80F water—warmer than normal underground water and probably geothermally heated. Still farther east, about 60 miles from the Pinacates near the border east of Sonoita, is reportedly a "boiling hot" well dug in the late 1800s.[13] Geologist Charles A. Wood has noted that the amount of heat flowing out of the Earth's interior (a good indicator of volcanic potential) increases across northwest Mexico toward the Pinacate area. Perhaps the Pinacate lavas will rise again.

Having guessed that the last major eruptions occurred sometime between 150,000 and 1,000 years ago, we still ask whether anyone witnessed them. This brings us to the history of Indian occupation in the area. When did the first human characters appear in this drama of fire-breathing volcanoes? This simple question leads into a cactus patch of archaeological controversy. Although most archaeologists place the first humans in North America around 12,000 to 10,000 B.C., when low sea levels opened the Aleutian land bridge from Asia, a few say that scattered earlier intruders also arrived as far back as 40,000 B.C. Interestingly enough, the Sonoran Desert heartland plays a role in the controversy.

Throughout North and South America, the oldest *well-dated* human artifacts come from the 12,000 to 10,000 B.C. period. These artifacts, from many sites, prove people did enter America from Siberia through Alaska and rapidly swept across the continents. In the earliest example of environmental damage to the American frontier, they apparently hunted big mammals, such as the mammoth, to extinction.[14] Their stone tools include the big, beautifully flaked Clovis and Folsom spear points—named for the towns in New Mexico where they were found. These spear points were designed by pre-historic inventors specifically to hunt the big game. As the big mammals vanished from the landscape, these points vanished from the archaeological record, and were replaced by less distinctive, less easily dated tools.

In spite of the tidy story told by the big points and the verified dates around 12,000 to 10,000 B.C., a growing minority of archaeologists claim evidence of more primitive hunters who came thousands of years earlier. Their purported tools were much cruder—roughly shaped choppers and scrapers. Even the tools are controversial, and sites are scarce. Isotopic dating methods, such as the radiocarbon technique that dates carbon in organic materials, have yielded mixed results. Several sites have yielded ages as old as 20,000 B.C. or more, but critics say the dates are unreliable because of contamination of the carbon.

Perhaps, in summary, a few primitive hunters wandered North America before 12,000 B.C., and were overwhelmed—technologically and in numbers—by a new wave of immigration around 12,000 to 10,000 B.C. when a climate shift enhanced the Siberia-Alaska land bridge.

Throughout the Sonoran Desert, this argument swirled like a dust devil. One reason these regions are of such great archaeological interest is that the desert pavement of the Pinacates and other volcanic regions is

Saguaros *"have a stately look, like the pillars of ruined temples."* Mary Austin, The Land of Journeys' Ending, *1924.*

Ajo Mountains, Organ Pipe Cactus National Monument, showing light-toned layer of 50-My-old ash near summit. Sunset, January 12, 1980.

the perfect environment to preserve the ancient evidence. Tools lie for ten thousand years where they were dropped on the stable, pebble-covered surfaces, and millennia-old trails are easy to trace. The Pinacates are the best example; as Tucson archaeologist Julian Hayden wrote in 1976:

> *The Sierra Pinacate is unique among the deserts of North America in that all non-perishable remains of man's occupancy are preserved in direct association with the surfaces upon which they were deposited, undisturbed by erosion. This is as true of the earliest stone tools as it is of tin cans left by cowboys or campers.*[15]

Prehistoric rock alignments discovered by author's party, northwest of Elegante Crater and verified by Julian Hayden, August, 1970.

One of the first archaeologists to call attention to these earliest desert traces of humanity was the California researcher, Malcolm Rogers. From the 1930s through about 1960, he recorded crude, ancient sites scattered throughout the Mojave and Sonoran deserts of southern California, Arizona, and Sonora.[16] These ranged from rock alignments depicting giant figures (best visible from the air!) to so-called sleeping circles and clusters of crudely flaked stone tools. "Sleeping circles" are cleared areas, usually six to ten feet across and bounded by a ring of boulders. They may have been used as windbreaks for sleeping (sleeping out in the desert at night is much more comfortable if you have a shield from the wind and if you have some rocks to hunker against—try it). Alternatively, they may have been personalized

storage areas ("This is my stuff!").

Rogers worked out the classification scheme still used for naming these early desert cultures. The earliest he called the *San Dieguito* people, after archetype sites near San Diego. The dating of the San Dieguito culture was helped by discoveries in Ventana Cave, on the northeast edge of the Sonoran Desert, about 100 miles northeast of the Pinacates in the hills of the Tohono O'odham reservation. Ventana Cave was an archaeologist's dream.

It had a long history of human habitation, represented by orderly layers of soil containing bones and tools, with the oldest on the bottom. The earliest such layer contained San Dieguito tools, a Clovis point, and other tools. It dated within a millenium of 9350 B.C., consistent with the theory that San Dieguito people were representatives of the first Americans, who arrived around 10,000 B.C. As a result of these studies, most archaeologists agree the San Dieguito period lasted from a cool era around 10,000 B.C. until a hotter, drier period, called the *altithermal*, centered around 5000 B.C.

A dissenter from this point of view is Tucson archaeologist Julian Hayden, who was an associate and student of Malcom Rogers.

Hayden became the colorful, grand old man of the Pinacates, outliving other Pinacate pioneers of this century, such as Ronald Ives. With his white, bushy mustache, short white hair, and courtly manners overlying a tough, sinewy core, Hayden looks the part of a sheriff transported by some time warp from the 1880s. There is always a twinkle in his eye. There is even a twinkle in his mustache. Behind this facade, you sense answers to a hundred secrets of the desert. When I first talked to Julian about the Pinacates in the 1960s, I was a complete greenhorn. He knew it and I knew it, and the twinkle seemed to say, "You haven't even scratched the surface." Twenty years later, in spite of many hours in deserts and libraries, I'm still a greenhorn around Julian.

Hayden and Rogers had found old, crude stone

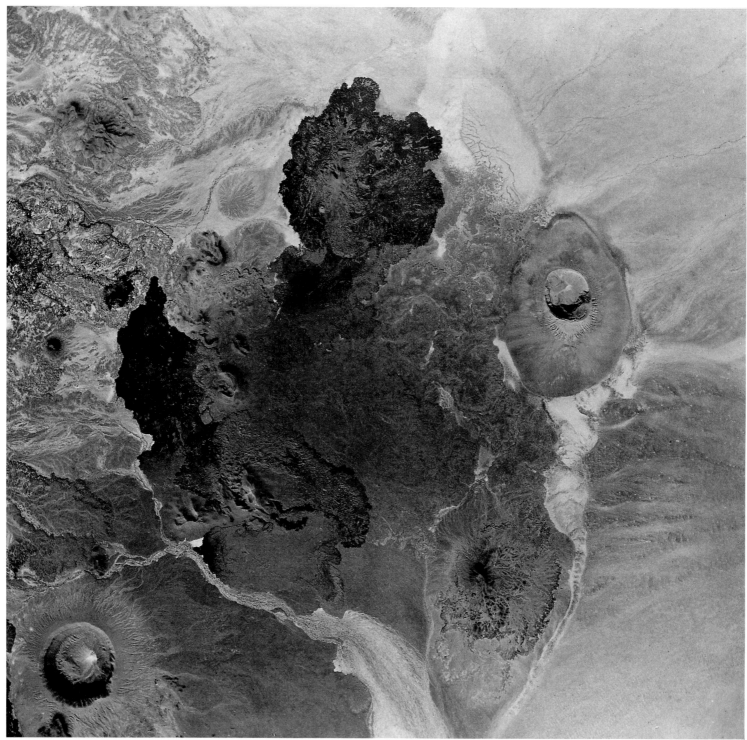

Aerial photo of the very dark, young flows between Elegante (lower left) and Cerro Colorado (right). Unidentified aerial survey, November 17, 1954.

tools with an unusually high degree of shiny surface stain called *desert varnish.* Rogers eventually designated these as just an early phase of San Dieguito cultural remains. Hayden, pushing the search into the Pinacates, found lots of these tools and concluded that they were distinctly older than San Dieguito. He joined a few other maverick archaeologists in the view that Southwestern hunters had arrived 30,000 years ago or earlier.

To understand his argument, remember that desert varnish is a shiny, blackish, varnish-like deposit that builds up (to the thicknesses of nearly 1/10 millimeter) on basalt lavas and other rocks as a result of chemical processes during thousands of years of exposure to desert conditions. It seems to form particularly during the hot, dry, "altithermal" conditions, perhaps primarily only within certain ranges of moisture and temperature.

Hayden found that the San Dieguito tools had a certain level of desert varnish but that the seemingly older tools had a distinctly thicker level of varnish, as if they had been through an extra altithermal period. Hayden called these the tools of the *Malpais* people, resurrecting a term that Rogers had earlier discarded. Hayden postulated an earlier, "Malpais Altithermal," a hot, dry period, peaking around 17,000 B.C., similar to today's desert climate, in which desert varnish formed readily. In the Pinacates, he attributed numbers of sleeping circles, trails, trailside shrines (rock cairns), rock alignments and intaglio figures (made by scraping aside the desert pavement, the thin gravel cover that is left behind as wind blows away surface dust) to the Malpais folk.

Hayden buttresses this work with his findings on dunes near Adair Bay. Here he found shells he interprets as food remains from ancient camps. The shells were dated as much as 37,000 years old or more.

Hayden's Pinacate explorations, which he often pursued alone in his battered old truck, have commanded universal respect, although his conclusions have been criticized. Indeed, in his important 1976 summary paper, he sardonically thanks "the unnamed editor who likened [an earlier draft] to the vaporings of Erich von Daniken [the pseudo-science writer of "ancient astronaut" fame], thereby outraging me to the point of writing the present paper." In the late 1980s, increasing reports of North and South American sites older than 12,000 years old seem to support Hayden's conclusions.

Only further patient exploration and isotopic dating will settle whether the first human beings walked into the Southwest as early as 40,000 B.C. (and saw the tail end of the cataclysmic eruptions?), or as recently as 10,000 B.C., when most of the major activity had ended. My own guess is that while there may or may not have been some pre-10,000 B.C. wanderers, Indians after 10,000 B.C. did witness fumarole or mild eruptive activity in the Pinacate area.

THE REST OF THE INDIAN HISTORY of the Sonoran Desert is a saga of human interactions with a harsh environment, and the creation of a now-lost civilization in the river valleys around its edges. By around 3000 B.C., the large mammals were extinct, and the "tool kits" of primitive Americans had recognizably different implements, including smaller projectile points and a new type of grinding mortar, in which rock-hard mesquite pods could be crushed by gyrating a pestle in a conical hole cut into rock.[17] The people who made these tools are called the *Amargosa* people.

Pottery, which was first manufactured in the New World around 3000 B.C., reached the Southwest around 200 A.D. That marked the end of the Amargosa lifestyle. Around that time, additional cultural influences from the advanced civilizations of central Mexico spread northward, bringing not only pottery but a more advanced lifestyle along the eastern river-borders of the Sonoran Desert, especially the Santa Cruz and Salt-Gila near Phoenix. Under these influences, the people of southern Arizona began producing beautifully painted pottery, finely worked turqouise and shell jewelry, and a fine system of canals, fed off the then-verdant rivers. Social influences from central Mexico also led to construction of ball courts that look like scaled-down football stadiums.

It may be interesting for modern sunbelt Arizonans to contemplate that only a millenium ago, "high" culture was flowing *north*, from the grand civilization of Mexico to the "third-world" country that is now the United States. The intriguing culture that blossomed as a result, for about a thousand years in the region of present-day Phoenix and Tucson, is called the *Hohokam culture* (ho-ho-kam, no accented syllable).

Throughout the Sonoran Desert, in the period of about 200-1250 A.D., Hohokam Indians built one-story brushwork "pit houses," partly dug into the soil. Hohokam towns during this period were clusters of these pit houses, often with a rough central plaza, an outlying ball court, and nearby cultivated fields and trash mounds. But near the end of the Hohokam period, by around 1300 to 1450, Indians of the eastern rivers began to construct impressive above-ground, multistory adobe buildings, like the ruins still preserved at Casa Grande. Many of these still stood in spectacular ruins along the Gila when Kino came through around 1700.

In contrast to the Hohokam flowering on the northeastern Sonoran Desert's riverbanks, survival was a harsher proposition in the western deserts, and the people of the desert heart remained country cousins, with cruder pottery and no substantial architecture.

The social situation in the Sonoran Desert, especially around 1200 A.D., was curiously like that of the Near East in Biblical times. Like the wandering Hebrews of the harsh deserts, the provincial Hohokam of the western desert had little direct influence from the glamorous urban centers of the Gila River—the Babylons of the Hohokam era.

Senita cactus, Ajo Mountains, Organ Pipe Cactus National Monument. In background is light 50-My-old ash layer over darker basalt. November 27, 1986.

Two mysteries of Hohokam archaeology are where the Hohokam came from and what happened to them. There are two theories of the source of Hohokam flowering. The first is that the Hohokam were invaders, probably spreading from northern Mexico, bringing advanced Mexican culture from the south. The second theory is that the Hohokam were not newcomers, but merely local Arizona Indians, whose culture changed rapidly as they adopted customs infiltrating from Mexico during trade. The debate over these theories continues.[18]

The desert dwellers of the Pinacate area never even made much pottery of their own. By about 700 A.D.,

Natural zen garden with senita cactus, brittle bush and barrel cactus, near Emilia Tank. January 22, 1983.

pottery-making technology had spread west down the Gila during Hohokam expansion, and reached the Indians of the lower Colorado River, known as *Patayan* people.[19] From about 1050 onward this drab pottery, made locally in the lower Colorado River area, was the main type appearing in the Pinacate heartland; apparently it was brought in by trade.[20]

In 1967, Hayden pointed out that, surprisingly, the *earliest* pottery in the Pinacate region was not the abundant, drab Yuma tradeware, but nicely painted Hohokam ware from the "Babylons" of the Phoenix-Tucson area. What were the urban Hohokam or their pots doing in the Pinacates? Hohokam jewelry of the

urban centers shows the answer: it is made of shell from the Gulf of California. Several lines of evidence show that the Hohokam made treks from the urban centers through the desert heart to the Gulf coast, to collect not only shells but salt.[21] First, trails, campsites, and pottery fragments testify to abundant traffic through the area. More importantly, Hayden pointed out that while petroglyphic rock drawings are fairly rare in the Pinacate area, two water tanks have petroglyphs in the Hohokam style, including figures of shells. One is at Tinaja Romero near a trail across the southeast side of the Pinacates, and the other is a Hohokam village site about 55 miles to the north, in the Growler Mountains west of Ajo, on a main trail from the Hohokam heartland. The second line of evidence is the fact that the Tohono O'odham, or Papagos, of the last century have made their own salt pilgrimages to the sea across these same networks of trails. Hayden's Indian informants told him that the Papagos traveled "fast and light" across the desert heart, and collected their salt without the help of the local desert Papagos of the Pinacates, who remained haughtily aloof. Probably the salt journeys of historic times are a tradition carried over from Hohokam times. The aloofness of the Pinacate locals might explain why the Hohokam made the trip themselves, instead of depending on trade.

WHAT HAPPENED TO THE HOHOKAM? This question is even more controversial than the question of where they came from. In 1539, when Marcos de Niza came through only a century after the last of the Hohokam multistory buildings, the Indians had abandoned the huge adobe structures, and were living only in scattered villages of mud and brush structures. By the time Kino discovered Casa Grande in the 1690s, it was a haunted house, the subject of cryptic legends.

Archaeological evidence shows that something crucial happened around 1400 to 1450. The Hohokam

attitudes of his contemporaries, Pumpelly quotes an outrageous passage from a contemporary publication, *Arizona and Sonora*, by one Sylvester Mowry:[31]

> *A steady, persistent campaign must be made [against the Apaches]. They must be surrounded, starved . . . surprised, or inveigled—by white flags, or any other method, human or divine—and then put to death. If these ideas shock any weak-minded philanthropist, I can only say that I pity without respecting his mistaken sympathy. A man might as well have sympathy for a rattlesnake . . .*

We should wince at this, but we should also realize that just as the historic natives of our region suffered at the hands of our forebears, the last remnants of the prehistoric natives suffer at our hands. Time and commerce have destroyed many traces of the Hohokam, the grandest prehistoric civilization of the Sonoran Desert. Newcomers, from Spanish ranchers to American developers, have plowed and paved their plazas and ball courts. Explosive sunbelt growth in recent years has seen village sites that were mapped by Kino and excavated in the 1920s or 1930s deeded over to builders for housing tracts or shopping centers. In addition, the Central Arizona Project—the aqueduct, the distribution canals and the feeder lines—has eaten up hundreds of Hohokam and earlier sites.

BECAUSE THE DESERT HEART remained a backwater, isolated from the Hohokam rise and fall, the history of its people was simpler. Hayden concludes from artifacts that the historic Indians of the Pinacate area, who were called *Areneños*, or Sand Papagos, were direct descendents of the ancient Amargosans, and that these same people lived in the desert heartland throughout the Hohokam occupation to the north.

As Spanish and Anglo newcomers moved into their desert, the "untamed" Indians were driven farther and farther into the untamed outback. The Sand Papagos

Dark and light mineralogies. The Sierra Blanca Mountains at the south tip of the Pinacates offer startling contrasts of dark basalt flows (foreground) abutting old, light-toned, eroded granites. February 19, 1989.

developed a reputation as a fierce breed. Many sources identify two main groups, one centered around Quitobaquito, and a westernmost group in the Pinacates and dunes. The westernmost Sand Papagos, including a band who holed up at Papago Tanks, were considered the worst of the lot, and a threat to travelers in the region. Not without some respect for their gritty persistence, Hayden in 1967 called them the *Pinacateños*. Stories of the Pinacateños give us new respect for the craft and knowledge of the tough Native Americans—knowledge completely lost to modern urbanites.

Lumholtz tells of an old Indian hunter who used to be able to run after and overtake deer. The deer tired quickly because their feet grew sore on the rocks; he would then shoot them with his bow and arrow. Both Hornaday and Lumholtz recount stories of how the Indians used to hunt sheep in the craters. Spotting sheep grazing on a crater floor, the Indians would gather near the most natural exit, and then send one of their party down to scare out the sheep. As the animals fled, the hunters felled them with arrows and even with clubs. Hayden has described a curious custom of the Sand Papago, who apparently made careful cremations of piles of bones of animals they hunted for food—a custom perhaps related to their reverence for mountain sheep horns, mentioned earlier. In 1985, Hayden reported that most of the well-preserved cremation sites he had recorded in the '60s had been "scattered and trampled by cattle, horses, burros, cowboys, and tourists."

An eyewitness account of the Pinacateños was recorded in June, 1854, when Col. Andrew Gray led his railroad survey party on a dash across the Pinacates and the Gran Desierto dunes to the coast at Adair Bay:

In this naked spot [of Adair Bay] I found a band of Indians [Papagos] almost in a state of nudity, living on fish and crabs caught in the salt creeks and lagoons of the Gulf; and a sort of root, which was ate [sic] after roasting upon hot coals; . . . the vegetable itself, when first gathered and cooked, was very luscious, and resembled in taste the finest sweet potato, only far more delicate. It was very abundant in the hills, all, except the top buried in the sand, apparently attached to some other root.[32]

Botanist Gary Nabhan, in his 1985 book on Sonoran Desert plants,[33] tells more details of this unique delicacy of the desert, growing in what Gray called "the most desolate and forlorn-looking spot for 80 miles around the head of the Gulf." More than a century and a half earlier, Manje had mentioned it, describing Indians in this region "eating roots of wild sweet potatoes." None-

theless, Gray was credited with discovering this amazing plant, because he sent a specimen to the famous botanist John Torrey, who identified it as a new genus, *Ammobroma Sonorae,* commonly called *camote.* Nabhan recounts that although government studies were made in the 1930s to see if it could be cultivated in desert regions, it defied domestication. A parasite, its germination apparently depends on a delicate sensitivity to the presence of an appropriate host plant at an appropriate distance.

Peter Brady, who traveled with Gray's expedition, commented that even among the young Indians of 12 or 14 "their teeth were all decayed and were level to the gums." Nabhan claims this observation was made when Brady was "somewhat aroused by the beauty of the thinly clad maidens," but I find no reference to this in Brady's reminiscences. When Gray sent the newly discovered camote to Professor Torrey, a reason for the decay became apparent. Torrey found strong acid in the plant, and both Torrey and Brady theorized that this acid damaged the natives' teeth. Nabhan allows this as a possibility. But crusty old Thomas Childs, who was married to a Sand Papago woman, claimed to have solved the mystery from first-hand knowledge:

I know what caused it. Those Indians ate their . . . clams raw, and opened them with their teeth. They were worn down from eating those clams.

Nabhan interviewed elderly Tohono O'odham on both sides of the border, who recalled the roaming life of their youth, a richly varied life that changed from season to season and even from one year to the next, depending on weather and rainfall. They might head to the ocean for fish, then plant fields in the Pinacates where water runoff would produce a crop, then move on to the green banks of the Gila River.

Another source of information about the daily life of these Indians was Thomas Childs, mentioned above, who lived at Quitobaquito around 1903-07,[34] and recorded his reminiscences.[35] Childs tells of an Indian legend that gives a more eerie picture of hunting—the kind of Sonoran Indian tale echoed decades later in the bestsellers of Carlos Castenada, some of which had Pinacate-area settings. According to Childs' tale, in times of dire need for meat, the Indians would ask their elder-brother-god, I'itoi, for an old ram for which he had no more use. Then they would leave an arrow in a cave (the sacred cave near the summit?) and go to a certain large rock on the east side of the Pinacates. Here, an Indian would sit and wait. Soon, an old mountain sheep would approach, and would not run away "as he came for that purpose." When the sheep came close enough, it could be shot with an arrow.

Indian informants told both Lumholtz and Childs about the old main camp of the Sand Papagos, called *Sunset Camp.* It lay near the sand margins north of Chivos Tanks, between Moon Crater and Papago Tanks and was the campsite discovered by Lumholtz.

As best we know, the Pinacateños did only minimal farming, as contrasted with the eastern Papagos, who maintained extensive fields near Tucson. Lumholtz describes one agricultural site, near Suvuk Tank, on the southeast edge of the Pinacates. Nabhan recounts locating this site from an airplane with Julian Hayden. Then, following Hayden's advice, Nabhan talked to the Romero family, who even today occasionally plant tepary beans there. They get a healthy crop if the rains are right, and if the runoff from between the lava flows drains into the field. Another ancient agricultural site was eight miles west of Papago Tanks, according to Childs. Success of such agriculture depended on locating just the right environmental niche where a combination of soil and topography caused nature to do the farmer's work. The long-lost transition from hunting to agriculture— the revolution that our European-descended schoolbooks say happened 10,000 years ago—was happening here in the Sonoran Desert only a century ago. Records

of these techniques shed valuable light on how human societies made the transition from roaming tribesmen to settled farmers and city dwellers.

According to Childs, the Pinacateños wore long hair, plastering it with mud occasionally to kill lice. "When they point to some distant spot," Childs tells us, "it is mostly done with the chin. Other Indians made fun of their accent, calling them people 'who talk like Chinamen.'" The feeling was mutual.

The ratty, surviving bands of Pinacateños became increasingly known as unsavory characters at best, desperados at worst. Travelers along the Camino del Diablo were still not safe. Childs says that two old Papagos told him in 1884 that members of their band of 100 to 150 had killed '49ers on the Devil's Highway for the tobacco and buckskin bags they carried. In 1854, some of the more peaceful Sand Papagos from around Quitobaquito were hired to guide Gray's expediton, but the party was menaced by unfriendly Pinacateños.[36]

In 1858, placer gold was discovered about 85 miles north of the Pinacates on the Gila River, at a boom town called *Gila City.* Sand Papagos and Mexicans worked there for some years, earning a few dollars a day. One day some of them killed a cow and the owner's cowboys chased them back to Quitobaquito. This flight brought some of the Sand Papagos back to the Pinacate area where they tried to settle around Quitobaquito, Sonoita and Ajo.[37]

Lumholtz recorded that it was generally felt to be impossible to capture Sand Papago desperados once they reached their lairs in the Pinacates. Yet in response to some of the troubles of this period, the Mexicans sent troops who killed some Sand Papagos and rounded up many others, deporting them to Caborca. Others fled to the dunes, to Yuma and to the gold digs along the Gila River.[38]

In the 1890s, some Sand Papagos killed two Mexicans during their siesta near Quitobaquito. A Mexican posse from Sonoita tracked this group into the dunes

Very large bedrock mortar, margin of Tule Tank in the Cabeza Prieta
Mountains. October 20, 1985.

west of Papago Tanks and killed them, sparing only a little girl who was brought back to Sonoita and raised there.[39]

Even during Lumholtz' visit in 1910, he reported that ". . . the sand people were not a pleasant lot to deal with. They were rapacious and probably merciless to strangers." If they were unpleasant, they were at least colorful. A tale is told about old Quelele, the Indian who guided Lumholtz to the Papago sacred cave near Pinacate Peak. In his younger days in the late 1800s, Quelele had been arrested by a Mexican officer and ordered shot for some offense. The Mexican asked his name. The arrogant Papago answered "Quelele," and explained that it was the name of a northern Sonoran buzzard. "I'm a Mexican buzzard," he added. "I eat dead Mexicans!" Impressed by his arrogance and moved by some tradition of the Old West, the officer ordered him released. "Whoever talks to me like that deserves to live!"

Another interesting old Indian lived not in the Pinacates, but at Quitobaquito, where he was an informant of Lumholtz. He was known as José Juan. Lumholtz describes him as a medicine man, reputed to be 115 years old, and certainly looking 100. His son, Augustín, had a silver mine in the Cabeza Prieta Mountains—a source of much local lore. One tale was that pure silver had been melted there and cast into bullets, mistaken for lower grade metal. Cipriano Ortega, famed for the story of the golden bell of Sonoita (Chapter 4), so pressured the Indians around the turn of the century to find out the location of Augustín's mine that he drove most of them away from Sonoita.[40] Some came to live with Childs in Quitobaquito, while others drifted to Ajo.

The Sand Papagos' legend lingered on. As late as the 1950s, long-term Sonoita resident, Don Alberto Celaya, who transmitted much verbal history to later researchers such as Hayden, and who was a nephew of one of the posse members, considered that the Pinacateños had been "*Como Apache,* brutal, suspicious,

Prehistoric bedrock metates on margins of Papago Tanks. November 27, 1987.

and hostile to all but the Yumas, their friends,"[41] while Sand Papagos at Quitobaquito were peaceful.

The last Pinacateño survivor was an Indian hermit, Juan Caravajales, usually known simply as Caravajales. He was apparently one of those who had been driven from the area around 1850 and eventually returned with his wife.[42] Childs met him and his wife on a trip to the Gulf with José Augustín, probably in the 1890s. When Lumholtz visited the area in 1910, Caravajales was still a hermit, well known in the area. Lumholtz met him and left this record of the last native of the Pinacates:

He owns a burro and a horse and plants a little maize, besides raising a few squashes and watermelons [probably at a site not far from Papago Tanks]. He catches fish on the coast also, but camotes, the "roots of the sands," form his principal means of subsistence. In fact, he lives almost entirely on these camotes, and is able to find them out of season. He often goes without food for days, which does not trouble him, as he is the proud possessor of a canteen and in his travels is never without water. He confided his secrets and domestic troubles . . . When his wife left him a few years before, he decided to go back again to live in the médanos [dunes] where he was born. Once a year he visits Sonoita to see relatives and to get drunk. There is no harm in the elderly man, but neither is he sympathetic. He is thin, rather bald, and almost completely deaf, but seems to be healthy. Recently he had been in Quitovaquita [Quitobaquito] for two days and had remained without eating during that time; then he had ridden to get the camotes for three days more without food.[43]

Although Lumholtz apparently thought Caravajales eventually died in the desert, a granddaughter of Tom Childs, researching Sand Papago history in mid-century, interviewed various old Papagos and learned that Caravajales had come walking into the Sand Papago community on the Gila, near Gila Bend, around 1912. He taught the residents some of his techniques of desert agriculture and eventually died there some years later.[44]

Thus ended 10,000 years of Indian occupation in the Pinacates.

The ghost of Juan Caravajales rose again half a century later in a more charming context. Hayden tells how he once encountered a group of Mexican ranch workmen erecting a line cabin near Papago Tanks. One of the workmen was a good-looking young man, who came to be nicknamed El Novio. He proudly showed off the cabin and exclaimed that he liked the area and the cabin so much he was going to bring his fiancée, be married, and live here. Months later, Hayden happened on the same group sitting around a table in the Grijalva ranch headquarters, north of Papago Tanks. El Novio looked despondent, a little tipsy, on the verge of tears. "What's the matter?" Hayden asked. El Novio described how he had brought his sweetheart to the spot. She took one look at the landscape around Papago Tanks, and, having never been bitten by the Pinacate bug, saw only stark desolation. She promptly left.

Hayden drew on his Pinacate lore to help. "Do you know who Papago Tanks is named for? Sometimes its called Tinaja del Indio!" Hayden explained how, long ago, Juan Caravajales had brought his wife to live in the same region; how she had become tired of it, and left him; how Papago Tanks came to be named for this lone Sand Indian. "Just think, El Novio, you may live here alone, too, and some day they may name a tank after you: Tinaja del Novio!" Hayden describes how, as he left, the young man had been transformed. He sat with a smile, sighing to himself, "Tinaja del Novio, Tinaja del Novio . . ."[45]

Many of the pioneering 20th-century explorers of volcanoes and Indians have departed. Malcolm Rogers, who charted the stone circles and intaglios, was hit by a car and killed in 1960. Ronald Ives, the crusty geographer who made the first detailed maps, sleuthed among old Spanish documents, and studied the volcanic stratigraphy, died in 1982. An interesting story connects them in death. Rogers' associate, Julian Hayden, scattered Rogers' ashes over a favorite hill overlooking Celaya Crater. When Ives died, the modern Pinacateño guild of Hayden, Bill Broyles and Ives' friend Arnold Hudson, of Flagstaff, scattered Ives' ashes in the same area, so that, as Hayden remarked, they can argue into eternity their theories of the ancient desert.

Any modern traveler has the potential to continue the spirit of Hornaday, Lumholtz, Sykes, Rogers, Ives and Hayden. It involves knowing something about the place you are going, instead of blundering ahead in the hope of being entertained, oblivious to the nuggets of mind-gold you are missing under your feet. We all have the choice between discovering and destroying.

We can *look for* things.

Still there, to take one example, is the sacred cave of the Papagos, the sun shining down through cracks in the roof to form random spotlights on the shadowed floor below. The latest report I can find of Indian materials there was by a travel writer, Wilson McKenney, in 1950. Inspired by Lumholtz, he climbed the peaks on an unseasonably hot October day—his thermometer read 126F (surely in the sun!). Lying in "disordered confusion" in the cave were 96 prayer-sticks, about 12- to 20-inches long, crudely painted in reds, brown and greens. They looked like "spokes knocked from a gaudily painted child's wagon." Betraying Anglo ethnocentrism, he estimated that "probably less than a dozen men have seen the sacred cave," by which he meant white men, ignoring the generations of Indians who had come and any women who may have reached the cave by that time. He ruminated, "it is an obvious conclusion that Elder Brother has led the survivors of *Papaguería* out of the giant sand hills beside the lava-formed tinajas to reservations and habitats more favorable to man." Interesting, how we credit Elder Brother with the effects of rampaging Europeans, who, in the sardonic view of Mary Austin,[46] "massacred the game . . . ; cast down the shrines, seeking buried treasure; built nothing, preserved nothing, roared muddily through the land, and ran out like Western rivers, in the sands of a time that shows every disposition to forget them."

Shell petroglyphs on basalt, Tinaja Romero, Pinacates. January 22, 1983.

Journal entry. Exploring Indian trails east of Papago Tanks. November 28, 1987. *Coming down off a cinder cone we think may have been climbed by Kino, our party stops at a cluster of a dozen prehistoric pottery sherds within 15 feet of each other.*

There are more signs of prehistoric activity. Each of the three groups of pools along the wash has bedrock mortars among its water-sculpted rocks. Hiking along, we continue to find trail segments and sherds. One broad terrace farther upstream reveals shells, obsidian flakes, sherds and a mano or grinding stone. Nearby, one of my friends spots a roughly finished triangular basaltic projectile point, about an inch and a half long.

Ventana Cave, on the Tohono O'odham Indian Reservation, Arizona, site of human occupation from 9350 B.C. until modern times. Cave is a deep rock overhang at the foot of the cliff. February 22, 1981.

Along the trail is a row of crude rock structures, two to three feet high. I speculate that they may be prehistoric hunting blinds but later, Julian Hayden informs me they are Anglo hunting blinds. He knew the man who built them in the 1920s—a Major Brady from Mesa, Arizona.

No one comes here anymore except cows.

When I was ten, we used to go to my grandfather's farm after the field had been plowed, and collect arrowheads. Now it is a different story. I sense the transience of things. What to do with the mute remnants of our prehistoric and historic life—pottery sherds, projectile points, grinding stones, petroglyphs, rock alignments? Let them stay! Collecting them is not only illegal, but pointless. The dusty artifacts moldering on a million mantles and in a million dresser drawers and in a million showboxes in closets are adding little to anyone's life. Even museums can't use donated artifacts, collected without documentation. Capture them in another way! Photograph them, sketch them in your collector's notebook, muse over them, or write a poem about them on the actual site—take them back in your mind. But leave them. Toss them back under a bush, like the true fisherman who throws back the ones that are too small.

Remember in any case that it is illegal to remove specimens from public lands including the Mexican Pinacate Federal Reserve. Remember, too, that it is illegal to transport ancient artifacts across the border.

At the dawn of the space age, we live in the last century of human history when the cast-off artifacts of our ancestors—their bones and buried cities—are littering our planet. Most have been picked up, cataloged, museumed, or shelved. Most of the urban ruins have been paved over, instead of being enshrined in parks. We have the chance to save only these last places where one can go walking and realize so clearly that we are all standing on the shoulders of those who went before.

In our generation, landscapes are like flowers. They are transient. You have to enjoy each one for what it is now. Gaze well. Tomorrow, next decade, it may be gone.

8. Craters and Lava Flows

. . . lava like galvanized iron, on each side of which there were smooth sandy beds . . . the lava pocketed with soils apparently of extreme richness, for in them were leafy trees and lawns of real grass, starred with flowers . . . looking the more wonderfully green because of the blue-black twisted crusts of rock about.

[In another area] the basalt which ran out . . . was a coarse bubbled rock . . . The sand-laden winds had ground its exposed surfaces to a pitted smoothness like orange-rind, and the sunlight had faded out its blue to a hopeless grey.

T. E. Lawrence
Seven Pillars of Wisdom, 1935

THE SPOOKIEST FEATURES of the Pinacate landscape are the craters that pock the lavas. Craters exert a peculiar fascination for me. Something is odd about huge circular symmetry superimposed on nature's chaos. It is something odd, to walk through nature at her most random, among the twisted forms of lava flows, and presently find yourself within a circular symmetry seemingly scribed by the gods. Craters make private amphitheaters, lost sanctuaries.

From Manje's "big hole of such depth that it caused terror and fear" in March, 1701, to Hornaday's "magnificent, grand Vesuvius in the desert" in November, 1907, these cavities inspire dramatic expressions of awe among onlookers.

The ten major craters listed in Table 1 are circular features several hundred yards to three-fourths of a mile across. They range from the yawning cauldron of 800-foot-deep Elegante, to the flat, silted-in pancake of Díaz. As an assembly of volcanic cavities, they are unique in North America.

Elegante is a vast, dark amphitheater, resounding with unearthly echoes. The ochre ash beds of Cerro Colorado turn glowing golden-crimson at sunset.

Mighty Sykes is even more fearsome than Elegante in its basalt-dark depths, while nearby MacDougal is sunnier, flat-floored by bright sediments, and sports a green central garden. The smaller craters, like Kino, have rounded rims, where a traveler stands for a several moments before sensing that something strange has happened here to arrange these hills in a perfect circle.

Table 1: Major Craters of the Pinacate Mountains*					
Name	Diameter		Depth		Approximate**
	Meters	Feet	Meters	Feet	Age (years)
Elegante	1,200	3,940	250	820	149,000
Sykes (Grande)	700	2,300	220	720	Young?
MacDougal	1,100	3,610	130	430	185,000
Cerro Colorado	750	2,460	4	13	Youngest?
Molina (Cloverleaf)	150	490	30	100	Undated
Kino	800	2,620	20	66	Undated
Moon	450	1,480	0	0	ca.340,000
Celaya	550	1,800	80	260	Undated
Badilla	350	1,150	10	33	Undated
Lynch	300?	1,000?	20?	60?	Undated
Díaz	800	2,624	0	0	Undated

*A list subjectively arranged in order of "spectacularity."
**Based on Lynch's (1981) work, except for Cerro Colorado.

Previous page: Ropy "pahoehoe" lava on the Ives Flow. November 25, 1985.   *Sunset in Cerro Colorado Crater. February 9, 1985.*

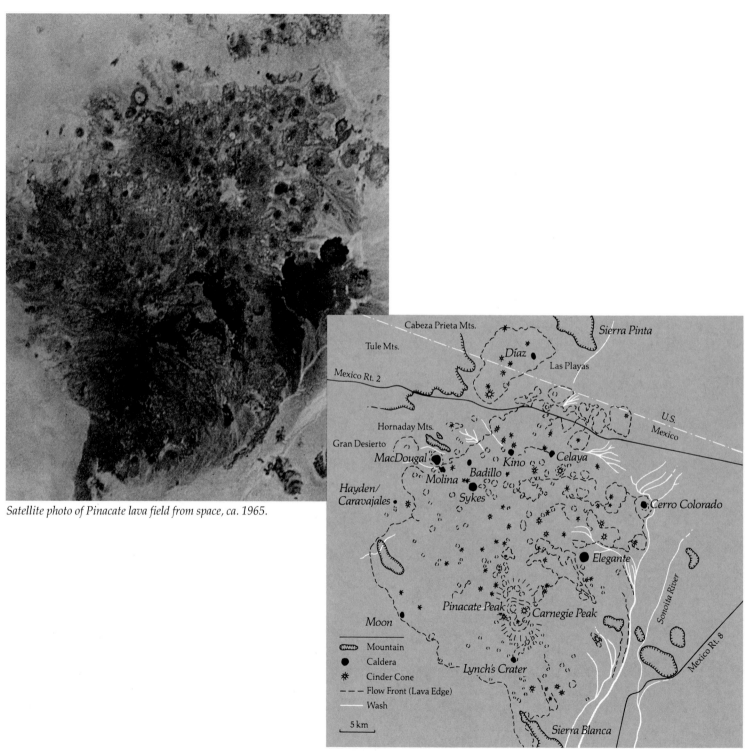

Satellite photo of Pinacate lava field from space, ca. 1965.

Map labels:

Cabeza Prieta Mts.

Tule Mts.

Díaz

Sierra Pinta

Las Playas

Mexico Rt. 2

U.S.

Mexico

Hornaday Mts.

Gran Desierto

MacDougal

Kino

Celaya

Molina

Badillo

Hayden/
Caravajales

Sykes

Cerro Colorado

Elegante

Sonoita River

Pinacate Peak

Carnegie Peak

Moon

Mountain

Caldera

Cinder Cone

Flow Front (Lava Edge)

Wash

Lynch's Crater

Mexico Rt. 8

5 km

Sierra Blanca

Sketch map identifying craters, summit peaks and other features.

146

But for the accidents of history, Elegante and Cerro Colorado might have rivaled Half Dome and Old Faithful in fame among nature lovers. Yet they are virtually unknown and even circumstances of their discovery are clouded. They were obviously known by Indians, who left artifacts in them. One of Kino's expeditions stumbled on some depression, although it was probably not one of the major craters. Chapter 4 mentioned rumors, circulating after 1850, of holes in the Pinacates that "went clear down to Hell"; the craters must have been known locally by then.

Lumholtz[1] records that Nogales mining engineer Ygnacio Bonillas visited Sykes Crater in 1882, and that although Elegante was "little known among the very few Mexicans who visit the Pinacate," it had nonetheless "been mentioned to me as the largest and most beautiful of all the craters here," proving that Elegante was known before Lumholtz visited it. Ives[2] credits Bonillas with "apparently discovering many of the great calderas," and remarks wistfully that "the Bonillas notes have not been found." Bonillas, a true Pinacate pioneer, does not even have a major crater named after him! Although Bonillas apparently passed on much of his information to the colorful Sonoita law officer, Jefferson Davis Milton, there is no clear record of crater visits by Milton prior to his trip with the MacDougal-Hornaday party in 1907.

Most of the crater discoveries are credited to the MacDougal-Hornaday expedition, because they published the first measurements and reports. Though Milton was helping to guide them, it was apparently accidental that they stumbled on MacDougal Crater; Milton in fact may not have known the exact approach to MacDougal Crater, which, with its low rim, is not spectacular until you traverse the final ten yards.

The lava flows of the area have a long history and a wide distribution. For example, northeast of the Pinacates and south of Ajo, the Growler Mountains reveal layer after layer of basalt. Basalt denotes a dark type of lava defined by its composition, and is one of the most common lava types. The basalts of the Sonoran Desert were not building the towering volcanic cones indigenous to Hollywood movies set in 2,000,000 B.C.; rather, they spread fluidly to make broad flows called *flood basalts.* Flood basalts cover tremendous areas in various parts of the world, including the American Northwest, where the Columbia and Snake River valleys expose flows that cover more than 100,000 square miles. The familiar grey patches on the moon, which make up the facial features of "the man in the Moon" are also flood basalts, making the vast extraterrestrial shore to which Neil Armstrong and subsequent astronauts carried the first wave of human exploration to another world.

Flood basalts form when the lava is very fluid, due to high temperature or high gas content, or both. The eruptions usually come from long cracks, or fissures. Fissures have formed in the Sonoran Desert as Baja California is slowly dragged north and west by the forces of plate tectonics.

Fresh basaltic lavas are generally blackish in color, but browns and reds are created by the rusting of their iron-rich minerals during conditions of intermittent rainfall. In contrast to the brooding dark lavas, many older, eroded mountains rising from the desert sediments of the Pinacate region are bright, tan, granitic rock.

What forces actually drive the lava out of the ground? This has been studied at the Hawaiian shield volcano, Kilauea, which has dimensions similar to the Pinacates. If one could descend into Earth, one would encounter partly melted zones at some depth. Geothermal regions have such zones at shallower depths than other regions. Kilauea's lavas, for example, originate in a partly melted zone 30 or 40 miles down. Melted and charged with gas vapors, the magma has lower density than the solid rock between it and the surface. By Archimedes' principle, therefore, the weight of the heavy rock pushes down and squeezes the light magma upward. When rock fractures occur during earthquakes, they are soon filled by lava worming its way toward the surface. Here and there this magma collects in pockets, or *magma chambers* a mile or so below the surface, where it may await its moment of glory during an eruption.

Once flood basalts spread over the landscape, the fissure vents are hidden. But in three-dimensional reality, the fissures extend to considerable depth, and erosion often reveals the sheets of basalt that froze underground on their way to the surface. These vertical or slightly inclined tabular sheets, usually a few feet thick, are called *dikes.* Dikes can often be seen in crater walls, road cuts and the faces of faulted cliffs. When erosion washes away the weaker surrounding rocks, the dikes are left standing like ruined castle ramparts. These are common in the Pinacates.

As lavas erupted during the last few million years to form the proto-Pinacate "Santa Clara Volcano," fluid basalts spread for tens of miles. Each eruption formed a new layer, but sometimes long periods of inactivity stretched between eruptions. Thus, in places where we can see cross sections of the layers, such as the inner cliffwalls of Elegante Crater, a keen-eyed observer sees signs of erosion on the top surfaces of each flow.

As the Santa Clara vents continued erupting, basalt flows accumulated into a gently sloping pile thickest at the middle—the characteristic dome shape of a shield volcano. Coursing down the gentle slopes, from century to century, came dark, ribbon-like lava flows—black, brown, red—frozen into motionless rivers. Who knows what early wonders—strange arches, turrets, pits, and twisted sculptures—were buried by the lavas? The stage was set for creating the features we see today. Their form would depend on the nature of the particular magmas of the final eruptions.

Many factors determined what happened during specific eruptions. If the magma has a lot of dissolved gas, it spews out of any accessible vent under high

Massive squeezeups in "aa" lava northeast of Elegante Crater. Pinacate Peaks in background. November 27, 1986.

pressure, like agitated beer. If it has a lower gas content, it may flow more smoothly. If it is highly basaltic, it may be very fluid. But if it is more granitic, which means it has a higher silica content, it tends to be more viscous and stiff, sometimes piling up or blocking its own vent, leading to explosive outbursts.

Nature seems to like two distinct kinds of basalt flows. They have picturesque Hawaiian names, after their Hawaiian prototypes. In an *aa* (pronounced ah'-ah) flow, the surface freezes while the bulk of the flow is still plastic and flowing. Jagged surface clinkers, from fist-size to gigantic house-sized blocks, break apart, upend, or slide over one another. Often, during the flow, the molten lava is not even visible; the flow looks like a slowly moving pile of jagged, cindery fragments. A few days' hiking on the stuff can wear out a decent pair of boots. T. E. Lawrence (better known as Lawrence of Arabia) described similar lava in *his* desert: "like scrambled eggs gone iron-blue, and very wrong . . . sharp as insect bites underfoot."[3]

Ropy "pahoehoe" lava, Ives Flow. November 28, 1985.

A *pahoehoe* (pay-hoy'-hoy) flow is the other extreme. Here, the lava is fluid and congeals in smooth surfaces, reminiscent of molasses. Fresh pahoehoe has a glassy sheen, lost after the surface is weathered. As the lava spoozes out of the ground and runs downhill, it may pile up; smooth folds form, one against another, usually a few inches in diameter. The result looks like a coiled lariat, and is called *ropy lava.*

Other kinds of eruptions may produce no lava flows. If the ejecta spews out in small particles, they suddenly solidify as they strike the cool air, forming ashes or cinders. If not carried too far by the wind, they may pile up to build a cinder cone. If the particles weld together because of heat or moisture, they form deposits known as *tuff.* All of the large craters of the Pinacates have ashy or tuff rims, testifying that such material was the last to erupt out of the vents that formed craters.

Thus we see the volcanic landscape as a geologist sees it. The Pinacates abound in examples of both aa and pahoehoe flows, as fresh as if they slithered over the ground yesterday. Ropy lava lies in coils here and there as if giants had cast aside lassos.

Cinder cones rise like giant anthills where individual vents sprayed fountains of fiery cinders hundreds of feet into the air. And then there are the craters.

The process of formation of the large Pinacate craters is controversial. Even the term, "crater" is controversial because it implies many things to many people. Worse yet, it implies nothing precise to a geologist. It conjures up the image of a great pit, but says nothing about how the pit formed. So the word gets used for all sorts of formations. People casually refer to "craters" at the tops of cinder cones; "craters" formed by tremendous volcanic collapses; "craters" caused by limestone sinks; "craters" blown out of the ground by volcanic explosions; and "craters" blasted out of the moon, Earth, and other planets by huge meteorites from space. Willy Ley, the early prophet of space travel, railed against the "dunderhead who thought 'craters' would be a . . . convenient name" for the lunar depressions.

I use the term *crater* to refer primarily to roughly circular volcanic structures with *negative* relief, i.e., whose floors are below or nearly even with the surrounding ground level. Some observers loosely use the word "crater" to refer to cinder cones, but these have *positive* relief; the vent is often marked by a small summit depression whose floor is above the ground level. I reserve the term *cinder cone* for these, though I will sometimes use the term *summit crater* for the small pit at the top.

The only confusion remaining comes from the few structures that occupy a middle ground—the bane of scientific classifiers. Some cinder-cone-like structures develop such wide vents that they resemble collapsed craters; aided by partial collapse, their *summit craters* grow perhaps half as wide as the cone and may have a floor near or below ground level. Fortunately for our semantics and classifications, these intermediate-style craters are few.

How did the giant Pinacate craters form? To discuss the origin of a crater we must be clear about its original shape. Erosion and filling has produced their *present,* rounded interiors. Even Elegante, the finest of all, presents an evolved shape. On the rim, the weak tuff beds have worn back to form a gentle inward slope, like a shallow funnel, all the way around. The gentle inward slope ends abruptly in a 200-foot vertical drop down the layered basalt cliffs. This ends in another gentle slope forming a shelf around the bottom of the crater. The shelf consists of debris that fell off the wall, plus lakeshore deposits from a prehistoric lake that once shimmered in the bottom of Elegante. The floor of Elegante, the bottom of the ancient lake, is a gently curved bowl of alluvial soil. A central thicket of vegetation marks the low point where water collects.

The vertical basalt walls give the best clue to the original shape. The original profile of Elegante—and probably all the craters—must have been cylindrical, with black basalt cliffs towering above a depressed floor of jumbled, collapsed rubble, or a puddle of molten lava called a *lava lake.* At the top of the basalt lay the raised rim of tuff and ash and ejected boulders, also sectioned by a vertical inner face. It looked like an immense drill hole with a raised rim.

This is not just speculation; many fresh craters in Hawaii have this appearance. They are called *pit craters,* and they are common on shield volcanoes like the Pinacates, as noted by volcanologist A. Rittmann:

These craters are flat depressions with very steep, perpendicular, or even overhanging walls, which tend to collapse along peripheral cracks as they are undermined by the lava-lake. They are thus subsidence craters of a special kind, which are designated pit craters, and whose occurrence is restricted to shield volcanoes.[4]

Pit-crater formation and evolution have actually been observed in Hawaii. At one remote spot, during a period of volcanic activity, the roof of a subterranean lava-filled rift collapsed with a loud report and a tremendous burst of smoke, producing a deep pit with slightly overhanging walls. This example, however, was only 50 to 70 feet across. Growth to larger sizes adds complexity. A few miles away, at Kilauea Volcano, is the most famous pit crater, Halemaumau, a central attraction of the Hawaii Volcanoes National Park. In May, 1924, underground water made contact with the magma chamber under this crater, producing huge volumes of underground steam. These caused cataclysmic explosions that sent up dust clouds of pulverized rock 20,000 feet into the air, and boulders up to half a mile. Wall rocks were shaken loose, broken and ejected. No molten lava was ejected—only steam, dust and rocks.

As the walls collapsed, Halemaumau's diameter was enlarged from 1,400 to 3,000 feet, while the outline remained circular. Lava flows soon covered the floor, sometimes ponding into molten lava lakes, with a thin crust that looked like rock, but laced with cracks exposing the molten lava, that would give off an eerie glow in the night. The vertical cliffs show a cross section through flat-lying basalt beds, closely resembling the inner walls of Elegante and several other Pinacate craters. Today, one can see new cracks and fissures all around Halemaumau's rims, as if the walls are ready to collapse again with little provocation. Indeed, Halemaumau looks like a smaller Elegante without its gentle rim of tuff and without its bowl-shaped floor of eroded soil.

Observations of Hawaiian pit craters might seem to settle the question of how the Pinacate craters formed. But the Pinacate craters are bigger than most pit craters, and surmounted by low rims of ejected ash and tuff. Their raised rims of beige tuff remind us that simple collapse is not the whole story; material was blown out, too, and piled up to form a shallow cone. The distinction between craters formed by collapse and craters formed by explosive activity has long been important to

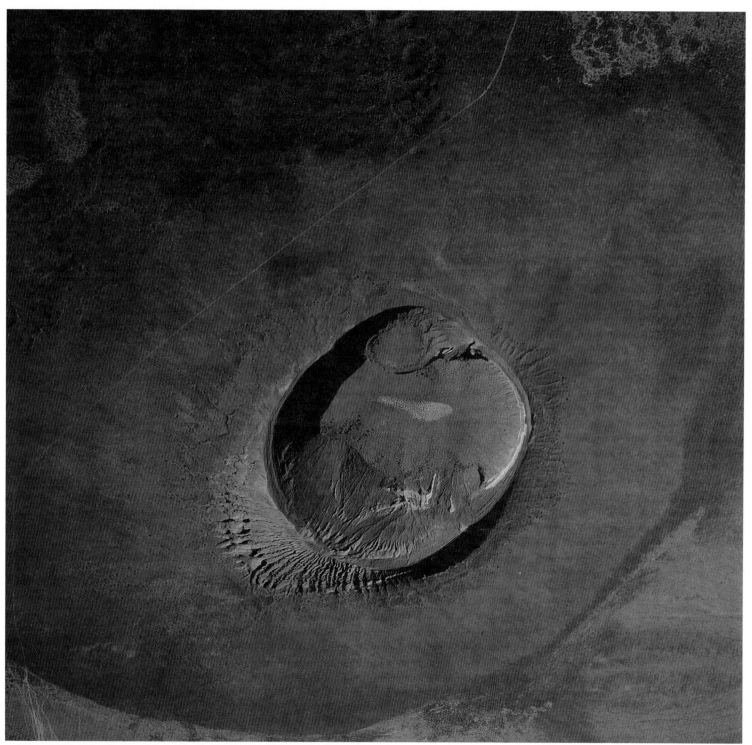

Vertical aerial view of Cerro Colorado Crater, showing highly eroded ash and tuff in south wall and secondary "pancake" crater vent in north wall. April, 1969.

volcanologists, and has caused much controversy in the Pinacates. Did the Pinacate craters go "crunch," or did they go "bang"?

AMONG LARGER CRATERS this distinction was established by the volcanologist Howell Williams. His terminology describes a spectrum of types, ranging from a *caldera*, caused entirely by collapse, to an *explosion crater*, where the hole is formed by blowing material outward. An important type of explosion crater is the *diatreme*, in which gas-charged magmas from great depth erode the mouth of the vent into an ever-widening funnel-shaped opening.

Much of the argument about Pinacate craters is whether they are calderas or diatremes. Surprisingly, however, one of the first modern papers to speculate about their origin proposed that Elegante was caused by a meteorite impact! Amateur naturalist Allan O. Kelly,[5] inspired by a 1951 popular article on Elegante by Wilson McKenney, visited the crater late that year. He pointed out the similarities to the shape of Meteor Crater, about 260 miles to the northeast, and noted that a magnet would pick up magnetic material on both craters' rims. Unfortunately for this idea, the shape similarity is coincidental, and Ives pointed out in 1964 that magnetic rock fragments are "a normal desert phenomenon." Interestingly, my reprint of his article, which I believe arrived in the 1960s, contains a handwritten note signed by Kelly: "I have long since given up hope that Crater Elegante is . . . meteoritic . . ."

The conflict between the caldera theory and the diatreme theory began as soon as modern volcanologists studied the area. Cal Tech geologist R. H. Jahns, writing in a 1955 fieldtrip guide,[6] pronounced the craters "small but otherwise typical collapse calderas . . ." He made an exception for Cerro Colorado, which he viewed as a diatreme. In a companion article, University of Arizona geologist F. W. Galbraith[7] argued that things were not so

Brittle bush growing around lava boulder ejected from Elegante Crater. February 9, 1985.

clear-cut. He cited an opinion by geologist Eugene Shoemaker, who had studied eroded diatremes in northern Arizona, that the Pinacate craters were diatremes, with Cerro Colorado being only the best example. The others, he believed, had been enlarged by collapse of parts of the walls.

Ives, in his 1964 summary of the region, sided with Jahns, stating that "the great craters . . . can be classified as typical collapse calderas."

At about this time, some geologists speculated that the ancient Sonoita River had run across the broad flats north of the Pinacates, instead of down the east side. So a theory arose that ground water from this ancient stream got into the magma chambers and caused explosive, crater-forming outbursts, spread across the northern flank, where several craters appear. In this view, the craters are a type of explosion crater involving ground water, called a *maar* (from a German word for lake, because many European examples are water filled). The classic maar is formed as water hits the magma, turns to steam, and causes an explosion driven not by volcanic energy, but by steam pressure, like that of an overheated boiler. But the northern Sonoita rivercourse is now widely regarded as "mythical," to use a word applied by geologist Daniel Lynch, and the theory of maars aligned along an ancient river has been more or less discarded.

In his 1972 doctoral dissertation, geologist James T. Gutmann pointed out that the volume of debris on Elegante's rim was "much smaller than the volume of the crater," leading him, too, to the collapse theory. He proposed that Elegante's eruptions culminated with a catastrophic blast of ash from a magma chamber in contact with water-bearing sediments beneath the crater. Collapse resulted quickly. The crater, he summarized, "in some respects resembles a maar, but is in fact a small collapse caldera."

The 1981 doctoral dissertation of geologist Daniel Lynch cast him as the angry young man of the field, aggressively challenging the earlier experts. He called parts of Gutmann's geological presentation "bizarre." At the same time, Lynch, following the code of Old West graciousness toward adversaries, named the prominent rise on Elegante's southeast rim "Gutmann's cone."

The conflict came over the magma's location and withdrawal. Lynch placed the magma chamber much deeper than Gutmann, and ridiculed Gutmann's model of collapse as too much like an elevator descending. Instead, Lynch argued, the magma erupting from depth eroded the throat of the vent to nearly the crater's present dimension, like a diatreme, and collapse was only a final effect in widening the crater. Steam from ground water helped drive the eruption, Lynch said; he called the craters *hydrovolcanic features*.

At some point, the geologists begin arguing over details. We know that the Pinacate craters are volcanic sites where giant eruptions blew out substantial volumes of ash. Cerro Colorado may represent this stage in fairly pristine form. In other craters, such as Elegante

and MacDougal, collapse was an important subsequent process. The degree of diatreme activity before the collapse may be forever lost to us.

Lacking more dated rocks, we can only speculate as to which of the craters formed first. Lynch's limited age data are included in Table 1. Probably there are unseen older calderas buried by lavas and desert sands. Within a few years, there will probably be radioisotopic dating of all the craters and their associated flows. Only then will we know just when and how "Hell boiled over in the Pinacates."

We can imagine what an observer might have seen, had anyone been present 150,000 years or so ago. A large vent is erupting. Dense columns of white steam laced with black, sooty smoke rise high over the Pinacates for many days. They are visible for a hundred miles. Dark curtains of ash rain out of them. Fire fountains a hundred feet high play around the vent. By day they are pale red against the landscape; at night they light up the undersides of the clouds, as if Lucifer left a door open. Occasionally the vent ejects volcanic bombs—rocks trailing delicate traceries of smoke. The activity grows more violent; the grey ash cone, colored by yellow and white sulfur deposits, rises higher. The vent in the cone, hidden by smoke, widens steadily, reaching a width of a few hundred feet. Multiple vents develop, as at Cerro Colorado, where a secondary circle forms one wall, or at Molina Crater, with its cloverleaf shape. Through the vents, the volcano exhausts the stuff of its life. In the midst of earthquake and fume, perhaps over a period of days, the walls collapse with a mighty roar, perhaps in several episodes. The highest part of the cone disappears, sending a roiling smoke plume thousands of feet into the sky. After the smoke clears, a vast pit is exposed. White vapors from steam vents play around its walls and slopes, looking like ghosts crossing the landscape on moonlit nights. During the next few decades, subsequent eruptions and earthquakes in and around the crater may widen it as parts of the walls fall into the

Hadean floor of lava ponds and rubble islands.

During ensuing millennia, rains erode the craters, washing much of the soft tuff deposits from the rim into the interior, thus softening the crater's rim. The lava cliffs remain vertical. During the last ice age, 13,000 years ago, heavier rainfall creates lakes, filling the floors of at least some of the craters. Sparkling in the sun, the circular lake of Elegante becomes a welcome stopover for wildfowl migrating from the glacier country of the north. At last, strange mammals arrive, who kill the mammoths and dress in their skins. The climate warms and dries; lake bottoms turn to playas and become abodes of dusty lizards.

THE CRATERS HAVE INDIVIDUAL PERSONALITIES. Cerro Colorado, visible from Mexico Highway 2 as a pink cone in the green, saguaro-studded plains, is unique in shape, color, and origin. It is one of the most pleasant to visit. It best presents diatreme features, with its double vent and surrounding high walls of stratified tuff. The ring-shaped wall, with its asymmetric crest, rises 360 feet above the desert, but the floor is only about 13 feet below the surroundings. A hike around the outer edge of the rim, where erosion has gullied the soft tuff slopes, is an adventure in a wonderland of miniature, tilted canyons and remnant pinnacles. Late eruptions draped tuff beds over part of the rim and inner wall, where they make a giant's ramp into the interior. Perhaps some of these tilted strata sagged into the interior during an abortive collapse; huge sections of wall are poised at an angle, about to fall. The secondary crater on the low, northwest wall makes a pretty pancake, easy to descend, and contrasts with the high cliffs on the east. One can scramble over the low rimwall that divides the pancake from the rest of the vegetated floor of Cerro Colorado proper. Of all the craters, Cerro Colorado has the most enticing interior, a secret, walled desert garden. Sometimes cows from nearby ranches wander in this volcanic park, perhaps feeling sheltered by the surrounding walls. It is one of the few Pinacate pastures where cows look happy.

Hikers, too, can amble among bushes and groves and little dry washes to the towering vertical wall of the east inner rim, littered along its base with collapsed fragments and talus.

This west-facing cliff transforms itself at sunset into one of the grand vistas of the Southwest. It is as if its stalwart, sunburned face had absorbed extra color from each of the sunsets of the last ten thousand years, and has this one last minute each day to give it back.

Elegante and the other craters differ from Cerro Colorado. Their rims are lower. Their walls are formed by cliffs of basalt rock, while Cerro Colorado has no massive basalt beds. Most have deeply depressed floors, and several of them can be entered only arduously.

Largest of the craters, Elegante stands alone on the east flank of the shield. True to its name, it displays most dramatically and symmetrically the major crater features: vertical cliffs of cross-sectioned basalt beds; a shoulder of beige tuff on the rim; a broad, gently sloping outer apron of cindery debris; a disturbed wall profile, which turns out on examination to be an old cinder cone cut in half during collapse of the crater itself. As you walk up the gentle outer rim, you pass many boulders that were thrown out of Elegante during the eruption, often splatting into still-pasty tuff beds. Many of these "fossilized splashes" can be seen where boulders landed 149,000 years ago.

The bowl-shaped floor, containing the ancient lakebed deposits, is marked in its central low spot by a green patch of dense vegetation. This is a feature common to most of the craters, but is somehow surprising when first observed. To reach and return from Elegante's private garden is not easy. The gently inward-sloping tuff beds are easy to descend, but then one stands at the top of the sheer basalt cliffs. They are only broken by gullies here and there. On the east side, just

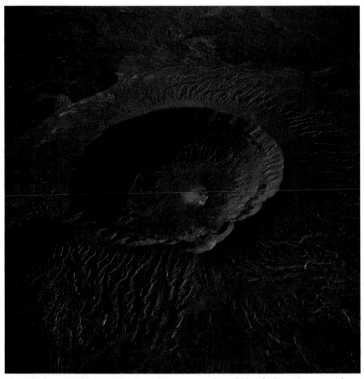

Aerial view of Elegante Crater. Note apron of eroded-ash deposits around the crater. April, 1969.

A last dramatic feature of Elegante: on the east wall, north of Gutmann's Cone and not far from the ladder, is a striking dike of basalt, protruding like a strange, prehistoric wall in defiance of erosion. Jahns measured it to be 28 inches in maximum thickness and concluded that the lava was thrusting up and outward from Elegante's center when it entered an underground fracture and solidified. Later, erosion exposed it.

MacDougal is the huge depression reached by the MacDougal-Hornaday expedition on November 13, 1907, after they passed through "MacDougal's Pass," on the northwest side of the Pinacates. MacDougal is the westernmost of the craters. Lynch found an age of 185,000 years, based on a basalt sample that he interprets as contemporaneous with the MacDougal's formation. Orangish dunes from the western Gran Desierto overlap its flanks. It is the shallowest and most inviting of the three giant craters, Elegante, MacDougal, and Sykes. The dark-brown walls enclose an attractive flat expanse of orangish soils studded with saguaros, bushes, and a central drainage patch that bursts into flowers in the spring. As in Elegante, the basalt cliffs are capped by a gentler, receding layer of eroding tuff.

Second largest of the calderas, MacDougal is easy to enter, though more than 400 feet deep. Its wall is broken here and there by subordinate, sectioned craters. After descending a cliff-hugging trail, you cross a wide apron of eroded talus and gain the flat floor. Here I am never without a weird feeling, being surrounded by 360° of cliffs. The visible universe is suddenly finite. Godfrey Sykes made the first *recorded* descent onto this floor in 1907. In 1974, geologist C.A. Wood published magnetic and gravity surveys that allowed him to estimate MacDougal's subsurface structure. He inferred the existence of a massive column of basalt—solidified lava in the buried eruptive vent. He estimated it to be about 880 feet across, or about one-fourth the diameter of the crater, and buried under about 500 feet of dust and sand.

A few miles east of MacDougal, amidst the hills

north of the cross-sectioned vent called *Gutmann's Cone,* at the base of the tuff, is an old rickety ladder that was once the standard route. In the niche that holds the ladder, behind its weathered, nailed boards, is the remnant of a still-older ladder made of small logs wedged into the walls. It probably dates from the Lumholtz era. During my first visit in the early 1960s, we climbed down the ten or twelve feet of ladder and picked our way down the steep, rubbly hillside to the floor, passing a rattlesnake on the way. I had heard that route described as the only way down, and had repeated this statement later, to embellish my accounts of my own death-defying adventures in Elegante. To my chagrin, my 14-year-old daughter scampered straight down among rocks and gullies of the southeast wall in record time in 1985.

Three lobes of the "cloverleaf." Molina Crater. April 25, 1964.

called *Phillips Buttes*, lies the rugged crater, Sykes, which is nearly a clone of Elegante. Sykes preserves more of the steep original volcanic cone than any of the other calderas, as if only the central part of the original volcanic cone collapsed to make the crater. Its rugged profile makes it seem as young as Elegante, but it is undated. When you approach, you see not the inconspicuous low mound of other craters' rims, but an imposing, steep-sided grey plateau among the neighboring reddish cinder cones. As you walk up the outer flanks, the rise steepens until it becomes a tiring ascent. At the crest you discover with a shock that the "plateau" is not flat-topped, but a vast cavity. Ives calls it "a mountain with a hole in the top."

What a hole! Steep on the outside, Sykes is also exceptionally steep inside and the hardest of the craters to enter. Hikers on one expedition I joined used ropes to help them clamber 700 feet down. Coming back up, they were often on all fours. Being higher in the hills than the other craters, Sykes has less windblown tan dust to soften and partially bury its floor and rim approaches.

Seeking a hill that Kino and friends climbed near here in 1701, I climbed the tallest of Phillips Buttes, which rises just above the rim of Syke's Crater on its west. The climb seemed perilous not only for its steepness but also for the chollas that cover the slopes—a peril also attributed to these hills by Hornaday. Here I confirmed not only a view of the sea, but also a view into yawning Sykes Crater, which appears as a vast, shadowy cavity whose bottom is hidden. It looks truly fearsome and unique from this viewpoint, fitting Manje's description of "a big hole of such depth that it caused terror and fear." Unfortunately, there is no evidence that Kino and Manje ever climbed these hills or saw this view, even if it matches their reaction.

Between MacDougal and Sykes lies the multiple crater which the 1907 expedition named *Molina,* after a Mexican government official. Shape is its claim to fame. Sometimes called *the Cloverleaf*, it is a coalescence of

Aerial view of Sykes Crater. ca. 1970.

three or perhaps four separate vents, each trying to make its own crater. Galbraith regarded it as most like Cerro Colorado in formative process, because of the multiple vents; the external appearance, however, is very different because Molina's rim is low. Molina's individual cloverleaf lobes are the smallest of the Pinacate craters, and reveal the characteristic vertical cross section of basalt layers. Further work might clarify how much collapse was involved, or whether such small pits are the work of explosive venting alone. The lobes of Molina are separated by low-slung saddle ridges of rubble. It is hard to imagine how these graceful, symmetric ridges were created by the competing violent eruptions!

Running across the north flank of the Pinacates, on a line almost due east from MacDougal, are three intermediate-sized craters, pleasant in prospect and rarely visited. They are a matched set, shallow, similar in size and form. Badilla, westernmost, displays three cones along its circumference that have been sectioned by its rim. Kino, in the middle, has a similar sectioned cone on its south rim, with bedded ash layers sloping out of it. Surrounding Kino are several curving faults forming low cliffs facing the crater. They suggest the beginnings of a collapse that might have made Kino rival its bigger cousins. Celaya, to the east, is the largest in diameter. Badilla, Kino, and Celaya are more subtle than the big craters. You might wander their rims for some moments before sensing their design and realizing that you are like an ant on the edge of a dinner plate.

Moon Crater, a loner, is isolated west of the Pinacate Peaks, at the margin of the sea of lavas and the sea of sands. It is a lovely feature from the air, with a heart-shaped rim and a central cone, unique among the craters. Lynch's data show that the crater punched through 340,000-year-old basalts. It must be younger than that, but its worn appearance suggests it might not be much younger. Wood's magnetic survey led him to conclude that the cone is underlain by a massive plug of basalt, which is no surprise. Curiously, he also concluded that a second column of basalt wormed its way nearly to the surface just south of the central peak, under the flat floor. Evidently, it never erupted.

Moon Crater's discovery is an example of the Pinacates' strange interconnections, this time across generations. As with other craters, there were probably two discoveries: the first by a local desert rat, and the second by an Anglo explorer who put the crater on the map. According to Hayden,[8] a local Mexican, Filiberto Perez, was known in the area as El Viejito. Visiting the southwest Pinacates as a youth, he had seen a piece of basalt with gold-bearing quartz. Living his later life in San Luis, he remained intrigued, and spent 45 years poking around that part of the Pinacates in search of gold. He was active in the area in the 1940s. He had identified Moon Crater and called it *Volcán de Chichi*, referring to the beautiful central cinder cone. He was using Mexican slang, one meaning of which is breast. El Viejito's discovery never became widely known.

The rediscovery involved the Sykes family. Godfrey Sykes, hardy geographer of the Hornaday expedition, had two sons, Glenton and Gilbert, already mentioned. Living in Tucson, the sons became colorful Southwestern figures in their own right. They followed their father's tradition of curiosity about everything in nature. For example, once I camped under the stars with them in the traditional Sykes family camp spot near the rim of Sykes Crater; this camp spot must have gone all the way back to Godfrey and the MacDougal-Hornaday expedition. Out of the blue Glenton wandered over to ask, "What do you think of the Big Bang theory these days?" He knew I was an astronomer. Later he came back again. "What's the latest thinking on the Hubble constant?" The Hubble constant is a property of galaxies that tells something about the age of the universe. Glenton's irrepressible curiosity extended to all subjects, small and large.

It led him to a new crater. At about age 60, he led a Pinacate outing in the winter of 1956-57. It included photographer Tad Nichols, who published some of the first, and still some of the best Pinacate aerial photos; Arizona Desert Museum curator William Woodin, whose wife, Ann, wrote the Southwest classic, *Home is the Desert*; and astronomer Keith Pierce. Seeking recreation and adventure, they had driven to the seldom-visited southwest side of the lavas. Next morning they climbed a ridge and someone raised a question: "Sykes, what crater's this?" Sure enough, though Sykes and the rest of the party hadn't realized it, a shallow crater with a central cinder cone stretched before them. Sykes had never seen it. But he was supposed to be the guide! Recounting the story to me later, he said, "Well, I didn't want to disappoint them. I saw the cone in the center . . . it looked like a lunar crater you can see through a telescope, so I said, casually, 'Oh, that's Moon Crater,' as if I knew all about it." Astronomer Pierce blessed the name and it stuck.

Panorama of Sykes Crater as seen from Phillips Buttes. November 29, 1987.

Sykes is usually credited with the discovery, mostly because the story of El Viejito and Volcán de Chichi has been virtually unknown. Sykes remained modest about it. One time when Sykes told me the story he concluded with a shrug, "Well, it was there a long time before we found it." Ives[9] remarked ruefully that he had walked twice within a few hundred feet of Moon Crater without detecting it.

The region around Moon Crater is fascinating; a short hike from the crater takes you through the contact zone between lava and the Gran Desierto, where strange vegetation tries to gain a foothold on dunes marked by tiny footprints of beetles and rodents, and where you wonder what other volcanic wonders have been buried by sand.

I had a hand in the recognition of two newly discovered craters—or should I say, crater-like features.

The first is south of the Pinacate Peaks, in the Ives Flow, which runs south-southwest down the flank of the volcano. In November 1985, Dan Lynch led a group of us, including Pinacate photographers Tad Nichols and Pete Kresan, and Glenton Sykes' daughter Georgie Boyer, onto the Ives Flow, where he pointed out several collapsed vents. Another visit in April 1989 clarified some of the relationships, but there was still inadequate time for a proper survey. Nonetheless, in the midst of this flow several collapsed vents approach the status of true collapse craters, and give intriguing clues about the formative processes of the other craters. All of these collapses look relatively young, in that they are floored by the original jumbled heap of chaotic broken boulders. Lacking the bright, smooth floors of windblown dust that have accumulated in the other craters, they do not show up in aerial photos.

Patterns in rock. Fractured basalt at the rim of large sag depression
in Ives Flow. November 28, 1985.

The southernmost of the vents we visited is the best: a tangled complex of collapse depressions, probably exceeding 500 feet across, surmounted by a large spattered cone on the southwest rim. I refer to this as Lynch in Table 1. It is perhaps more of a potential crater. Had these events continued to develop, the whole complex might have coalesced and collapsed into one large caldera. The complex of depressions has several lobes, like Molina, but much more irregular in outline and surface roughness. One eastern lobe is an immense, boulder-floored pit, awesomely rough and deep. The main lobe is shallower, surrounded by walls perhaps 30-feet high. One has the impression at this and other nearby vents that the lava withdrew at some stage of the eruption, causing the surface layers to sag and then collapse in tumbled rubble.

A mile or so to the west, still in the Ives Flow, is a depression where the sagging seems to have been frozen in midprocess. The basalt is fractured in interesting patterns around the rim, but sagged smoothly into the interior instead of breaking into higgledy-piggledy chaos.

The other crater discovery came earlier. In the 1960s, with my graduate-student friends from the Lunar and Planetary Laboratory of the University of Arizona, I made foolish forays in my two-wheel drive car to study the otherworldly lavas and craters of the Pinacates. Here was another planet on our doorstep. During the first manned orbital flights, the black stain of the Pinacates showed up prominently against the bright, cloudless desert in the photos taken by astronauts. One day, I noticed on one of these that just where the northern lavas cross into Arizona, a small circular bright spot resembled the bright patches in the floors of the major craters. Could a crater have escaped notice on our side of the border while sightseers explored the more vivid Mexican lavas?

In April, 1968, planetary scientist Dale Cruikshank and I made a car trip to the region. At the cost of a broken radio antenna, snapped off by a lurking palo verde along the dirt road, we reached what we thought must be the feature—an open sandy area with nearby tuff beds and volcanic bombs that indicated nearby eruptive activity. Later, back at the office, Cruikshank turned up aerial photos that gave stereo coverage of the area: now we could study three-dimensional relief. Our joy in our discovery was shortlived: we could see that we had been in the wrong area, an irregular open space adjacent to the spot we had been seeking. The stereo revealed that our true target was indeed a single shallow structure with a rim all the way around.

We were now encouraged enough to give our feature a name—*Díaz*, for the first European traveler in the area. If Melchior Díaz traveled El Camino del Diablo on his way to the Colorado, he may have passed within a hundred yards of his "crater."

On May 5, we made a flight over the area and we spotted both our "false Díaz" and the "true Díaz." "True Díaz" had very little relief, but was well-defined as a ring-like ridge in the basalt flows. Armed with our new aerial photos we returned by car and were able to walk a few hundred feet north of the Camino to the nearly flat pancake of Díaz.

The evidence as to the true nature of Díaz is enigmatic. My colleague, geologist Charles Wood, noted in his 1972 master's thesis[10] that a 1970 unpublished map[11] showed Díaz as a "tuff ring filled with alluvium." He and I visited it in 1973, when we observed symmetric sloping of the tuff beds around the crater, and he obtained magnetic measurements. These he interpreted[12] to show a central magnetic disturbance like that in MacDougal, suggesting a buried, basalt-filled vent. He concluded that Díaz might be either a "typical Pinacate crater completely sand filled, or . . . an aborted crater that only sagged and didn't collapse." Its true nature awaits further exploration.

After our success in recognizing and finding Díaz from astronauts' orbital photos, Wood went on to a

NASA position that involved studies of more orbital photography. One day he called excitedly. There was another Díaz-like feature. It was a circular dark ring surrounding a bright patch, like Elegante's cindery rim with its bright, dusty floor. The "floor" held a dark central spot, resembling Moon Crater with its central peak. Unbelievably, the new, potentially undiscovered crater was only a few hundred yards from highway Mexico 2. On our next trip we breathlessly set out from the side of the road to discover the new crater. At the position of the dark rim we were fighting our way through dark, thick vegetation on level terrain. At the edge of the crater floor there was no depression whatsoever; we found ourselves on the edge of a circular playa of cracked, dry mud, absolutely flat. The "central peak" turned out to be a field of grain being cultivated by a farmer taking advantage of the natural drainage toward the playa's center. Ever since, we refer to this spot, one of the flattest areas of the Pinacates, as Wood's Hole.

THE ENIGMATIC CRATER-LIKE STRUCTURES provide additional missing links between true collapse craters and partly collapsed vents and cones. The first is a peculiar shallow saucer located in very rough country across a lava chaos northwest of Elegante. Lunar researcher Alan Binder and I once hiked in it during the early 1970s to evaluate for NASA what kind of geologic observations could be obtained by scientist-astronauts during brief excursions on the last Apollo flights. We asked ourselves: if you have been able to study a feature only from space photos, what can you learn when you have, say, only two hours on the ground? We were able to pass on some suggestions: a tiny input into the vast program that was Apollo. The second feature lies between Kino and Celaya and is an unusual, shallow, half cinder cone, forming an inconspicuous C. To my knowledge, both features first were recorded on aerial photographs by Tad Nichols. It seemed appropriate that

Aerial view of Kino Crater and surrounding lavas. September 14, 1972.

Kino's principal two aides, Carrasco and Manje, who first explored the Pinacates with him, should be honored with named features near Kino Crater, and so we began to use these two names for these features. As a mnemonic aid, Carrasco's name went to the C-shaped structure.

Wood assigned a name to a third feature that may be a missing link between cinder cones and craters. It is a compound cone with an outer rim, but the interior is nearly filled by an inner cone, as if a wide, shallow crater formed, only to be nearly refilled by buildup of a second cone. Located at the extreme west flank of the lavas six miles southwest of MacDougal (114°42′E; 31°53′N), it was pointed out to Wood by Julian Hayden. Wood named it *Hayden* in his 1972 thesis. In a second University of Arizona master's thesis published a year later, environmental researcher Larry May gave this cone the name *Caravajales,* after the turn-of-the-century Papago hermit of the Pinacates. This cone/crater invites further study.

Aerial view of Díaz Crater (foreground) with dunes in middle distance and profile of Pinacate shield volcano on horizon. September 14, 1972.

The Pinacate cinder cones offer a universe of their own. Many have their own special presence, depending on the geometric quirks produced by eruption and erosion. My favorite is one of the Phillips Buttes, the hills west of Sykes Crater. They were explored by Sykes and John Phillips on November 15, 1907, and later named for Phillips.[13] One of the buttes is flat-topped and seemingly undistinguished when viewed from nearby. An aerial flyby, however, reveals that the flat top contains a remarkable summit crater—a shallow, flat pancake in which lies a central garden surrounded by a bright tan playa, surrounded in turn by pepper-red cinders washing down from the raised rim. It conjures an image of a Mexican fried egg sitting in its griddle.

The modest climb to this summit reveals another one of the Pinacate's hidden treasures: nature's hilltop zen garden of cacti and adobe. Within the shallow craterlet, the playa has a hard-baked surface, flat as a parking lot, with a striking geometric pattern of worn cracks. The re-creation of this crackled playa after each major storm

would be interesting to observe. The view across the Gran Desierto to the west is hardly credible: the flat colors under high sun look like a huge painted backdrop, not a real landscape. New Mexico photographer Jody Forster and award-winning New Mexico painter Peter Nisbet, both of whom have worked extensively in the Pinacates, call this crater a natural sanctuary. We hope that it will remain always in its extraordinary natural state.

Journal entry. A day at Elegante and Cerro Colorado. February 9, 1985. *Most of the 17 miles south from Mexico 2 to Elegante is a smooth cinder road with a soft hump in the middle. But 100-yard segments, including the early stretch up onto the lavas, are rough with lava blocks or rutted washes. The roads are ever-changing. Today, the road does not arrive at the whitewashed-boulder-lined, can-and-Pampers-littered parking lot that I remember from a few years back. The parking lot seems to have vanished, and the road slopes up the gentle east rim, all the way to within 50 feet of the true rim. This is larceny, I think, robbing the newcomer of the growing excitement of the walk up the rim, and the stunning reward: making that last breathless step to discover the ground dropping away in front of you, into an abyss.*

The silence of Elegante. On the rim, you are exposed and the wind hisses, stirred by the heating of air in the crater perhaps, threatening to blow off your hat. But as I climb down the treacherous slope below the rim, and sit on a boulder to muse, I am struck by the silence. Zephyrs, the occasional cry of a hawk, but no sound from outside the crater wall. It is its own, enclosed world.

From the rim crest, I look outward. The slope leads down into the surrounding green desert. Today is overcast: little breaks of blue sky and a pale greenish-blue horizon. A cold, grey, diffuse light flattens the landscape. The slope is dotted with blue-green brittle bush, the favorite guest of Sonoran Desert basalts. Among them are gold-green palo verdes, dark green spots of mesquite in the distance, light yellow-green saguaros sticking up, far out on the desert plain. Horizontal, dark reddish-brown lines in the distance mark lava flows rising above the multi-green carpet of desert plants. Jagged blue peaks line almost the entire horizon.

Later we drive to Cerro Colorado, where the road, just as at Elegante, now climbs up on the rim, within 50 feet of the edge. Sonoran Desert writer Joseph Wood Krutch discovered a law of human nature: modern travelers always travel as fast as they can.[14] I propose a corollary: they have to drive as close as they can to what they want to look at, and they don't start looking until they get there—as if nothing is worth experiencing except designated "sights" that have already been discovered by someone else. Between Elegante and Cerro Colorado we have to go slow and we try to do better: every spot is interesting if you just look. But the car is the enemy of the sightseer.

We select a camp spot in a declivity adjacent to the west rim. As we investigate this spot I discover two Mexican coins lying in the tuff beds, a 1974 peso and a seven-sided 1977 ten-peso piece. Heavy coins, from the days when the peso still amounted to something; now they rush to mint 100-peso coins, and by the time they get them out they are still worth only a nickel. I stash the coins behind a little brittle bush in the mouth of a 1-meter-scale cavelet on the eroded inner wall at the top of the north rim. Someone else can find them again. The treasure of Cerro Colorado.

Again, the silence. Facing the interior, you hear your ears ring. I'm struck as I hike the rim by being an insignificant mite, crawling on the face of a larger creation. I climb over lips of broken tuff, steps a foot thick, where individual beds are exposed, slanting back away from the crater, only to be surmounted by another bed. These make stairstep terraces to climb over as I ascend the sloping circumference of the rim. I become aware of something. Though I climb over seemingly chaotic jumbles, as perceived on the ten-meter scale I survey cautiously as I walk along, an occasional sweep of the eye reveals that these jumbles are part of a mighty, circular pattern. Soil joins to form crags, crags extend to steps, steps to curving terraces, terraces to vast arcs that sweep off into the mighty circle of the caldera. There was a focus somewhere

Beautifully formed twin cinder cones and transitional crater/cinder cone referred to as Hayden or Caravajales. ca. 1970.

to one side of my path, in the middle of Cerro Colorado. From this focus, nature produced a symmetry, a pattern. I can only climb around one jumble at a time. Do ants sometimes perceive that the jumbled grains they climb over are part of some giant pattern—a square sandbox or the circle of a concrete planter? Many of us humans would like the jumble of our daily lives to add up, somehow, to some mega-pattern, when seen at a distance . . .

On the north rim, I sit waiting for a break in the grey clouds, so I can see a more spectacular late afternoon light on the east wall. Little breaks of sun come, but not wide enough to light the whole east wall's curve. It is growing cloudier, darker. I hear my daughter's 13-year-old voice from across the crater floor, singing to herself. The acoustics of this great amphitheater are fine. She is happy, exploring among the clefts and slumped blocks of the lower south wall, nature's playground. Her unself-conscious music is sweet and pure.

Once when we visited the Grand Canyon I came on her sitting on the rim by herself, gazing off across the multi-colored walls of light, singing America the Beautiful.

5:15 P.M. As it gets darker and cooler, crickets have started to chirp along the rim.

5:30 P.M. Dozens of swallows are soaring against the sky over the crater, whistling and calling. They swoop around and around, waiting for the right moment to dive into their holes in the cliff.

5:40 P.M. The air is alive with birds and their songs. Finally the sun comes out in the last few degrees of sky between the clouds and horizon—beyond the westernmost edge of the storm-cloud system hanging over the Sonoran Desert. The crater wall lights up with a burst of amber gold. In the distance, on the darkling plain beyond the crater wall, the saguaros are suddenly being hit full on by sunlight. Proud and erect, they leap into brilliance. Their vertical sides glow olive-gold, while the tangled palo verdes and mesquites are lost in a maze of grey-violet branches and shadows. The light on the vertical east wall of Cerro Colorado gets brighter and more intense by the minute, reaching a flushed climax. And then as the sun sinks behind a distant cloud, a hundred miles away, the color fades faster than it had appeared. High overhead, low clouds of grey and high clouds of white overlap in the sky. As the sun disappears in a glow of orange-pink mist at the horizon, tinges of pink play across the undersides of the low, grey clouds for perhaps two minutes, and then vanish. Unconcerned breezes play on among the palo verdes, not yet alerted that night is coming.

The cynic in me whispers an unwelcome thought: had Cerro Colorado been on the U.S. side and become a National Park, some administrator seeking the greatest touristic and entrepreneurial opportunity, would have leased space for "facilities" nearby. A grand old rustic lodge with its parking lots would dominate the area. Two miles down the road, where those saguaros stand, would be the campground full of snow-bird trailers, and Cerro Colorado's rim would boast a little overlook stand with a Kodak Picture Stop. Substituted for the loss of intimate experience would be the fact that many more people could have seen the wonder of Cerro Colorado. Tourists would flock to this platform ten minutes before dusk, trailing their candy wrappers, and all watch during their alotted ten minutes at sunset, grabbing their 1/125 second photo-chemical memories. Young lovers with chewing gum would gaze arm in arm with a briefly renewed sense of wonder, kids would say "neat" and drag Moms back to the room in time for whatever the New York networks had discovered would sell that season, and decent, portly oldsters would grouse as to why their spouse wanted to drag them here when they could have gone to Florida.

The swallows settle into their holes for the night.

9. The Curious Case of Monsieur Pinart: New Light on Three Mysteries

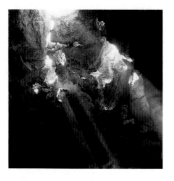

At the camp all day long. Bad day—sand storm covering us. The mules have disappeared. We are here without water and five leagues across the sand from the coast. This is not pleasant due to the semihumid heat. In the morning I ascend the little calcined black hill in front of us, and from the summit I can perceive perfectly the . . . bay, a circular form which makes a gulf. Muri, my guide, whom I sent after the mules, returns at 6:30 without them. What a day; my God! . . . thin sand covers us and enters our noses and eyes . . .

Freely translated from the diary of Alphonse Pinart, camping in the Gran Desierto, March 15, 1879

NOW THE STORY GETS MORE PERSONAL, because I have an adventure to relate. This is an adventure of libraries, old manuscripts, and old trails. Chapter 5 mentioned that a French geographer and linguist, Alphonse Pinart, traveled through the Sonoran Desert and across the Pinacates in 1878-79. Pinart kept a diary at this time and later published an article about part of his trip. I have saved Pinart's story for its own chapter for two reasons. First, the details of his diary and his trip came to light only during the writing of this book, through events that I will recount. Second, Pinart recorded some of the earliest evidence about three Sonoran Desert mysteries mentioned in earlier chapters: the mystery of a lost mission; the mystery of the identity of the great hole that caused terror and fear to Manje and Kino, somewhere in the Pinacate lavas in 1701; and the mystery of the most recent volcanic activity in the Pinacates. Pinart's clues to the latter mysteries can be appreciated only after our discussion of the region's fiery volcanic history, in the preceding chapters. Pinart's writings shed new light on the Desert Heart—or rather old light, an eyewitness's report hidden until now in a time capsule from 1879.

Alphonse Pinart was an Indiana Jones of the 1800s, one of the breed of 19th-century scientist-adventurers who lived drama and danger in the quest to bring back nothing more than knowledge, notebooks and sketches. Yet little is known about him. One thin book, published by the Southwest Museum of Man in Los Angeles in 1966, tells about his life. Even it notes that ". . . accurate information about him, his travels, adventures, and many publications, was quite difficult to obtain."[1]

Born in 1852, Pinart was only 27 at the time of his Sonoran explorations. His life was a story of brilliant early success, followed by declining fortunes. His father, who had founded an ironworks, died when Pinart was a boy, apparently leaving him with considerable wealth. Pinart developed an interest in languages and a yearning for the most exotic parts of the world. An abbé whom he met at age 15 encouraged him, especially in studying the relation of Asian and Native American languages. Apparently he first came to America at age 17, and his later career involved three principal areas: the lush South Pacific islands, freezing Alaska, and the blazing Sonoran Desert.

In his early career he was fantastically productive

Previous page: Inside a lava tube. Shafts of sunlight shine from ceiling crevices through dust kicked up from flow. Ives Flow. March 11, 1989.

Aerial view of dunes and bushes in the Gran Desierto, west of Moon Crater. ca. 1969.

and ambitious. He was a voracious observer, recording the lay of the land, river courses, structures of mountain ranges, and climate. He kept diaries and notebooks of his travels and collected specimens for European museums. He transcribed by hand lengthy documents of historical interest if he could not collect them. After a period of study in a region, he published scholarly papers in geographic journals. In addition he was a linguist, and he made dictionaries and published studies of native languages in the regions he traveled.

His first big success came after he set out for solo explorations of the Asian-American land bridge—the Aleutian Islands—at age 19. After a year of travel and collecting, he returned to France where he prepared exhibits of ancient artifacts and presented speeches and articles on his observations. He was a sensation. One contemporary sketch of the handsome, young, bearded explorer described him as a cross between the celebrated African explorer, Stanley, and D'Artagnan, of musketeer fame. Various professional societies elected him to membership and the Société de Géographie gave him a gold medal for the most exciting discoveries reported in 1873. In that year he began publishing a series of books on exploration, purchasing books for a massive library, and voyaging to new destinations including Russia, Easter Island, and America. In early 1876 he traveled along the Gila River and through Tucson. This journey he described in a major 1877 article for the *Bulletin de la Société de Géographie;* it led to his interest in further exploration of the Sonoran Desert.

Pinart's Southwest expeditions were not the modern multiman scientific efforts, planned in advance with shipped-in supplies. Rather, he was usually a lone naturalist, traveling with burros, a servant and local guides. In his article about Arizona, he described the "petite ville" of Phoenix, with 300 inhabitants, the Casa Grande ruins and the Gila River, "here a quarter mile wide, its bed full of islets covered with cottonwoods and other trees," a far cry from today's trickling, barren stream.[2]

But now Pinart's fortunes began to wane. He had attracted support from the French government, but with happy-go-lucky nonchalance, he did not always end up in the part of the world where he had said he was going. Further, he was no money manager. With admirable but short-sighted enthusiasm, he had spent most of his inheritance on his publications, library and travels. By the late 1870s, when he made his Sonoran Desert trip, he was in financial ruin. But in San Francisco, just as he was leaving for Sonora, he met a wealthy and beautiful young woman of 21, Zelia Nuttall. He married her in 1880 and was temporarily reestablished. Soon he was traveling and spending liberally, but the marriage was dying. By 1883 he had to auction the precious books of his library to raise cash, and by 1888 Zelia divorced him. She went on to gain fame as an analyst of Aztec and Mayan manuscripts. Although Pinart's publishing projects were seriously scaled back, he continued publishing papers, albeit on a less ambitious scale. He lived his last years, after 1900, relatively withdrawn, but did have a second marriage in 1907. His reputation declined so much that he was little known when he died in 1911 at age 59. Partly because of his obscurity at the end of his life, his work on the Sonoran Desert and the Pinacate region never appeared in English and languished almost unnoticed.

During his trip on the Gila and through Tucson in 1876, Pinart was intrigued by the Mexican side of the border. His enthusiasm for adventure never seemed dimmed by personal circumstance. Impoverished in the fall of 1878, Pinart still set out from San Francisco to explore the Sonoran Desert and the Pinacates.

His trip occupied the winter of 1878-79, and he published part of this "Voyage en Sonora" in the *Bulletin de la Société de Géographie* in 1880. His record of this trip was filled with observations of life and landscape in the desert Southwest during that shimmering lost moment of transition between ancient times and 20th-century civilization.

Ocotillo blossom along Pinart's route. Ives Flow. March 11, 1989.

contained little decipherable information. But from the 1960s to the 1980s, as I worked on drafts of this book, I was haunted by the thought of unstudied extensive eyewitness descriptions of the region in the 1850s.

In August, 1988, I discussed this with Julian Hayden, who told me how Ives' footnote came about. Southwest researcher Paul Ezell had got wind of the diary around the 1950s, and had obtained from the Bancroft Library a microfilm of the pages about the Pinacates. Ezell, a friend of Hayden, had then asked Hayden's wife, Helen, to translate it. Helen Hayden had struggled valiantly to translate the rough French handwriting from the pale and somewhat scratchy microfilm. Helen had since died, but Hayden recounted to me from his memory that the diary contained colorful passages about a smoking cave and Pinart's loss of his burros during a storm. Helen, Hayden said, had been able to translate only a part of the diary, and had given up on the illegible remainder.

Hayden told me he was the source of Ives' information, having passed this news to Ives when Ives was writing his 1964 article. Ives' erroneous date must have been merely a typo or misunderstanding. Still, I applaud Ives for inserting his flawed footnote, because it sent me off on a new and fascinating quest.

Hayden had no copy of the Pinart manuscript, and said his wife had returned it with the translation to Ezell. By a twist of fate, Ezell had died in California only weeks before, and I learned that boxes of his Arizona papers had been sent to the University of Arizona Library's Special Collections, only a few blocks from my house!

Now I felt I was hot on the trail of something too good to ignore. Did the boxes contain the missing Pinart manuscript? Peter Steer, of the Library, made a heroic effort going through the newly arrived boxes, but found only an illegible negative of the microfilm. I was about to give up, but a few weeks later, in September, I received a message from Peter. Two new boxes had arrived. There, at the bottom of the last box, under some

I can set the stage for Pinart's story by recounting my own relation to it a century later. Ever since reading Ronald Ives' classic 1964 article about the Pinacates, I had fretted over a footnote in which Ives reported that "a French traveler" named Pinart had "visited the region in the 1850s." Still more intriguing, the footnote said that Pinart had left "a quasi-legible diary . . . now in the Bancroft Library" at the University of California, Berkeley. This was virtually the only reference to Pinart in all Pinacate literature, and unaccountably, it garbled the facts. For one thing, Ives placed the trip two decades too early. Also, Ives' wording made me believe the diary prehistoric sherds collected by Ezell, appeared a more legible positive microfilm of Pinart's handwritten journal, and at the very bottom, in an envelope with Hayden's name, a typed copy in French of an article Pinart had published in 1880 about this same trip, "Voyage en Sonora." At the same time, I learned that Arizona historian James Officer, at the other end of the university campus, was already planning to publish a translation of the entire 1880 article, which covered a wider region of Sonora, beyond the desert heart. Officer, however, had not seen the diary version. I told Officer of my interest in the diary and suggested our interests could be complementary; the diary might shed more light on his article, and vice versa. In return, he gave me a copy of the original French article as it appeared in the 1880 *Bulletin de la Société de Géographie.*

Thus, in the space of a week, I was able to assemble for the first time since Ezell's efforts both the obscure 1880 published account and the original field notes from 1878-79.

The next question was how to get this mass of material into good English. I do not read French. By chance, a colleague in my office at the Planetary Science Institute was a sunny, young Belgian astronomer, Dominique Spaute, a native French speaker who had obtained her doctorate in Toulouse, had arrived in America only two years before and was interested in everything. Would she be interested in translating a century-old unknown diary by a fellow European traveler? *"Oui, certainement."*

During the next weeks we got together, armed with our maps, dictionaries, and copies of the microfilm in various degrees of contrast to bring out the faint handwriting. We worked eclectically, sometimes with the material spread out on the living room floor or sometimes, on a favored spot on the backyard grass. One time, during a scientific meeting in the Bay area, our working spot was a bench in Golden Gate Park. Domi (as she is known) read haltingly and I typed into my

Hornito on east margin of Ives Flow. November 27, 1985.

laptop word processor. Within weeks Domi had learned to read Pinart's handwriting, and words that had originally been indecipherable now began to make sense. Pinart's Sonoran diary was peppered with local Spanish words, but my wife, Gayle, a desert expert and a Spanish speaker after Peace Corps years in Peru, stood by to help with those, and the diary began to come alive. Often we could cross-check with the 1880 article, which was based in part on the diary, although the two manuscripts turned out to be complementary, not redundant. Domi later made a complete translation of the 1880 article for Officer, and we confirmed that the diary contained many episodes not in the article, while the article expanded on episodes merely annotated in the diary.

In late 1988, I was able to visit the Bancroft Library in Berkeley for the first time. This amazing institution houses a vast collection of Southwest and other materials assembled by the historian H. H. Bancroft, including

Top: Pinart's sketch of Pinacate from nearly due east along Rio Sonoita.
Bottom: Pinart's sketch of Pinacate from the south on the Ives Flow.

Traced by author from enlargements of sketches in Pinart's original sketchbook.

a large mass of Pinart materials from various parts of the world. A friendly computer led me to a Pinart file on Sonora, and twenty minutes after filling out some forms I was holding in my hand Pinart's original two, brown, five-by-seven-inch, cardboard-bound Sonoran diaries, containing the pages we had been translating from microfilm. Ezell had obtained only the diary pages on the Pinacate region, but these two little volumes described the whole trip from San Francisco onward. And there was more! In addition to his other talents, Pinart sketched beautifully, and along with the diaries were two sketchbooks of pencil drawings, rendered along the trail. To my disappointment, Pinart made only two of his less finished drawings while he was actually crossing the Pinacates, but the sketchbooks contain many charming drawings of the missions in many Sonoran towns, petroglyphs and views of mountains and villages. In addition to the diaries and sketchbooks, there

were some less colorful notebooks cataloging materials in missions and notes on local officials—the detritus of Pinart's passion to record anything that might be interesting to future historians.

In presenting the following account of Pinart's journey, I have combined somewhat free translations of both the 1878-79 diary and the 1880 article, to make the account as readable as possible.

Pinart's expedition through the Sonoran Desert began with a sea voyage in 1878 from San Francisco to Mazatlán, whence Pinart struck north, leaving "civilization" behind at Caborca, as he said. Around Caborca, Pinart heard of the salines, or salty ponds along the coast, southwest of the Pinacates, to which generations of Hohokam and Papago had trekked to collect salt. Pinart resolved to visit them, but was told not to try to cross the dangerously barren desert directly from Caborca. Rather, he would be guided along the same, ancient route that Father Kino had taken, north to Sonoita, then west along the Sonoita River to Quitobaquito. Like Kino in 1698 and 1701, he would then travel south from here along the riverbed, skirting the east flank of the Pinacates, then trek west across the southern Pinacate lavas. From the southwest edge of the Pinacates he would cross the dunes of the Gran Desierto to the coast. Hence Pinart was to produce the first modern field diary we have from within the Pinacate lavas— a unique record.

Near Caborca, Pinart commented on several of the famous *trincheras,* or walled hills. Twentieth-century controversy about their purpose had not arisen, and Pinart described them without reservation as "walls in dry rock, having served as fortification . . ." Here, he also sketched abundant petroglyphs, which he called *hieroglyphic paintings.* Furthermore, he gave an early account of the methods used by Papagos to construct their houses, which he described as "clean . . . dug in about 0.25 (meters) . . . 5m in diameter and 1.6m in height at the center." Around the depressed floor, a framework of

The Gran Desierto dune field crossed by Pinart. April 8, 1977.

arched poles was erected and covered with brush tied in bundles. The style was reminiscent of the Hohokam pit houses of a thousand years earlier.

An old Papago guide named Babatoa led Pinart from Caborca to Sonoita. Babatoa said he would find a second guide at Sonoita to take Pinart across the Pinacates. Leaving the river valleys near Caborca and moving north toward the heart of the desert, Pinart was aghast at the landscape. "All this country is an immense plain, arid, presenting as vegetation only . . . palo verde, a few stunted mesquites, etc. The region is pitiful. Things can barely live there . . . From this plain . . . rise . . . hills, peaks, and mountains which form a chaos." In spite of his negative reaction, he shared the 19th-century faith that things could be improved. "Once watered, these lands are very good for cultivation."

No guide was found at Sonoita, about which Pinart had little to say, except for commenting on a nearby "Campo American."

Finding no guide, Babatoa cheerfully took Pinart on to the little settlement of Santo Domingo, "a rancho (with a) few huts . . . located around a little pond . . ." A party of 25 or 26 Americans was just departing for Ajo.

Pushing on down the Sonoita riverbed, they passed the ancient campground called *Agua Salada* and a fork in the trail marking the departure of the Camino del Diablo toward the right. They turned left, down the Sonoita until "Muri . . . makes us stop at 6:30 and digs a hole in the riverbed beside a mesquite and brings us back some water . . . only a little salty." Muri had to dig about 30 inches.

Here Pinart began to remark on the extinct cinder cones, or *craters* as he called them, along the route, and he made a rough sketch showing the cones with the Pinacate shield rising in the distance, a lava flow visible on its slopes. Now Pinart was approaching the Batamote Hills, on the lower Sonoita River. More than a week earlier, in Caborca, Pinart had already described an extraordinary rumor he had heard about the Pinacates—

Senita cactus and fruit. Ives Flow. November 28, 1985.

the first known record, I believe, of the lost mission of the Pinacates.

> *Around the middle of the Pinacate exists the pozo Batamote where it seems that there exists a little rock wall and a little trail. It is from this point that the famous report has come, which tells that a few years ago someone discovered the ruins of a mission or church and houses . . . in the state in which the fathers abandoned them.*

What can we make of this rumor? First, as a historical record, it is exciting in that it is one of the earliest records of lost-mission legends. It presages Lumholtz' similar record of rumors by three decades. "Among Mexicans," Lumholtz relates, "there is a persistent rumor of an abandoned mission somewhere in the sand-dune country east of the Colorado River, showing foundations of walls near a spring . . . and an old smelter . . ." Lumholtz recorded the rumor that a man looking for his lost horses out of Tinajas Altas had stumbled upon the ruin near the Cabeza Prieta Mountains, but that according to other rumors, the ruin was on the lower Sonoita River, near the eastern edge of the Pinacate lavas. Kirk Bryan, the geologist who studied the region's resources in the 1920s, said the same stories were still current at that time. Julian Hayden wrote to me that "By my day, the location was thought to be west of Papago Tanks somewhere out toward the dunes." The supposed mission was even given a name: *Church of the Four Evangelists.* Hayden recounts one specific report of a discovery of the mission foundations, which he traced to an outcrop of columnar basalt, entirely natural, but giving the impression of a tile floor flanked by columns.

Pinart's account of a lost mission at "Pozo Batamote," or Batamote Well, gives us a clue to the origin of these stories. It shows that the earliest recorded site revolved around a place called *Batamote.* Writing in Caborca, miles to the south, Pinart said this was supposed to be in the middle of the Pinacates, but the place name "Batamote" is used for the region on the edge of the Pinacates, on the lower Sonoita River, around the Batamote Hills, where Kino and Manje recorded a substantial village and had baptized the ancient-looking Indian woman. Water was usually available by digging in the Sonoita riverbed. Thus, the earliest-known version of the lost-mission story places it on the lower Sonoita River, not in the Gran Desierto dunes. We can thus speculate that the rumor circulating in Caborca was a confused amalgam of accounts of the eastern Pinacate area. In particular, it combined the still-visible ruins of the old mission at Sonoita and a belief that Kino or some successor had established a little mission at the Batamote village site. The belief that Batamote (or somewhere) still had a "lost"-mission ruin like that at Sonoita

may be the explanation of the first of our three desert-heart mysteries—the legend of a lost mission in the Pinacate area, the legend that reached its most eloquent fruition in Esquer's *"Campos de Fuego"* fantasy.

Pinart's servant had a fever and left their party on March 12. Pinart and Muri made another camp in the Sonoita riverbed and by March 14 they were on the south flank of the Pinacate lavas, climbing up and down over lava hillocks, "calcined and black." At 9:30 A.M. they arrived at "a little plateau where . . . there is a ravine and a tinaja." So far, Muri had led Pinart on exactly the route along which Kino and Manje had been led two centuries before, testifying to the persistence of Indian routes and Indian memory. The tinaja was probably one of the tanks near the modern Cuervo Tanks, site of an Indian settlement, and probable site of Kino's stop. As if to confirm the persistence of Indian tradition, a group of red-turbaned Papago *Mezquitaños* presently arrived from the coastal salt ponds, like ghosts from the past.

Pinart and Muri soon departed the water tank to cross the vast Ives Flow, the same region where Kino, Manje, and Salvatierra had mused on the volcanic forces that had produced this awesome terrain, and where Manje had recorded his cryptic note about the great hole that caused terror and fear. By astonishing coincidence, Pinart unknowingly raised a different mystery of his own in exactly the same region.

Climbing down the plateau, we find the bed of black lavas which, descending from the volcano, throw themselves toward the sea. From the plateau, we clearly distinguish the dunes of the coast. The flow that we traverse for a league and a half [resembles?] pudding. We pass and visit at the S.E. an opening still in activity filled with sulfurous cinders, warm, from which [come] some sulfurous vapors. Also on the left—offering of arrows—fear of Muri to descend . . . —from this little eroded crater descends some lava pudding-like, inflated, of recent origin.

Pinart is asserting, in this somewhat fragmentary diary passage, that he visited an active vent, warm and emitting sulfur fumes! Our amazement comes because, as we saw in the last two chapters, the Pinacates are universally regarded as completely dormant. According to conventional wisdom, no hot vents should exist anywhere in the field. A modern reader of the diary is frustrated by the fact that Pinart lapses into fragmentary notes separated by dashes. But any doubt about what he is asserting is removed by the article he published a year later in the French geographic bulletin. Fortunately, this is one of the incidents he chose to describe in more vivid account:

From this last encampment we have to pass over an immense lava flow, which . . . is no less than three leagues across. This flow is located on the south part of the volcano and descends from the crumbled edges of the principal crater. One would imagine being in the middle of an agitated sea, from which the high waves were transformed by an unknown phenomenon to their present state of immobility and solidity. In the middle of that sea, a few secondary cones have formed, which have, themselves, poured out eruptions of lava onto the ancient layer; one of these cones is still in partial activity. The opening of this little crater is filled in with sulfurous and warm cinders; on one of the sides is a cave from which escape abundantly some very sulfurous vapors.

I ventured into that cave, breaking in up to the middle of my leg each step that I take. At the bottom is a little opening, hardly big enough for a man to pass, and from which the vapor escapes whistling. What astonished [me] the most was that on a flat rock located at about the middle of the cave, I found a quantity of objects deposited by the Indians as offerings to the spirit of this place. There were arrows, shells of various types, and heads of

bighorn sheep. I interrogated my guide, Muri, about this, but I couldn't get anything from him; he was standing as if petrified, trembling in his limbs, and not daring to go further than that rock into the cave.

So, in exactly the same area where Manje wrote of a great hole that caused terror and fear, Pinart's guide shook with fear in front of a cave that supposedly housed an active vent as well as an Indian shrine! Is it possible that a fuming vent really existed in the Pinacates as recently as 1879? Could the fearsome cave be related to Manje's fearsome "big hole"?

There is an observation that supports a positive answer to both questions. The southwest quadrant of the Pinacates, though crossed by ancient Indian routes, has been the least-explored quadrant in recent times, so it is the region where such features might have gone unrecognized. This is where the relatively fresh-looking Ives Flow runs down the mountain's broad flank toward the dunes. In the middle of the Ives Flow rise at least three low ridges with collapsed summit vents. These appear to have been sources of secondary venting within the Flow, just as Pinart mentions. The centers are collapsed into chaotic, rubble-filled pits, smaller and more irregular than the classic craters to the north. In the walls of these pits are striking, yawning caves: lava tubes exposed in cross section as the lavas collapsed.

I suspect that one of these features marks the cave that Pinart described. The trail that Pinart, Manje and other travelers followed from Cuervo Tanks across the Ives Flow to the sea passed within some hundreds of yards of these caves. Rechecking this area in 1989, I found that one of the largest caves, in the wall of an impressive collapsed vent near the center of the flow, contained bighorn sheep skull fragments and charred wood fragments. Although any artifacts it might have contained had been removed, it fit Pinart's description, even including some large, flat lava slabs near the middle of the entrance. Thus, I conclude that this cave, or one like it along the trail to the salt ponds, may have been known as an important shrine, perhaps second only to I'itoi's cave near the Pinacate summit. This would give, finally, an explanation of the mystery of Manje's "big hole of such depth that it caused terror and fear," a description apparently recorded in the middle of the Ives Flow. What Manje recorded was one of the collapsed vents or caves now known (through Pinart's description) to have been a shrine at which Kino's Indian guides would have stopped. Ironically, if this theory is right, in all of Kino's and Manje's visits to the Pinacates, they missed the large craters that make the area famous.

The real question is whether Pinart's description bears on the mystery of the last eruption in the Pinacates. Conceivably, in view of the known geothermal activity in the area, hot vapors from underground conduits might have been escaping through a vent in the back of the lava tube that Pinart visited.

On the other hand, Julian Hayden[3] has suggested a completely different interpretation, which he developed when Helen Hayden translated as much as she could of this passage. Hayden recalled that Don Alberto Celaya, the aging Sonoita resident who guided Lumholtz to some of the Pinacate features, had told stories of how his uncles had explored a lava tube in this part of the Pinacates. Finding old Indian firebrands in the cave, they lit them to explore the cave's dark recesses. The tube was caked with bat guano, and one of the explorers dropped a torch, igniting the guano. It smoldered for years and the column of smoke was well known in the area. Apparently a number of these guano fires were subsequently started. Hayden inferred that Pinart had unknowingly stumbled into Celaya's cave or one like it, presumably in the waning stages of the fire.

After I had explored some of these caves in 1989, I talked to Hayden again and he described a cave *he* had visited in the area some years earlier. He called it a "great

View across the Ives Flow toward Pinacate Peaks, along route of Pinart, Kino and Manje. November 28, 1985.

tube with collapsed central cavern," which led far eastward where it tapered to an end. It "had burned long ago," was "deep in guano ash," and contained Indian offerings that were partially charred. Hayden felt that this tube, which may be the same one I saw, was Pinart's cave, though he refers to other burned-out caves in the area, including one found by University of Arizona geologist Larry May. Hayden remarks that many of these used to contain offerings and that one yielded an Indian *atlatl*, or throwing stick, radiocarbon-dated at about 1500 B.C., while another nearby tube yielded a musket ball.

Hayden's idea is that the heat and fumes were not volcanic at all, and Pinart was misled. This theory is much more consistent with the current view that the Pinacates are totally dormant.

Nonetheless, there are some counterarguments in favor of Pinart's active vent. First, Pinart could hardly have been more explicit. Discussing an opening still in activity, as warm cinders, sulfurous fumes, and whistling vapors from a vent, he leaves no doubt that he really means to describe active volcanic fuming. Second,

View out of the mouth of a small lava tube. Ives Flow. November 28, 1985.

he gives no evidence of fire in his cave, which should have been obvious from ash and soot deposits. Third, he does not remark on the Indian artifacts being charred, although they might have escaped charring if a fire had merely smoldered in the guano. Of course, they could have been added in the few years between the supposed fire and Pinart's visit, though Indian activity in the area was slight by the 1870s. Fourth, Pinart specifically says the fumes were sulfurous and coming through a vent in the rear of the cave, not seeping up from warm floor deposits.

It is all quite a mystery. Perhaps we can accept Hayden's theory with the modification that fumes from one burned lava tube had migrated through a network of tubes and were being emitted from an opening in the rear of Pinart's unburned tube. Yet this does not explain the "hot cinders" that Pinart reported. At the very least, Pinart's report reopens the question of the date of the most recent volcanic activity in the Pinacates. It seems to support the possiblity that Indian legends of the area refer to eruptions or venting within the last thousand years or so. Possibly, Pinart has given evidence of con-

tinuing volcanic venting in the Pinacates. At any rate, the curious case of Monsieur Pinart's cave deserves further exploration on foot throughout the great sea of billowing lava that forms the Ives Flow. Perhaps one day more evidence will come to light to clarify whether an active vent really existed in March of 1879.

By the evening of March 14, Pinart and Muri and their burros had trekked on across the lavas and descended into the sands. The day had been cold and windy. The next day was even worse. Strong winds blew the sand and inspired the passage at the beginning of this chapter. Some of the burros wandered away and Muri spent much of the day in fruitless search. They left this camp at 3:30 A.M. on March 16, following a difficult, grey trail with their remaining mule sinking and slipping at every moment. Soon they came upon a Sand Papago family camped on a sandy terrace:

> *What can those poor devils live on in this desert . . . The Areneño Papagos number very few today, and speak a dialect somewhat different from that of the Papagos but so little is the difference that at the next instant I can barely detect it. It is a matter of pronunciation and intonation rather than anything else.*

This verifies Thomas Childs' recollections from some years later that the Areneños were considered by the other Indians to speak peculiarly.

Finally, they arrived at a water hole, and then the saline lagoons, that Pinart took to be ancient depressions or craters that the sea had filled during an epoch of high water level, leaving evaporite salt deposits. Pinart described the salt deposits as "having a thousand colors," but was "disappointed with the saline after the descriptions that I had been given by a person flattering them." As if to make up for the disappointment, the ever-observant naturalist recorded an unusual March shower of meteors "more numerous from 9 to 11, a few of them being very bright."

daughter, Georgie Boyer, who has driven in to join us. She entertains us with stories of her father, Glenton Sykes, who complained that too many people were "food fussies," and boasted that "if it doesn't walk away, I can eat it." With this inspiration, we settle into a good Thanksgiving dinner of baked beans out of a can (there is never a better Thanksgiving dinner than a few cans of beans in the Pinacates), and I locate Halley's comet, a gossamer fuzzball in the blackness of the Pinacate firmament, near the Great Square of Pegasus. My companions are glad to see it so well; the city lights have robbed them of the night sky.

These lava plains, where we have hiked today, are like a great sea—a sea of four-foot frozen waves—each with its own valley and crest. You can see forever. When you are in a house, or an alcove in the hills, or a little shady spot under a tree, the universe seems hemmed in to just that scale. Here, you see for miles, a sea of ridges of lava, and yet, as you walk across the pahoehoe, each ridge, each niche, is different—its own little universe. Here, a twisted bit of lava protrudes; here a beautiful coil of ropy lava; here a little "kipuka" with bushes and flowers—an island of soil left by the lava stream; and here is a collapse opening into a lava tube 15 feet wide, big enough to crawl into. At night, in bed, thinking about this scene, I have vision of the scale of complexity in the universe, and a sudden surreal metaphoric dream takes shape, in which each little pocket in the lavas is a person, with his or her own personality, and the sea of people goes on, mile after mile, forever—repeated scenes, all unique.

Journal entry. Return to the Ives Flow. March 11, 1989.
When I came here in 1985, I hadn't known of Pinart's diary and hadn't known that this was the area he crossed. Reading his diary, I was inordinately pleased by the analogy we both made with the surface of the open sea . . . a kindred spirit from the past. I remembered the collapses and caves of the vents that Dan Lynch showed us, and made connections with Pinart's fuming vent and with Manje's terrifying "big hole." I looked at photos I had taken in 1985. Black cave openings beckoned. Perhaps these features really are out there somewhere in the

"[The cloudless sunset] is the broadest, the simplest, and in many respects the sublimest sunset imaginable—a golden dream with the sky enthroned in glory . . ." J.C. Van Dyke, The Desert, 1901.

Dusk at camp in the Pinacates. ca. 1969.

Ives Flow, I began to think. The whole area deserved another look.

So my friends and I have returned to Lynch's camp for a blitzkrieg one-day reconnaissance of the Ives Flow. We set out through the thicket of bizarre hornitos, and 2/3 mile or so past a large cinder cone into the center of the flow, in search of (a) Pinart's cave of fumes and hot cinders, which he said was located southeast of the trail and in the side of a vent, and (b) Manje's big hole. With these goals in my mind, and with Pinart's and Manje's diaries in my hand, I feel I am experiencing this landscape more keenly than when I was at the same spot 3-1/2 years ago.

On the way to the vents our party looks for signs of Indian trails across the lavas, and finds none, save for a 1 x 3 inch plainware sherd. The vents are roughly as I remember.

The first prominent example as we head southwest is a prominent dark ridge. Reaching its top, one finds that its whole center has collapsed to form an elliptical east-west crater perhaps 70 yards long and 30 yards wide. There is no flat floor, only a tumbled-down mass of massive basalt boulders. From almost any spot on the wall, prominent black cave entrances yawn on opposite walls—10 feet and more in height. These fit Pinart's description.

We explore the various lava-tube entrances one after one. The large cave on the southeast wall becomes a favorite candidate for Pinart's cave. It has an entrance as much as 30 yards across, partly blocked by masses of rock that have fallen off the rims. The floor is coated by powdery dust. My friend, physicist Floyd Herbert, probes back into the cave with a weak flashlight. He estimates he has gone 50 yards back, where the cave is 4 feet high and 10 to 20 feet wide, but no end is in sight. This is the largest cave we see and one that might have attracted Indian attention. Bones, mostly of small animals, are abundant. In keeping with Pinart's description, we find evidence of visitation, burned sticks, and a bighorn skull fragment and horn among the rocks near a flat rock at the rubbly entrance. All of the caves are as much as 20F cooler than the 90F outside temperature, and some of them have a distinct breeze blowing outward. This breeze (the "wind" that disturbed the Tohono O'odham?) probably comes from the temperature differential between the deep passages and the warm surface rocks. Could Pinart have smelled some sulfurous fumes wafted out from below? Or did he merely mistake the musty, organic smell of the cave for sulfur?

A possible discrepancy between this cave and Pinart's description is his mention of "breaking in up to the middle of my leg each step that I take," as if he were walking on thin, fresh, pahoehoe crust. Nonetheless, Floyd reports that the powdery dust let him sink in up to his ankles; perhaps that was Pinart's meaning.

On the outer sloping rim of this vent, we note another match with Pinart's description: pudding-like pahoehoe dribbles down its slopes.

Continuing south-southwest past a big red cone on our right, we hike perhaps another 2/3 mile to the top of a dark mound that looks like a ridge. This is the first of the complex of collapses that make the feature I called Lynch's Crater. This whole complex abounds in two categories of structures possibly relevant to Manje's big hole. First, there are many more caves, some sloping gently downward and others more vertical. These are usually exposed in the sheared-off walls of the collapsed vents. Second, some of the collapsed vents themselves form mighty depressions that may have inspired terror in the Spanish travelers. This is especially true of the pit forming the easternmost lobe of Lynch's Crater. A view from the rim shows an enormous, almost V-shape collapsed chaos, probably over 100 feet deep and perhaps 100 to 200 feet across.

No single feature is a conclusive match to either Pinart's cave or Manje's hole, but the weekend survey has convinced me that we are on the right track—that we have been walking close to the features that so impressed Pinart a century ago, and Manje nearly two centuries before him.

10. New Times

The mood of the desert is never sad. It is either entrancingly smiling or terrifyingly grand; radiant in its ephemeral garb of flowers and in the golden silence of its bare plains and tinted mountains; awful at night when hell is let loose, storm rages on the heights, the cloud is alive with forked lightning, and the heavens reach in incessant thunder.
  But it is the smiling mood that leads the unwarned or unwary astray . . .
                                                                    Raphael Pumpelly
                                                                    My Reminiscences, 1915

The faith of the desert was impossible in the towns. It was at once too strange, too simple, too impalpable for export and common use . . . The scream of a bat was too shrill for many ears . . .
                                                                    T. E. Lawrence
                                                                    Seven Pillars of Wisdom, 1926

FOR MUCH OF THE 20th CENTURY, the heartland of the Sonoran Desert went largely ignored. From the 1870s into the early 1900s, scattered mines and struggling ranches persisted here and there. The most productive mine in the area was just north of the border, on the east edge of the Sonoita Mountains. This site produced gold, silver, copper and lead. According to old accounts, it had been worked in the 1870s and '80s, and was sold in about 1890 to Cipriano Ortega, the colorful border character who installed the "golden" Wellton bell for his wife. Ortega called the mine *La Americana* and extracted a reported $14,000 worth of ore, which he processed at his ranch south of the border. Then he sold the mine in 1899 to local merchant M. G. Levy. Levy renamed it the Victoria mine, for the wife of one of his storekeepers. It yielded another $30,000 for him. The mine changed hands in later decades, with lesser yields, until mining in the area was prohibited in 1978.

Mining and ranching on the American side was affected by American land-management policies. In the early years of the century, much of the desert on the American side came under the care of the Department of the Interior. In 1937, Organ Pipe Cactus National Monument was established to preserve some of the unique vegetation of the area. It is a quiet and beautiful Monument, stretching about 30 miles along the border. Writer Tom Miller, in his book *On the Border*, describes its founding as "due more to hard-drinking politicians than to selfless wilderness preservationists." Miller asserts that it was established partly at the behest of Phoenix legislators who wanted a paved road that would facilitate visits to Rocky Point and Mexico's cheap liquor.

Mining was prohibited in the Monument when it was established, but was permitted again in 1941 because of the war effort. It continued at scattered sites until the mining prohibition in 1978. Similarly, ranching was banned in the Monument, but in this case the story is more complicated. Around 1915, an old rancher named Lonald Blankenship established a ranch with a

Previous page: On the beach, east of Puerto Peñasco. November 28, 1986.   *Caborca mission towers. April 3, 1976.*

house, windmill, corrals and some 300 cattle near the border at the south edge of what would become the Monument. This complex was purchased in 1919 by Robert Louis Gray, a cowboy from southeastern Arizona. Other struggling cattle ranches were active in the area at sites such as Bonita Well and Dripping Springs. By the 1920s, Gray's sons were the dominant ranchers. Their activities covered all of the present Monument area. But when the Monument was established, the Park Service cited longstanding rules that prohibited grazing in national monuments. Now a long legal battle began between the federal government and the Gray family, who considered themselves betrayed by a monument they found misguided at best. From the house at Bates Well, wrote Henry Gray, "There is not an organ pipe cactus to be seen..." The battle over permits and threatened lawsuits ended only when the last of the Gray brothers died in 1976, ending cattle ranching in the area.[1]

A similar story was repeated at Quitobaquito, except this time with Native American residents. Juan José was a Papago medicine man who lived in the area off and on from 1860 until the time of Lumholtz, and he was followed by José Juan Orosco, a medicine man and hunter, who maintained grazing rights around Quitobaquito until his death in 1945. According to historical material cited by botanist Gary Nabhan,[2] Orosco's son, Jim, negotiated with the Park Service to sell the rights to the land for $13,000. According to Nabhan, there was a feeling among the older Tohono O'odham that Jim had no right to sell the land, which had been used by the tribe for centuries. Nabhan faults the Park Service for disregarding history: by 1962, it had destroyed José Juan's house and other historic structures in the area to create the present bird sanctuary.

West of Organ Pipe Cactus National Monument, the land stretching along the border became the Cabeza Prieta Game Range. *Game Range* was a name that echoed the worldview of Hornaday, Sheldon, and others who focused on the bighorns and other animals for sport as

Barrel cactus near Cuervo Tank. March 12, 1989.

well as study. Now they would be protected and efforts would begin to rebuild the dwindling populations of desert bighorn sheep and pronghorn antelope.

From the 1930s to the '50s on the Mexican side, the Pinacates remained a lost oasis, wild and relatively untouched, except for occasional hunting safaris. Scattered ranching and grazing persisted, and by the 1950s, individual woodcutters and rock cutters journeyed into the area with battered trucks. They created a maze of ill-defined dusty roads, whose courses changed according to fortunes of flood and season.

In 1942, Barry M. Goldwater made a trip along the Camino, exercising his considerable photographic skills. Some of his photos were published in 1943.[3] Ironically, this American pleasure trip followed by only a year a tragic journey in which seven of a party of nine Mexicans died in the area. Leaving Sonoita for Brawley, California, in August, they attempted a shortcut across the little-used Camino. Their truck stalled in the sand 17 miles east of San Luis, south of Yuma. Another traveler found them after they had been stranded without food or water for four or five days; the local sheriff reported that one man had slashed his own throat, and another, his wrists.

The modern Mexican highway, Mexico 2, was extended east-west across the north side of the Pinacates in the '50s, replacing the older road that paralleled parts of the still more ancient Camino del Diablo. Buses roar west along Mexico 2 from Sonoita toward Mexicali—commerce for Baja. American fishermen roar south on Mexico 8 toward a weekend in Rocky Point. The unknown Pinacates offer little of interest to these hurried passersby. Sand and cinders are blasted by the sun. As a result, the Pinacates, hub of the Sonoran Desert, remained remarkably unchanged even as the 20th century changed much of the outlying Sonoran Desert from dust to concrete, from floodplain to farm—from quiet desolation to noisy recreation area.

During the mid-century, the new breed of hardy academics—spirtual descendents of Lumholtz—began their explorations. In the '30s and '40s, geographer Ronald Ives was carrying out his gritty studies of northwestern Sonora's landscapes and history, mapping routes of ancient expeditions with little more than dusty diaries and determination. Archaeologist Julian Hayden soon followed, roaming the Pinacates during the '50s and '60s in his battered truck, studying archaeology and altithermals. Desert writer Randall Henderson[4] published an account of a visit to the floor of Elegante in 110F heat in 1951.

But now a strange transformation began, unique to the 20th century—the century of entertainment. The Pinacate country, scene of deaths and desperaton, became a setting for family outings. According to notes and photos in a little book published by southwestern scholar Lawrence Clark Powell, his erudite friend Duncan Brent and photographer William Aplin explored the Pinacates by Jeep with their families, probably in the 1950s.[5] Outdoor writer Ann Woodin devotes a chapter of her 1964 desert book to the first of their many family camping trips to the Pinacates, "enveloped by enormous solitude," apparently also in the 1950s.[6]

Writers of fiction also discovered the Pinacate wonderland. Not counting Esquer's *Campos de Fuego*, Zane Grey was first to mine these hills for romance. His 1913 *Desert Gold*, cited earlier, recounts a chase across the Pinacates.

> *The fugitives were entering a desolate, burned-out world . . . [The] red lava seemed to have flowed and hardened only yesterday. It was a broken, sharp, dull rust color, full of cracks and caves and crevices, and everywhere upon its jagged surface grew the white-thorned choya.*

Following in Zane Grey's footsteps, Louis L'Amour made his 1966 western hero, *Kid Rodelo*, trek across the same country.

> *The Pinacate country was all about them . . . outcroppings of jagged lava and the cholla. It was ugly country . . . Far off he could see a bighorn watching from a volcanic cone.*
>
> *The old gods lurked among the mountains . . . and the Pinacate was a place of the gods, as all such solitary places are apt to be.*

Another Pinacate novel touched closer to home. One of our Pinacate expeditions included a writer friend

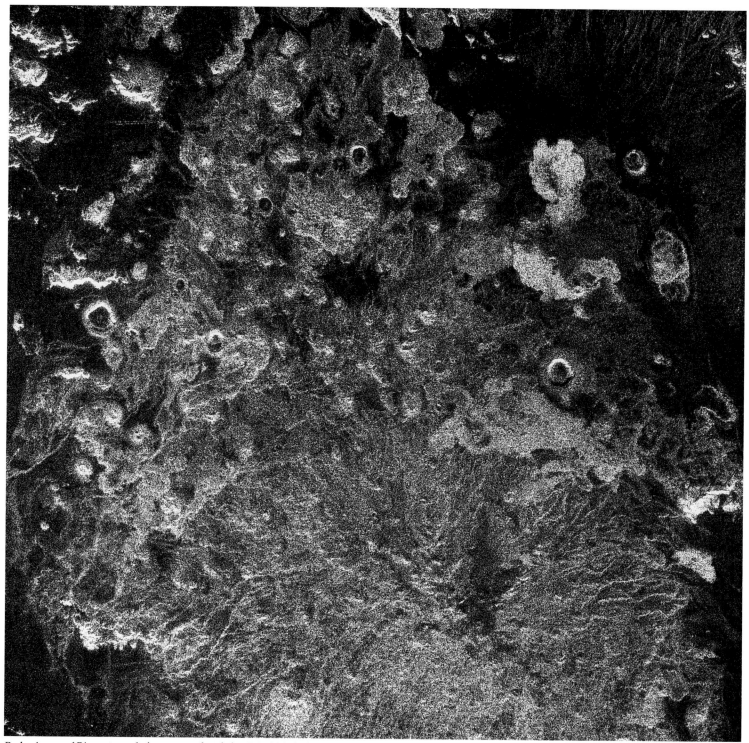

Radar image of Pinacate made from space shuttle by SLR (side-looking radar) experiment. Brighter areas reflect more radar, generally being rougher. Foreshortening compresses southern half (bottom), but dramatically reveals northern craters and rough lava flows. Compare upper right quadrant with aerial photo on page 130. (NASA, Jet Propulsion Laboratory, courtesy Susan B. Yewell.)

example, in a 1966 paper about Mars, I published aerial photos of dust-filled MacDougal Crater. Again in 1973, after I served on the Mariner 9 mission that first photographed dunes and wind-streaked, dust-veneered lava flows on Mars, I was able to publish aerial photos of similar features in the Gran Desierto, where prevailing winds have masked the dark lavas with a layer of orange dust. In 1976 the Viking landers gave us the first closeup photos from the *surface* of Mars. They showed that in terms of landscape, the arid Martian volcanic deserts are practically clones of the Pinacate regions of the Sonoran Desert! There are places in the Pinacates where you could be plunked down in a spacesuit, and not know if you were on Earth or Mars, except for the blue sky, a few scattered plants, and Earth's heavier gravity.

Comparisons of this sort have continued as researchers have analyzed geologic features of other distant worlds. A recent example involves a new technique, imaging radar, which bounces radar signals from an orbiting craft off a surface, and then uses the return signal to construct an image of the surface. The resulting picture, which looks like a fuzzy aerial photo, contains information about the roughness of the surface at the scale of the radar waves, typically a foot or so. One radar study of the Pinacates and adjacent Gran Desierto was published in 1985 by Ronald Greeley and four other geologists from Arizona State University in Tempe. The images revealed the craters and even the smooth, once-mysterious playa that we had named *Wood's Hole*. Such images have laid the groundwork for interpreting radar images of the planet Venus, sent from American and Soviet probes. These probes have used radar to map Venus, because Venus' surface is completely obscured by thick clouds. The clouds block photos, but pass radar waves. Once again, Pinacate-like lava flows and shield volcanoes are among the features revealed.

Astronauts training for the first lunar landings came to the Pinacates in 1965 and 1970 to get a feel for what they might encounter on the still-unknown craters

Dunes and basalt boulders on the surface of Mars, photographed by Viking-1 space probe, show a remarkable resemblance to desert heart landscapes at the contact between the Gran Desierto and the Pinacate lavas. (NASA.)

and plains of the moon. Among the sites they visited were Elegante, Cerro Colorado, MacDougal and other craters. Near the rim of one crater, they succumbed to an urge that has hit countless other travelers of the Southwest. On a bit of flat-lying bedrock they scratched their own petroglyph. It is an astonishing entry in nature's logbook, because it means that this desolate area now contains a continuous record of American history, from the first American hunters at least 10,000 years ago to the first men to reach the moon.

In a little-recognized link, these same astronauts fertilized the environmental movement when they transmitted pictures and descriptions of Earth from space a few years later. Seen *en route* to the moon, Earth became a precious blue marble, floating in a black void. On Christmas Eve, 1968, astronaut Lovell radioed from lunar orbit that the "vast . . . loneliness of the moon . . . makes you realize just what you have back there on Earth." Astronaut Anders, who had visited Cerro Colorado in 1965, saw Earth as "the only color in the universe—very fragile . . . it reminded me of a Christmas tree ornament."

As the environmental movement mushroomed at the end of the sixties, proposals for improved preservation were revived. In June, 1971, the Fish and Wildlife Service, which administered the Cabeza Prieta Game Range, proposed to convert 744,000 of the 860,000 acres of the Range into a wilderness area,[11] a strongly conservationist designation that restricts roads, vehicular traffic and other activities.

A 1971 newspaper review of the situation[12] noted ironically that this would be ". . . calling a spade a spade, something akin to designating Chicago a city. It is wilderness right now . . . about as barren and hostile a land as exists anywhere." Most important was the part of the proposal that suggested extending the Range west by 183,000 acres to include the historic Tinajas Altas Mountains and Tanks, and their associated graves and prehistoric sites. At a hearing in Yuma, the paper reported, the wilderness proposal was favored by the Arizona Wildlife Federation, the Sierra Club and the Wilderness Society, but opposed by mining companies, hunters, "four-wheel-drive types" and the Yuma County Board of Supervisors, who complained that there is already too much federal restriction of land in their county.

By this same time, the Game Range had come to be called—in the literature of its own administrators[13]—the *Cabeza Prieta National Wildlife Range,* and a proposal was being formulated to change the name again. On March 21, 1975, Public Land Order 5493 changed the name of the Game Range to Cabeza Prieta National Wildlife

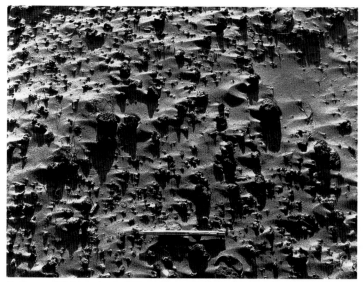

Patterns of light and wind. Prevailing winds in the Gran Desierto make wind tails behind each inch-sized lava pebble in an area of poorly developed desert pavement. Similar features have been photographed in gravel on Mars. April 8, 1977.

Refuge. The subtle semantic changes—from *Game Range* to *Wildlife Range* to *Wildlife Refuge*—reflected changing public sensibilities.

The proposals to create an international park with Mexico, or to create a U.S. wilderness area, or to add the Tinajas Altas to the existing Refuge, still languished. In spite of this inaction, a 1980 management study of the area, prepared by the University of Arizona, was able to conclude that the area at that time was being administered as a *"de facto* wilderness area in order to prevent degradation of wilderness qualities."

Organ Pipe Cactus National Monument, pristine and peaceful as it may still appear, began to experience its own problems. Long regarded as one of the most isolated monuments, it was now threatened by the burgeoning growth of nearby Sonoita, Mexico, the associated agricultural areas, and the heavy traffic on Mexico 2, only a few hundred yards from Quitobaquito. Water use for Mexican irrigation near Sonoita increased fivefold between 1978 and 1986, depleting ground water

Apollo 14 astronaut Alan Shepard, Jr., trains among Pinacate lavas and craters for his later walk on the moon. Astronauts wheeled the lunar rickshaw with them to carry samples and instruments. February, 1970. (NASA.)

Apollo 14 astronauts' petroglyph. May 7, 1987.

and increasing pesticide concentrations in the area. When 50,000 bees were placed in a colony 50 yards north of the border in the Monument, 80 percent of them died within the first year from pesticides being used in ejido farms south of the border.

If the impacts are noticeable now, what of the future? The population of Sonoita is expected to continue to rise, from 18,000 in the 1980s to 35,000 in 2000. As a result of these trends, in 1986 the Monument was listed as the major resource-management problem facing the western region of the U.S. Park Service.[14]

There is a delicate problem here. American environmentalists who see the dangers realize, at the same time, that it is impolite at best and hypocritical at worst to criticize their Mexican neighbors. Having risen to at least transient prosperity on the backs of pesticides and pollution, Americans can hardly criticize their southern cousins for seeing some of the same short-term benefits. The questions of how to proceed challenge our creativity and neighborliness.

THE WHOLE STORY OF CONSERVATION in the Sonoran Desert is complicated by military use of the area.

Since World War II, the American desert from the Wildlife Refuge north to the present Interstate Highway 8, some of the most scrubby land of the area, has been used as a bombing and gunnery range. Pilots practice air-to-air and air-to-ground maneuvers. The range today, suitably named after former Arizona Senator Barry M. Goldwater, is administered by the U.S. Air Force. Drivers along I-8 can often see jets zooming at steep climb angles or swooping low along the south side of the highway. The pilots are notorious for supersonic runs over Tohono O'odham villages in the reservation bordering the range. In spite of the Indians' repeated complaints about noise and broken windows, and repeated orders to avoid this behavior, the problem has continued for years. At a gas station adjacent to I-8, I witnessed a pilot roar directly overhead, a few hundred feet off the ground, banking spectacularly with wings

of the border evolve a symbiosis that would guide the distant bureaucrats: a more active partnership between the desert rats who know the land and the office-bound planners who study maps and wield dollars or pesos.

Sometimes a leaf floating downstream gets caught in an eddy and moves backward. For a while the desert heart seemed to be evolving into a peaceful reserve for naturalists' studies and visitors' wonderment. This evolution fostered an optimistic image: a healthy and urbane civilization, caring for its exotic wildernesses. But in the '80s, a decade of violent undercurrents below a facade of pseudo-urbane glitter, the desert heartland got caught up in backward eddies of greed.

A violent traffic in drugs, guns, and human beings has increased in the desert heart.

One day in 1980, in strife-torn El Salvador, a group of Salvadorans paid about $1,200 apiece to *coyotes*, or "travel guides" who smuggle undocumented aliens into the United States. The group acquired Salvadoran passports and 30-day visas to go as far as Mexico City, but had no permits to enter the U.S. On June 29, 1980, they entered Mexico and continued north by bus as far as San Luis, Sonora, the border town south of Yuma. On July 2, two groups of 16 men, women and children headed out by pickup truck, east along Mexico 2. They arrived before dawn on July 3 at a secret staging area: a restaurant outside Sonoita. Because the Salvadorans had paid such a high fee, Mexican coyotes had agreed not just to dump them near the border, but to guide them across the border into the U.S., an unusual concession. Some of the group even had guarantees that if they were picked up by the border patrol, they would get a second trip into the U.S. for free. Indeed, this was the second attempt for at least two of the women. Spending the day at the restaurant, the men of the party celebrated their coming adventure; they drank heavily with their "guides."

That evening, the truckloads of wayfarers rendezvoused on Mexico 2 a few hundred yards south of Quitobaquito. Here, the coyote guides led the group of

Dune-buggy tracks in the Gran Desierto, in the region crossed by Kino, Pinart and Sykes. The Gulf is on the horizon. February 19, 1989.

nearly 40 easily across the fenced border to the historic pond. In spite of the availability of drinkable water at Quitobaquito, they had purchased at least 20 gallons of drinkable water at the restaurant. With many of the men tipsy at best, the women carried this burden. At 9 P.M. they started north into the pleasant night. No one had prepared them for the July weather they were getting into. Some of the Salvadoran women, in Latin cosmopolitan fashion, were wearing high heels.

By 10 A.M. the next day, July 4, they had finished most of the water and some of the party began feeling faint. By noon they were strung out along the trail, and the "guides" struggled to keep them together. They were paralleling Arizona Highway 85 across part of Organ Pipe Cactus National Monument, challenging one of the harshest environments in North America.

At this point one guide said he could find water, and along with three men and one woman, took four empty bottles and set out to the north. This party disappeared and the coyote was later believed to have escaped back to Mexico. By mid-afternoon, some members of the remaining party were becoming delirious. The party began to split up.

One woman and one of the coyotes died of thirst and exposure that afternoon or evening. By the next morning, a couple of small groups made it out to the highway and were picked up. At least one group, which included a coyote, apparently tried to protect the secrecy of the rest and repeatedly said there were no others left in the desert. Finally, later on the same day, they admitted that 30 others were still back in the desert. Aircraft and ground searchers soon located the remaining survivors and 13 bodies. Two of the dead were lying face down on their open Bibles. Monument officials reported that the temperature on July 5 had reached 109F, with the sunlit soil reaching possibly 150F.

The story began breaking in Tucson and Ajo papers at once. Interviews with the survivors indicated that some of the group had attempted to get moisture by chewing on cactus or palo-verde branches, or drinking shaving lotion and cologne that they carried with them in suitcases. Fights broke out over the precious moisture in their own urine. According to some of the surviving witnesses, who themselves were only partly conscious, some of the women who died had begged for a quicker death at the hands of the remaining coyote, who attempted to strangle them; but he died, too, and the details remain unclear.

By July 8, controversy erupted. Plans had been proposed to deport the survivors because they were in the country illegally. Church and community groups in Ajo and Tucson responded with plans to shelter them and fight deportation through legal proceedings. The refugees were described by an El Salvadoran embassy spokesman as agricultural workers, domestic helpers and businessmen. An editorial in the *Tucson Citizen* said, "Clearly, American immigration policy is in shambles."

On July 10, the *Citizen* interviewed a Salvadoran who was employed as a housekeeper in Los Angeles, and was the mother of several in the party. She had saved and borrowed to pay Salvadoran smugglers to bring her three daughters to the U.S. They were supposed to have come by airplane. Her three daughters, ages 13, 14, and 20, had all died in the desert.

The papers photographed survivors waiting in Ajo to be transported to the Pima County Jail. In a page-one interview on the July 11, some of them begged not be sent back to El Salvador, asserting, for example, that "it will be death on arrival . . . I will be one of those never released again . . ." *Newsweek* for July 21 reported that two surviving coyotes had been arraigned on federal charges of transporting illegal aliens. The case of the Salvadorans fueled the Sanctuary Movement in which southern Arizona churches organized an underground railroad to bring Latin Americans who they viewed as political refugees safely into the country. This culminated in Tucson in 1986, with the sanctuary trial where several leaders of the movement were found guilty by the jury. Most of the survivors of the 1980 death trek were reportedly scattered across the U.S. by the late 1980s, their cases pending in the best, Kafkaesque style.

Traffic in human beings was not the only contraband commerce passing through the desert heart. In the spring of 1982, a light plane, reportedly from California, blew up over the Pinacates. The pilot allegedly had a history of smuggling drugs across the border. According to Julian Hayden, who saw some of the wreckage, the plane had been sabotaged with charges that blew off the wings and tail in flight, leaving the fuselage and passengers to crash. Speculation was that the charges might have been triggered by radio from Rocky Point. Pieces came down over an area of several square miles and the pilots and passengers were killed. Julian took a poignant photo of a lunch bag from the plane, speared on the end of an ocotillo as it fell near the "Bat Cave" lava tube on the way to Moon Crater.

In the fall of 1984, the Tucson Public Library sponsored "Writers of the Purple Sage," a series of programs on the literature of the Southwest. One of their activities was a visit to the Pinacates in celebration of the classic books by Lumholtz and Hornaday and the novels by Zane Grey, James Hall Roberts, and others. On the approach to Papago Tanks, they encountered a camp of heavily armed men, who shooed them on down the road.

Some days later, a Tucson Pinacate buff, who had been with the library party, crept back at night and observed a camp of men armed with automatic weapons. He heard gunfire and believes he may have tripped an automatic sensor. He fled but later returned to observe people driving trucks into the camp and transferring goods. Speculation circulated that this may have been a gunrunning or marijuana smuggling operation; such activities have increased in connection with civil unrest in Central America. By January, the same source reported a camp of Federales at Papago Tanks; apparently they had cleaned house.

The '70s and '80s saw a proliferation of mysterious, isolated dusty airstrips, laid out in the flatter areas of desert pavement. The shady traffic in drugs and arms cast a pall of danger over Pinacate explorations. Researcher Bill Broyles who used to drive around freely in the Pinacates at night, gave up this luxury, not wanting to stumble by surprise into a camp of edgy merchants with whom he preferred not to do business. The desperados of the old westerns were reappearing in the Pinacates of the '80s.

Perhaps the regression toward unsavory activity in the Pinacates is just a phase. Perhaps the sweep of history will set things right. Perhaps relations between third-world and developed countries will evolve in a humane direction and we can invent new *social* mechanisms that will allow a cleaner commerce across borders, a commerce of joy and mutual benefit. Perhaps the dark traffic of desert nights and deadly back roads will wither away. The question is, how can we bend twigs in that direction? Where do we go from here?

The answer may be preservation at the cost of increasing bureaucratization. With the growing population of the Southwest, the days are gone when we can jump in our cars and expect to find pristine deserts with no rangers.

The 19th century was the century of discovery of the west; the 20th is the unique, final century when we can explore its unguarded, pristine natural wonders on our own terms, as individuals, in our cars. We want to pass on to the 21st century as much of that experience as we can. But the next century will be one of choice. There will be either an endlessly increasing bureaucratization and regulation, to keep the benighted masses from destroying natural areas, or a new public paradigm of respect for the land. If we can create a commonly shared naturalists' respect for the land, there will be less need for regulation.

Wilderness status for the Cabeza Prieta, and Mexico's Federal Reserve status for the Pinacates are a first step down the road, but the fork, between bureaucratization and awareness, looms ahead. One ranger is not enough to protect the Pinacates in the society we have created.

As for the future, plans are already afoot to declare the Pinacate wonderland a part of the United Nations Biosphere Preserve program. This is an international program to recognize and protect unique regions of our planet. Practical consequences of such an act remain to be seen. The more precious we recognize an area to be, the more people want to see it; the more people want to see it, the more rangers and rules we seem to need. The only way out of this vicious spiral is to *educate* the next generation of travelers to have a keener sense of place. Then, even as it becomes possible for more people to visit an area, they would exercise this privilege with more aesthetic and historic sense, gaining more pleasure and leaving less trace.

Saguaros in the sunlight. Along Mexico 2, north of the Pinacates.
January 12, 1980.

Journal entry. Johnson Space Flight Center, near Houston, Texas. March 17, 1987. *The Lunar and Planetary Science Conference is held each year at this time on the muggy campus of the Johnson Space Flight Center, south of Houston. The first conference was held just after the first Apollo landings, to discuss the rocks brought back from the moon. Among planetologists, it was called the Rock Festival. Astronauts used to attend; now there are sessions featuring debates between financially strapped NASA administrators and disgruntled scientists who want to know why we can't get back to the moon.*

Apollo helped the world shrink to a global community. European, Japanese, and Soviet scientists attend the Houston meeting. The Russians report on their mapping of Venus by radar. The Americans admire their mission and their sense of humor. Sasha Basilevsky says, "We have been doing systematic mapping of Venus. But you know that systematic work is not the best way to make brilliant discoveries." So he shows

a potpourri of Venusian Volcanoes and lava flows. At a ceremony the Soviets hand over to the Americans three cans of the latest radar data tapes; with their space program on hold, the Americans offer in return only a color photo of Mars taken 11 years earlier, during the 1976 Viking mission.

My thoughts run to the Pinacate manuscript I am working on, and the comparison between the lonely Pinacate lavas and the lava plains of the moon, the shield volcanoes of Venus, and the windswept dunes of Mars. Will exploration continue? It is our glory that we can't stand the thought of a place we haven't visited. It's our shame that we don't know what to do when we get there.

It is a brilliant sunny day in Houston and the conference has ended, and the impossible green lawns of the Space Center stretch and sparkle under a blue sky. I stop at the visitor center once more to see the shiny Lunar Landing Module towering in the hall, and the old space suits hanging in display cases, hunched over like cadavers in a medical lab.

The nearby Public Information Office offers an opportunity to seek information about the Apollo astronauts' visits to the Pinacates during their training.

I go in. Luck is with me. It is noon, and the reception area is inhabited by three crusty, grey men shooting the breeze and exuding experience. I ask about astronauts in the Pinacates.

"I remember that," says one.

"He went on that trip," explains his friend.

"Yeah, I fell in one of those craters," says the first.

"Who went with you—which astronauts?" I ask.

"Shepard was there, and . . ."

"Where did you go? Crater Elegante?"

"Yeah, that's it. Elegante. I could barely climb out of there."

"And Cerro Colorado?"

"Yeah! Cerro Colorado!"

The greying and balding men, tough as buzzards, reminisce with me about their glory days, when they were helping to train men to walk on the moon.

They send me down the hall to the photo room, where the latest NASA press-release photos await visiting journalists. Sparkling prints they are, of ceremonies and ground-engineering tests. There are no fresh photos of other worlds.

The space program has been a shambles since the Challenger catastrophe a year ago, and the file marked "current activities" is sad and thin. Like most recent days at the Johnson Space Flight Center, this is a dull news day. Rock music from a secretary's small radio provides noise but not much inspiration in the listless office.

As I scan the files, the enthused grey veterans return down the hall with contact prints from their personal files. Shepard and the other astronauts, as thin and as short-haired as college boys in the early sixties, with their cowboy hats on, climbing around Elegante and Cerro Colorado.

The young ladies exhume more prints, color-faded prints, 17 years old. Tests of the little stroller the Apollo 14 astronauts pulled around with them on the ancient plains of Fra Mauro.

It turns out, I learn from the pictures and the men, that there were at least two training trips in which moonwalkers hiked the Pinacates, one in 1965 and one in 1970. They were just two of many trips to volcanic regions—Hawaii Volcanoes National Park, Craters of the Moon National Monument in Idaho, Sunset Crater in Arizona—the kingdoms of mysteries and holes and twisted rocks. Now, adventures on the way to the moon are remembered only by a few veterans in NASA offices. Outside, the gift shop sells portraits of Krista McCauliffe.

Two-day dash to MacDougal Crater. May 7, 1987. *Tucson author Tom Miller, author of* On the Border *and other books, has been commissioned by a Phoenix weekly,* New Times, *to write about the Pinacates. With some misgivings I agree to guide him on a quickie hot-weather reconnaissance. I don't like the heat, and I don't want him to talk up favorite Pinacate sites as great boondocker spots for hordes of Phoenix 4-wheel drivers, but I trust Tom's sensitivity.*

I'm to meet Tom at Border Patrol headquarters in Why. I take a thermometer and the temperature is 70F when I start from Tucson around dawn. Kitt Peak's bloodless granite contrasts with the flushed copper-chocolate basalt hills held down with a myriad of yellow-green spikes: saguaros at dawn.

At 10 A.M. as I drive around Why looking for Tom, the temperature in the car is 92F. I haven't turned on the air conditioner yet. I park the car in the shade for ten minutes and when I return the temperature inside is 97F. As we cross the border and check in at Sonoita, the car sits parked in the sun for one-half hour, and when we return to it at 1:50 P.M., the temperature inside is 106F. We arrive near MacDougal Crater around 4 P.M. and the air conditioner keeps the inside of the car hovering around 90F.

The sun is still high at MacDougal and I feel I won't get any extraordinary new photos in this light; so I content myself having Tom take three shots of me on the MacDougal rim in black and white. Tom professes to know little of cameras. He wants to see the rock on which the astronauts scratched their graffiti. After exploring some new spur roads, we reach the area where I remember the rock. There it is, with a scratchy scrawl:

APOLLO 14
NASA 2/16/70

The inscription is an impromptu effort, not nearly as impressive as the craftsmanlike prehistoric rock art in the area. Spacemen may be able to get to the moon, but they don't know beans about making petroglyphs.

The rock appears as if it may be bedrock, and I hope it is; but I visualize some barbarian coming in here with a truck and trying to pry it loose to put in his front yard.

Night thoughts in Los Angeles. April 3, 1988. *I'm looking out of my hotel room window over Wilshire Boulevard in the heart of fantastic L.A. This is the end product, the destination that drove the whole thrust across the Sonoran Desert. Kino's dream. California. A million lights spread beneath my feet outside the window, but no stars are visible in the clear sky.*

I am reading one of Chuck Bowden's books about the Sonoran Desert. "A lot of American books these days begin with a sense of loss," he says. His book is devoted to loss.

The book features superb color and black-and-white photos. The color photos show only nature and are gorgeous: plum-colored crags at sunset and blue fogs of snow in the mountains. The black-and-whites feature human impact, destruction. Fences, bulldozers, dead deer.

I'm with him. I want to believe every word and every image-inspired implication. Yet something is not right. In a color view, the city is beautiful: lights scattered like diamonds below rocky ridges. But in the text and the black-and-whites, the city is ugly. The photographer stepped a literal or figurative three feet to the left to include this pile of rubbish in the foreground, or that bulldozed saguaro. I know; I've done it myself. How can we learn to feel things as they are and as they might be, without caving in to culture-clichés that make a single landscape lovely in this shot, ugly in the next?

Much environmental writing in the '70s and '80s, I finally realize, is hollow, full of sad words about the places that are being lost—the Glen Canyons of the world. Such writing is as manipulative as a propaganda bureau's press releases, because it makes you feel for the place without thinking about larger issues. Fashionable environmental books of the '80s are concerned with the author's responses, all id and ego, with no superego core. Modern environmental writers chase their own tales: there are great flourishes of feeling, but few solutions. Bowden himself says, "The modern environmental movement is a messianic mission . . . (but) the center of the movement is an empty barrel." In many books about a special place, there is only sadness at loss, no pursuit of images to a final big picture. No consideration of the people who wanted the houses built from the trees that were cut down. Was our spread across the continent evil? Should the colonists have stayed in Virginia? Should their ancestors have stayed in Europe? Should the Neanderthals not have crossed that first river? What should I do about this in my desert book? It's not fair to write a book or read a book about the atrocities perpetrated on your favorite acre without thinking about how we need to live our own lives to create the kind of society and landscape in which we want to live. Much of the Sonoran Desert is still relatively wild, and that gives us a chance not only to save it, but to learn from it. We in the Sonoran Desert are pioneers in a new world; what kind of civilization do we want to build here?

Epilog:
Ruminations on Environmentalism
in the Late 20th Century

At present, in this vicinity, the best part of the land is not private property; the landscape is not owned and the walker enjoys comparative freedom. But possibly the day will come when it will be partitioned off into so-called pleasure grounds, in which a few will take a narrow and exclusive pleasure only—when fences shall be multiplied, . . . engines invented to confine men to the public road, and walking over the surface of God's earth shall be construed to mean trespassing on some gentleman's grounds . . .

Henry David Thoreau
In the essay, "Walking," 1862

It's amazing what happens to a place if you leave it alone . . . It just goes its own way. It stays alive. It grows. It gets better.

Paul Theroux
The O-Zone, 1986

I FEEL SHAPED BY EXPERIENCING the desert heart. To walk the lava paths that Kino walked three hundred years ago and to see exactly the same deserted vistas that he saw was an extraordinary experience for one who had grown up in the used and weary east, where volcanoes had been unknown for a hundred million years, where exuberant foliage hid sedimentary rocks, where dark streams trickled over mossy rocks all year round, and where every verdant acre seemed to be someone's back yard, township or farm.

How can we preserve the desert-heart country so that others will experience what we have felt? The quote from Paul Theroux says something about this. The plea to leave a beautiful place alone is the traditional last chapter in an environmentalist's book about a favorite place. Let's give it wilderness status. Keep out those who environmental writer Barry Lopez describes as having "a flair for violence and a depth of ignorance."

Ultimately, however, we can't solve this problem by restricting access. Technology grows. What do we do in 2050 when the uneducated rich trade in their dune buggies for 'copters? We've got to change the paradigm in people's heads, not just the technology in their hands.

We've got to increase *sense of place*. That happens by a slow, generation-to-generation process of education: a spreading not just of facts, but of a mixture of facts and feelings about the land.

The key to the whole environmental challenge of the late 20th century is to overcome what I call, to reduce it to one word, *disconnection*. Modern urban sunbelt inhabitants no longer experience the original beauty of the Southwest, nor do they understand much of its history. This is a loss of roots. They are disconnected from the original reality of their surroundings.

We have arrived in an era when the latest and most expensive resort hotel opened in another magnificent volcanic setting—the Kona Coast of Hawaii—touts "fantasy" adventures on their resort grounds. For a fee, you can swim in their pool with dolphins or go on a carefully managed safari across their grassland slopes. Instead of a real adventure of the body or mind, you can pay extra and experience synthetic adventure. The builders of this hotel recently announced plans to build a resort just outside of Tucson, promoting the same sort of pretense. Staged adventure is disconnection. Fortunately, for the moment, the heart of the Sonoran Desert still offers the real thing.

How to define the difference between synthetic adventure and the real thing? It is the difference between the (active) mind that wants to *create* an experience, and the (passive) mind that wants to be entertained. A popular magazine of the last century brought this home to me in a monthly column it ran, called "Artist's Adventures." Its illustrators recounted their adventures as they went out to experience and capture the reality and beauty of the world. With the right mindset, more of us could be having "artists' adventures."

To avoid disconnection we need to realize we are building a civilization in this desert, and we must make not just economic, but aesthetic, choices about what it is to be like. To do this we must develop an aesthetic consciousness of what we want. Van Dyke said the power to enjoy through the eye, ear and imagination was as important as eating, "but there has never been a time when the world would admit it." This is a problem in building our Sonoran Desert civilization, because the American ethic of individualism has been translated into a legal system that generally gives short shrift to aesthetic arguments, whether they are about billboard displays or zoning changes.

This situation, in turn, has led to an energy-draining polarization—the age of the lawsuit. In the short term, instead of concentrating on education and sense of place, the conservationist *we* are forced into sense-numbing legal battles and public initiatives against the developmentalist *they.*

But the long-term battle is more important. It must be won not by triumphing in legal conflict, but by affecting the public paradigm—the unconscious values that shape how we look at the situation. We need to produce a generation in which the we-they polarization is reduced by a mutual pleasure in sense of place.

We need the victory of education that expands the American capacity to respond to beauty and nature. A needed step is to clarify our definition of nature.

Texas scholar Frederick Turner hinted at this in a remarkable essay.[1] He imagines for a moment that the Grand Canyon was formed as a result of strip mining or agricultural erosion. Promoting the contemporary environmentalist worldview, teachers might bring school children to the rim to witness this hideous scar, as children are taken to Auschwitz. Later, the children might be taken to the verdant stands of aspen nearby on the Colorado Plateau to enjoy the beauties of *nature.* If this parable repels you, then decide for yourself where the dividing line is between an "unsightly" erosion gully and the wonders of the Grand Canyon. Does beauty lie in the object or in its mode of formation?

One problem in formulating an improved environmentalism for the next century is defining nature in a way that avoids disconnection. It is a particular and subtle problem around Southwestern cities. As developers' bulldozers, like cancer cells, rip into the surrounding deserts, environmentalists respond with bumper stickers—"Sonoran Desert: Love it or Leave It Alone." Many of them seem unaware that the *natural desert* they lament is itself an altered product of decades of overgrazing and water depletion. The more natural desert, to which we respond so intensely in the desert heart, is missing around the cities, where the land has been raped, scraped, scrapped and left to regrow.

IS NATURE EVERYTHING OUT-OF-DOORS? Or is it everything before humans arrived on the scene? Or are we part of it? Turner dramatizes this issue by noting that while strip mines are a modern American environmentalist's nightmare, the poet W. H. Auden loved the strip-mined hills of Cornwall; similarly, the evocative Mediterranean landscapes, "with their olives, sages, thyme and dwarf conifers, are a result of centuries of deforestation, goat herding, and the building of roads and cities." What we call *nature,* in such settings, is not nature at all, but the hand of humanity.

Why are we uncomfortable with this? It is because we share an American mythic view of nature, derived in our frontier days, as something pure, untouched, something not yet explored. (Or perhaps something modified only by prehistoric Indians.) Eventually this evolved to the view that nature is good and civilization is bad. Thoreau flirted with this pessimistic view. Only a few pages after extolling a beautiful farmhouse: "Nowadays almost all man's improvements, so called, as the building of houses . . . simply deform the landscape, and make it more and more tame and cheap." Van Dyke came directly to this dark conclusion: " . . . there is nothing ugly under the sun, save that which comes from human distortion. Nature's work is . . . beautiful."

That view led to our present scheme of *walling off* wilderness areas to keep (bad) humanity out and thereby save nature—and then going on with business as usual outside the nature preserves.

WE CAN NO LONGER AFFORD THAT VIEW. In the next century, it won't work. *Saving nature* will not mean a long-term battle to preserve a *status quo,* though this is the way it is usually presented. Indeed, if we imagine that nature can be *preserved* in some magically static state, then we are doomed to unhappiness because nature itself loves change. Volcanoes destroy forests; asteroids fall out of the sky and destroy species. As we learned during the Copernican and Darwinian revolutions (but seem prone to forget in our 20th-century city-bastions), we are not Lords of Creation, but part of creation. We have to face that principle and build our environmentalism on it.

Saving nature means a sophisticated interaction with the changing environment, grounded in choices about what *we* want to do. Even if we literally wall off an area, acid rain and the coming greenhouse effect insure that the area will be altered by human activities. We can no longer settle for the idea that human

actions are bad and let it go at that. We must adopt responsibility for the role we play. More than in any previous decade, we must accept that we are an influential part of nature, and that therefore *we* must choose self-restraints and aesthetic principles–and we must put them into practice at the ballot box, the shopping mall and the investment firm.

The desert can teach how to make the aesthetic choices we need to make to shape our own lives and our own civilization, because the desert teaches simplicity. It teaches respect for common pleasures, such as running water in our homes. Thus it can teach each individual to take conscious pleasure in the conveniences that are really important to him or her. Imagine setting up life in a cabin in the desert, away from the city. Imagine trips once a week into town, to furnish your cabin with one carload each week of the luxuries and necessities of your life. You quickly can put yourself into the mindset of choosing what is important to you. It might seem a hard experiment, this life in the wilderness, but remember, a thousand generations of our ancestors went through it without any weekly "trip into town" and without any machines.

A conclusion that can be drawn from this is that we must learn how to choose what we want from our culture. We need to learn to reject what we don't want, instead of mindlessly developing a desire for everything the hucksters throw at us. We can take a more mentally active, not passive, role in drawing from our civilization what we want to make our own lives more pleasing. Through our thought-experiment, the desert teaches a zen-like rule for right-living in the 21st century: know and enjoy as much as possible; consume as little as necessary for a well-designed life, because it takes a lot of effort to "get into town" and buy all that stuff that you don't need.

It amounts to developing a new aesthetic sensibility in which we assess the value of things. Simplify, Thoreau said. Drawing pleasure from these basics is a needed preventive against being drawn into the disconnected, urban, consumerist frenzy.

To transform this sensibility into a public paradigm will involve public education policy. It requires something invisible and slow—a shift in personal values over a generation.

PERHAPS PUBLIC DEVELOPMENT of this new paradigm, or new aesthetic, or new environmentalism—whatever we choose to call it, could be approached through a new high-school-level course that could combine some present courses and aim at an improved and shared sense of place. When I grew up in Pennsylvania we learned about Algonquins, Daniel Boone, Fort Pitt and George Washington's forays as a young officer through our region; even Cecil B. DeMille, the pioneer of hype and sex, came through town to make a film about the French and Indian War. Why is it that kids and office-bound professionals of today's Southwest seem to know so little about the Hohokam, the ruined villages under their feet, the adventures of Coronado or Kino or the rest? Disconnection through lack of education.

Education about the land creates the ability to appreciate it. One of the most important statements of Thoreau is the key: "There is just as much beauty visible to us in the landscape as we are *prepared* to appreciate" (my emphasis). Being prepared to appreciate something is the same as getting knowledge about it.

Such a new course would combine aspects of history, geography, and economics. This course will be called *The Land*. Just as this book has pivoted about the desert heart as a hub, *The Land* pivots about the student's locale: his/her city, state, geographical area. *The Land* is 30 percent history, 30 percent geography/biology/climatics, 20 percent modern economics, 10 percent archaeology, 10 percent free-for-all. Students in the Southwest's version of this course will visit ancient ruins, retrace parts of the route of Coronado, cross the Camino del Diablo, climb Sunset Crater, descend Meteor Crater, trace a Hohokam irrigation canal, talk to the modern rancher, have the largest local developer take them to his latest project and explain it, meet with the Planning and Zoning Commission and follow a real-estate project through the approval-hearings process.

Students need to have three objectives when they study *The Land*. First, and primarily, to learn what *nature* really means in their area: what geology, landscape, plants, climate and natural history are native to the area and how they have been changed by us during the human history of the region. Second, to learn how to experience recreation in nature, but to learn at the same time how to sort out the most basic blessings of civilizations from its mere frivolities. And third, to learn that ecological awareness involves not just actions like recycling metal cans (although that is a necessary thing to do), but the whole array of positive choices about what you want to draw from your civilization, what kind of life you want to build and what kind of city you want to build.

Perhaps through such an educational initiative we can create a generation primed to have a richer personal aesthetic when it comes to the land. I would be happy if, when pondering the Sonoran Desert, tourists and administrators alike could see not just a patch of useless land awaiting the Latest Idea (be it military test, mining venture, resort development, RV playground, nuclear-waste site, etc.), but a geologically unique and nearly pristine remnant of a long past that will not end tomorrow. If this dream fails, then at least I want the future dune buggy blasters, joy-jet-riding picnickers and overly enthusiastic gunnery-range pilots to *know* what they are destroying—that it is not just another playground on the outskirts of the L.A.-San Diego-Yuma-Phoenix corridor, but a last piece of the old, real world.

But the dream may succeed. If people are connected to their land, not disconnected, they will not want to let it go.

Notes to Chapters

Note: All references are to books listed in the bibliography.

Preface

1. Quoted by Larry Evers in the introduction to a 1983 edition of Mary Austin's *The Land of Journeys' Ending.*
2. Austin (1903, reprinted 1974), p. xvi.
3. Austin (1924, reprinted 1983), p. 438.
4. Doughty (1931, 1983 edition), p. 91.
5. Powell (1974), p. 145.
6. Thoreau (1862, reprinted 1980), p. 174.

Chapter 1

1. Felger (1980).
2. Lumholtz (1912), p. 171.

Chapter 2

1. Cabeza de Vaca (1542, reissued by the University of New Mexico Press, 1983).
2. The legend is retold by Hallenbeck (1949). Bandelier (1886, 1981) traces it to a German geography of 1508.
3. Casteñada (1596) translated in Winship (1904).
4. Di Peso (1974), pp. 800-801 recounts that a nephew of Guzmán led one of the raiding parties and published a diary about the trip. Indian warriors he encountered fought in ordered ranks.
5. For example, see Bandelier (1890, reprinted 1976), p. 68ff.; Engelhardt (1899), p. 2 and Winship (1904).
6. Gayle G. Hartmann and I published a review of the problem in 1972, concluding from reported distances traveled, and from the common overestimation of latitude by the early Spanish explorers, that Asunción (probably with Nadal) made the trip and probably reached the Gila River.
7. See the translation and discussion of Bandelier's 1886 work by Rodack, (Bandelier, 1886, 1981). See also Rodack's 1985 discussion of his route and the precise location of the Indian site involved—probably either that called *Hawikuh,* or that called *Qaquima.* Today, both of these are ghostly ruins, mounds of debris, remnants of standing masonry walls, scattered painted sherds. Qaquima is topped by an active Zuni shrine—stone slabs about a foot across, with prayer sticks and other offerings. Hawikuh sits on the side of a low hill and Qaquima, at the foot of an imposing mesa.
8. Ives (1959), pp. 35-36.
9. Hayden (1972).
10. The late historian Ronald Ives remarked to me once that he had tried to find reference to Díaz' entry into New Spain on the passenger lists of ships and other documents, without success.
11. B. C. Hedrick (1978) discusses the mystery of Corazones' location and puts it on the Yaqui River.
12. Ives (1959). Several other fascinating older sources bear on the route and events of Díaz' trip. A near-contemporary account was written between 1540 and 1596 by one of Coronado's soldiers, Pedro de Casteñada de Nacera, and published in Seville in 1596. It is included in Winship's 1904 study of Coronado's expedition. Matías Mota-Padilla published another history from old sources in Mexico in 1870. In the text I have synthesized an account from these two sources. Ives reviews these and more recent sources, together with his own experiences on foot in the area in the 1930s and 1940s, in order to reconstruct Díaz's route and deduce his burial place. The league, used in the Spanish original text, is a notoriously variable unit, changing with time and author; in the translation here it is assumed to be 2.5 miles.
13. The indefatigable Southwest adventurer, Godfrey Sykes (of whom more later), in a 1937 paper gives descriptions of the "mud volcanics" and steam vents as they still existed here in 1911, and their somewhat altered status in 1933. Similarly, Ives (1959) describes how "hot mud still bubbles up from below, [and] steam and fumes spread over the area." My own visit in 1972 recorded children playing among muddy warm puddles among scattered modest houses and dirt roads in desolate mud flats at the foot of Cerro Prieto. The second area, described by George James (1907), has not been suggested as the site Díaz discovered, but remains a second possibility. James describes an incident there, when a state geologist broke through the crust near one bubbling crater and was immersed nearly to his shoulders in hot mud and water; he was pulled out and barely escaped with his life. The features were changeable; the ground was firmer and less active a few years later, in 1906. James indicates that both "mud volcano" areas were visited as early as 1850 by Americans.
14. Frank Lockwood and Donald Page (1930), in a history of Tucson, recount these stories, but give them little credence. Page mentions the Fray Marcos manuscript, but its existence is unconfirmed. Such stories may have been the motivation for an interesting hoax: An inscription of Fray Marcos' name and a 1539 date on a rock in Phoenix's South Mountain Park has been shown to be a fake, probably dating from this era (see Bartlett and Colton, 1940). The perpetrator of the fake and its motivation has hitherto been a mystery; but Arizona boosters' attempts to claim a pedigree might have been a factor.

Chapter 3

1. Kino's original diary was translated and published by Bolton (1948).
2. Kino, translated by Bolton (1948).
3. Ives (1966a), p. 63.
4. Lenon (1987).
5. Donahue (1953); Hallenbeck and Williams (1938).
6. Austin, Mary (1983), p. 318.
7. Hornaday (1908, 1983), pp. 129-130. Desert wanderer and art historian John Van Dyke had described the same "lava shadow-illusion" at unspecified lava beds of this region, in his 1901 desert book. Hornaday, who shared many of Van Dyke's enthusiasms, may have picked up the idea in this earlier book.
8. Ives (1966a).
9. Ives (1942), p. 237.
10. Manje (1954), p. 161. Why did Manje say that the eruption theory was not credible? Was he disputing Kino? It was not only credible, but true!
11. Salvatierra (1946), p. 177.
12. Hayden (1966), p. 199; Ives (1966a), p. 70.
13. Salvatierra (1946), p. 181; Bolton (1960), p. 460 combines the various diaries of Kino, Manje and Salvatierra to give a vivid description of this trip.
14. Bolton (1960), pp. 411, 474.

Chapter 4

1. Engelhardt (1899), p. 27.
2. Dunne (1955).
3. Dunne (1955).
4. Dunne apparently erroneously uses "miles" once in place of "leagues."
5. Ewing (1941).
6. Ewing (1941); Polzer (1968b).
7. Lease (1965).
8. Ives (1963).
9. Polzer (1968b).
10. From a 1792 chronicle by Juan Arricivita, translated and abridged by Coues, (1900).
11. Quoted by Engelhardt (1899), p. 51.
12. Summary of Arricivita by Coues (1900).
13. These are published in a series of volumes edited by Bolton (1966).
14. Ives (1984), p. 6.
15. Quoted by Coues (1900).
16. Quotes from de Anza and Font are from the volumes of diaries edited by Bolton (1966).
17. Ives (1984).
18. Ives (1984), p. 21.
19. Ives (1984), p. 21.
20. Ives (1984) gives more detail.

Chapter 5

1. Quoted by Hague (1978).
2. Hardy (1977).
3. Flint (1831, 1973).
4. Weight (1959).
5. Broyles (1982; personal communication, 1987).
6. Lumholtz (1912, 1971), p. 321.
7. Lumholtz (1912, 1971), p. 182.
8. Lumholtz (1912, 1971), p. 321.
9. Emory (1848, 1951).
10. Audubon (1905; 1984). The last quotes are from Audubon's daughter's introduction to the volume.
11. Salazar gave his reminiscences in the early 1920s to James M. Barney, who published the account in 1943.
12. Ives (1964).
13. Gray (1856, 1963). The 1963 reprint includes the amusing reminiscences of Brady.
14. Michler (1857), p. 115.
15. Lumholtz (1912, 1971), p. 147.
16. Pumpelly (1870).
17. McGee (1901).
18. Ives (1963).
19. Childs (1954).
20. Gaillard (1896).
21. McGee (1901), p. 137.
22. Childs (1949).
23. The date of the largest quake in the immediate Pinacate area is confused in the records. Ives (1966a), p. 65, refers to a "'temblor grande' felt in Sonoita about 1875, or 'when my grandfather was a little boy,'" as his informant put it. The 1887 quake, on May 3, was centered southeast of Nogales and is well documented, but may have been too far east to affect Sonoita. It shook the Nogales-Tucson area, opened large fissures, and changed the Santa Cruz River course; hence it may be the one referred to by Ives. A tabulation of Arizona quakes of this era, published by the Seismological Society of America, lists one on December 15, 1875, felt south of Phoenix on the Gila River.

Chapter 6

1. Van Dyke (1901).
2. McGee (1901).
3. MacDougal was a sometime companion of writer Mary Austin. Her book, *The Land of Journeys' Ending*, cited earlier, is dedicated to him. Loose ends come together.
4. Hornaday (1908, 1983).
5. Fontana, Introduction to Hornaday (1983 edition). There are further historical hints of friction with oriental immigrants in the area, some of whom may have come originally from railroad-building crews. The biography of Sonoita lawman Jefferson Milton (Haley, 1948) tells about patrolling this area in the early 1900s to pick up Chinese immigrants illegally coming in from Mexico. In a harbinger of tragedies that would occur later (see Chapter 9), Mexican "guides" offering to take them across the border sometimes led them to an area called *Chinamans' Flat* and murdered them. Twelve were found dead there by Milton. According to a 1978 talk by archaeologist James Sherman, Dolen Ellis reported to him that some years earlier, these graves had been disturbed and the bones reburied by officials. In his 1913 novel, *Desert Gold*, Zane Grey mentions illegal traffic across the border in this area: among the threats were Mexican "desert men. They could cross the line . . . and smuggle arms into Mexico. Of course, my job is to keep tabs on Chinese and Japs trying to get into the U.S. . . . I'm not so afraid of being shot up, though out in this lonely place there's danger of it." This quote may account for the Japanese wanderers encountered by Hornaday. Pinacate explorer Bill Broyles (personal communication, 1987) cites a verbal confirmation from a source in Sonoita that Japanese spies were active in the area at that time, and that similar stories involving Japanese navy personnel in the Puerto Peñasco area were heard just before World War II. The idea that the Japanese might have reconnoitered possible invasion routes into the Southwest through the Pinacate area is a little-known aspect of military history.
6. Lynch (1981).
7. Broyles (1987).
8. A predisposition in this direction must run in the adventurous Sykes family. Seven decades after Godfrey did a headstand on Pinacate Peak, his great granddaughter, Diane Boyer, was on a similar mountaineering hike in Canada. According to her mother, she spontaneously stood on her head in a fit of exuberence when the party reached the summit, *without knowing the story of Godfrey!* Informed of it, Diane made a point of a ritual headstand at the time of her first climb to the Pinacate summit.
9. Haley (1948), p. 382.
10. Daniels, though he fell from grace with the Hornaday party, was commemorated elsewhere in Daniels Wash, near Ajo.
11. Lumholtz (1912, 1971). Various quotes in this section are from this book.
12. Celaya in later years befriended Tucson archaeologist Julian Hayden, to whom he told this tale. Julian passed it on to me, June 26, 1989.
13. Lynch (1981).
14. The location of these intriguing materials is unknown to me. A few watercolors are reproduced in the book (Pumpelly, 1918).
15. Bryan (1925), p. 419. A 1980 report on the area, prepared by the University of Arizona School of Renewable Natural Resources, cites an article by Rees (1980) to say that "O'Neill's mule returned loaded with rich gold ore to the Legal Tender Mine," a site some miles east, now known as the Papago Mine, and searchers from there found that O'Neill had apparently drowned. Bill Broyles (1987, personal communication) reports interviews with old-timers (to be filed at Arizona Historical Society), saying that O'Neill was an old man and died of hypothermia during a cold and wet October, and that his body was found huddled against the rocks just south of the grave site; another interviewee recalled the time as summer.
16. Broyles (1987, personal communication).

17. Esquer (1928).
18. Sykes (1951; a more scholarly account is in his 1927 paper).
19. Sykes (1937).
20. Sykes (1944).

Chapter 7
1. Thomas (1963).
2. Hayden (1985, citing Castetter and Bell, 1942).
3. Fontana (1987).
4. Bennett (1977).
5. Ives (1962).
6. Ives (1964), p. 38.
7. Ives (1964).
8. Ives (1935, 1956, 1964). The quote is from the 1964 paper.
9. Shakel and Harris (1971). Shakel became well known in southern Arizona in the '70s and '80s as a dynamic environmentalist.
10. Ives' files are in the Arizona Historical Society, Tucson. Ives' photos cover many parts of the country and are inadequately indexed as of 1989. Some indexing has been begun on a volunteer basis by Bill Broyles.
11. Hayden, personal communication.
12. Hayden, personal communication (August 1988).
13. Haley (1948), pp. 157, 160.
14. Martin and Klein, 1984; Haynes, 1987.
15. Hayden (1976).
16. Rogers' classic book is *Ancient Hunters of the Far West* (Rogers, 1966).
17. Hayden (1969).
18. The best summary of the competing arguments about Hohokam prehistory is given by archaeologists Randall McGuire and Michael Schiffer (1982).
19. See archaeological studies of the Cabeza Prieta region just north of the border, by Fontana (1965), and McClellan and Vogler (1977), and in McGuire and Schiffer (1982).
20. Hayden (1967).
21. Hayden (1967, 1972).
22. Smith (1966, p. 25, translation of Kino's diary).
23. McGuire (in McGuire and Schiffer, 1982), p. 203.
24. Hayden (1967, 1987a).
25. See *Kiva* special issue on Tumamoc Hill, 45, Nos. 1-2, Fall, 1979.
26. Quoted by Johnson (1966).
27. McGuire (1982), p. 193.
28. Fish, et al. (1984).
29. Roberts (1966).
30. Anonymous (1927).
31. Pumpelly (1870).
32. Gray (1856, 1963).
33. Nabhan (1985).
34. Stiles (1978).
35. Childs (1954), and footnotes supplied by Childs' correspondent and editor, Henry Dobyns.
36. Gray (1856); Hayden (1967); Childs (1954), p. 32.
37. Childs (1954).
38. Childs (1954); Stiles, 1978.
39. The posse included uncles of Don Alberto Celaya, Hayden's friend and informant, and Sonoita resident, circa 1950, for whom Celaya Crater was named.
40. Haley (1948), p. 179.
41. Hayden (1967).
42. Childs (1954), p. 29.
43. Lumholtz (1912), pp. 333-334.
44. This information from Julian Hayden, personal communication (October 1985).
45. Hayden, personal communication (October 1985).
46. Austin (1983), p. 223.

Chapter 8
1. Lumholtz (1912), pp. 212, 234.
2. Ives (1964).
3. Lawrence, T. E. (1935) Ch. 32.
4. Rittmann (1962).
5. Kelly's (1952) article is an ironic reversal of the story of Meteor Crater, caused by a large meteorite impact in northern Arizona. The Chief Geologist of the U.S. Geological Survey, G. K. Gilbert, led a party there in 1891 and, misled partly by the nearness of volcanic formations around Flagstaff, pronounced incorrectly that this crater was volcanic, not meteoritic! This mistake set back studies of meteorite-impact craters by several decades.
6. Jahns (1955).
7. Galbraith (1955).
8. Hayden (personal communication, August, 1988). This information was passed to Hayden by Hayden's friend, Pinacate woodcutter José Navarro, pictured in Hayden (1985). Hayden said he never met El Viejito, because El Viejito erroneously blamed Hayden for the disappearance of a utensil El Viejito had left stashed in a tree.
9. Ives (1964), p. 26.
10. Wood (1972).
11. Donnelly (1970).
12. Wood (1974).
13. Hornaday (1908, 1983), p. 193.
14. Krutch (1961, 1986), p. 143.

Chapter 9
1. Parmenter (1966).
2. Pinart's Arizona article was first translated into English in a publication by the Zamorano Club. See Pinart (1877, 1962).
3. Hayden (personal communication, August 1988). Wood (1974), p. 154, also mentions this story, citing Hayden.

Chapter 10
1. Basset, Carol Ann (In press).
2. Nabhan (1987).
3. Barney (1943).
4. Henderson (1961).
5. Hoy (1970).
6. Woodin (1964).
7. Ives (1964), pp. 8-9.
8. Nabhan (1987), p. 96.
9. Barney (1943).
10. Rodack (1968).
11. School of Renewable Natural Resources, University of Arizona (1980).
12. Hoyt (1971).
13. U.S. Department of the Interior (1970).
14. Shaffer (1986).

Epilog
1. Turner, F. (1984).

Bibliography

Abbey, Edward (1984). *Beyond the Wall.* (New York: Holt, Rinehart, & Winston).

Anonymous (1927). "The 'Lost City' is Visited by Many People." *Ajo Copper News* (April?).

Arvidson, R. E. and T. A. Mutch (1974). "Sedimentary Patterns in and around Craters from the Pinacate Volcanic Field, Sonora, Mexico: Some Comparisons with Mars." *Geological Society of America Bulletin, 85, 99.*

Audubon, John Woodhouse (1905, 1984). *Audubon's Western Journal.* (Cleveland: Arthur H. Clark Co.; reprinted in 1984, Tucson: University of Arizona Press).

Austin, Mary (1983). *The Land of Journeys' Ending.* (Tucson: University of Arizona Press).

————. (1903, 1974). *The Land of Little Rain.* (Albuquerque: University of New Mexico Press.)

Bandelier, Adolph (1886, 1981). *The Discovery of New Mexico by the Franciscan Monk, Friar Marcos de Niza in 1539.* (Tucson: University of Arizona Press).

————. (1890, reprinted 1976). *Contributions to the History of the Southwestern Portion of the United States.* (Millwood, N.Y.: Draus Reprint Company).

Barney, James M. (1943). "El Camino del Diablo." *Arizona Highways* XIX, March 14.

Bartlett, Katharine and H. S. Colton (1940). "A Note on the Marcos de Niza Inscription near Phoenix, Arizona." *Plateau* 12, 53.

Bassett, Carol Ann (in press). *An Audible Silence: Organ Pipe Cactus National Monument.* (Tucson: Southwest Parks and Monuments Association).

Bennett, E. Fay (1977). "An Afternoon of Terror: The Sonoran Earthquake of May 3, 1887." *Arizona and the West* 19, 107.

Bolton, H. E. (1934). *Rim of Christendom.* (New York: MacMillan; reprinted 1960 New York: Russell and Russell).

————, translator. (1948). *Kino's Historical Memoir of Pimería Alta.* (Berkeley: University of California Press).

————. (1949). *Coronado, Knight of Pueblos and Plains,* (Albuquerque: University of New Mexico Press).

————. (1966) *Anza's California Expeditions* (New York: Russell and Russell).

————, editor. (1963). *Spanish Exploration in the Southwest.* (New York: Barnes and Noble).

Bowden, Charles (1987). *Frog Mountain Blues.* (Tucson: University of Arizona Press).

Broyles, Bill (1982). Desert Thirst: The Ordeal of Pablo Valencia." *Journal of Arizona History,* 23, 357.

————. (1987). "Adventure in the Pinacate." *Journal of Arizona History,* 28, 155.

————. (1988). W. J. McGee's "Desert Thirst as Disease." *Journal of the Southwest,* 30, 222.

Bryan, Kirk (1925). *The Papago Country, Arizona.* (Washington: U.S.G.S. Water-Supply Paper 499, U.S. Government Printing Office).

Cabeza de Vaca, Alvar Nuñez (1542), translated and reprinted in 1983. *Adventures in the Unknown Interior of America,* translated by C. Covey. (Albuquerque: University of New Mexico Press).

Casteñada, de Nacera, Pedro de (1596, translated and published in 1904). "Relación de la Jornada de Cíbola." In *The Coronado Expedition, 1540-1542.* (New York: A. S. Barnes and Co.).

Castetter, E. F. and W. H. Bell (1942). *Pima and Papago Indian Agriculture.* (Albuquerque: University of New Mexico Press).

Childs, Thomas (1949). Letter to *Desert Magazine.* October, p. 27.

————. (1954). Sketch of the "Sand Indians," as written to Henry F. Dobyns. *Kiva* 19, 27-39.

Clark, Kenneth (1976). *Landscape into Art.* (New York: Harper & Row).

Coues, Elliott (1900). *On the trail of a Spanish Pioneer: the diary and itinerary of Fransicso Garces in his travels through Sonora, Arizona and California 1775-1776.* (New York: F. P. Harper).

Davies, G. L. (1969). *The Earth in Decay.* (New York: American Elsevier Publishing Co.).

Di Peso, Charles (1974). *Casas Grandes, A Fallen Trading Center of the Gran Chichimeca,* Vol. 3. (Dragoon: The Amerind Foundation; Flagstaff: Northland Press).

Doughty, C. M. (1931, 1983). *Passages from Arabia Deserta.* (Middlesex, England: Penguin Books).

Dolph, James A. (1983). "Dedication to William Temple Hornaday." *Arizona and the West* 25, 208-212.

Donahue, W. H. (1953). "Mary of Agreda and the Southwest United States." *The Americas,* 9, 291.

Donnelly, M. F. (1970). Geologic Map: Sierra Pinacate Region, Sonora, Mexico—Arizona, U.S.A. (unpublished).

Dunne, Peter M. (1955). *Jacobo Sedelmayr.* (Tucson: Arizona Pioneers' Historical Society).

Emory, W. H. (1848, 1951). *Lieutenant Emory Reports: Notes of a Military Reconnoissance* (sic). (reprinted in 1951, Albuquerque: University of New Mexico Press).

Engelhardt, Fr. Zephyrin (1899). *The Franciscans in Arizona.* (Harbor Springs: Holy Childhood Indian School).

Esquer, Gumersindo (1928). *Campos de Fuego.* (Hermosillo: El Modelo).

Ewing, R. C. (1941). "Investigations into the Causes of the Pima Uprising of 1751." *Mid-America* 23, 138.

Ezell, Paul H. (1954). "An Archeological Survey of Northwestern Papagueria." *Kiva* 19, 1-26.

Felger, Richard S. (1980)."Vegetation and Flora of the Gran Desierto, Sonora, Mexico." *Desert Plants,* 2, 87.

Fish, Suzanne K., P. Fish, and C. Downum. (1984). "Hohokam Terraces and Agricultural Production in the Tucson Basin." In *Prehistoric Agricultural Strategies in the Southwest,* edited by S. Fish and P. Fish. (Tempe: ASU Anthropological Research Papers No. 33).

Flint, Timothy, editor (1831, 1973). *The Personal Narrative of James O. Pattie, of Kentucky.* (Cincinnati: John H. Wood; reprinted in 1973, New York: Arno Press).

Fontana, Bernard L. (1965). "An Archaeological Survey of the Cabeza Prieta Game Range, Arizona." MS in Arizona State Museum Library, Tucson.

————. (1987). "Santa Ana de Cuiquiburitac: Pimería Alta's Northernmost Mission." *Journal of the Southwest,* 29, 133.

Gaillard, Capt. D. D. (1896). "The Perils and Wonders of a True Desert." *Cosmopolitan,* pp. 592-605.

Galbraith, F. W. (1955). "Craters of the Pinacates." in *Southern Arizona Guidebook, II.* (Tucson: Arizona Geological Society).

Gray, Andrew B. (1856, 1963). *Survey of a Route for the Southern Pacific Railroad on the 32nd Parallel, for the Texas Western Railroad Co..* (Cincinnati: Wrightson and Co.) (reprinted 1963 with reminiscences of Gray's colleague on the expedition, P. R. Brady, Los Angeles: Westernlore Press).

Greeley, R. and others (1985). *Analysis of the Gran Desierto—Pinacate Region, Sonora, Mexico, via Shuttle Imaging Radar.* NASA Contract Report 177356.

Grey, Zane (1913). *Desert Gold.* (Roslyn, N.Y.: Walter J. Black, Inc.).

Gutmann, James T. (1972). *Eruptive History and Petrology of Crater Elegante, Sonora, Mexico*. Dissertation submitted to Department of Geology, University of Arizona.

———. (1976). "Geology of Crater Elegante, Sonora, Mexico." *Geological Society of America Bulletin* 87, 1718.

———. (1979). "Structure and Eruptive Cycle of Cinder Cones in the Pinacate Volcanic Field and the Controls of Strombolian Activity." *Journal of Geology* 87, 448.

Hague, Harlan (1978). *The Road to California. The Search for a Southern Overland Route*. (Glendale: Arthur H. Clark Co.).

Haley, James E. (1948). *Jeff Milton A Good Man with a Gun*. (Norman: University of Oklahoma Press).

Hallenbeck, Cleve (1949). *The Journey of Fray Marcos de Niza*. (Dallas: University Press in Dallas).

Hallenbeck, Cleve and Juanita H. Williams. (1938). *Legends of the Spanish Southwest*. (Glendale, CA: The Arthur H. Clark Co.).

Hammond, G.P. and Rey, A. (1940). *Narratives of the Coronado Expedition of 1540-1542*. (Albuquerque: University of New Mexico Press).

Hardy, R. W. H. (1829, 1977). *Travels in the Interior of Mexico, 1825-1828*. (reprinted in 1977, Glorieta: Rio Grande Press).

Hartmann, Gayle G. and William K. Hartmann (1979). "Prehistoric Trail Systems and Related Features on the Slopes of Tumamoc Hill." *Kiva*, 45, 39-71.

Hartmann, W.K. (1966a). *History of the Lunar Surface*. University of Arizona. Ph.D. dissertation.

———. (1966b). "Martian Cratering." *Icarus* 5, 565-576.

———. (1973). "Martian Surface and Crust: Review and Synthesis." *Icarus* 19, 550-575.

Hartmann, W.K. and Gayle G. Hartmann (1972). "Juan de la Asunción, 1538: First Spanish Explorer of Arizona?" *Kiva* 37, 93.

Hayden, Julian D. (1966). Letter to Editor on Kino's Explorations of the Pinacates, *Journal of Arizona History*, Winter, 7, 196.

———. (1967). "A Summary Prehistory and History of the Sierra Pinacate, Sonora." *American Antiquity* 32, 335-344.

———. (1969). "Gyratory Crushers of the Sierra Pinacate, Sonora." *American Antiquity* 34(1), 154-161.

———. (1972). "Hohokam Petroglyphs of the Sierra Pinacate, Sonora, and the Hohokam Shell Expeditions." *Kiva*, 37, 74-83.

———. (1976). "Pre-altithermal Archaeology in the Sierra Pinacate, Sonora, Mexico." *American Antiquity* 41, 274-289.

———. (1985). "Food Animal Cremations of the Sierra Pinacate, Sonora, Mexico." *Kiva* 50, 237-250.

———. (1987a). "The Vikita Ceremony of the Papago." *Journal of the Southwest* 29, 273-374.

———. (1987b). "Talking with Animals: Pinacate Reminiscences." *Journal of the Southwest* 29, 222.

Haynes, Jr., C. V. (1987). "Clovis Origin Update." *Kiva*, 52, 83.

Hedrick, B. C. (1978). "The Location of Corazones." In *Across the Chichimec Sea*, edited by C. L. Riley and B. C. Hedrick. (Carbondale: Southern Illinois University Press).

Henderson, Randall (1961). *On Desert Trails*. (Los Angeles: Westernlore Press).

Hornaday, William T. (1908, 1983). *Camp-Fires on Desert and Lava*. (New York: Scribner's; reprinted 1983, Tucson: University of Arizona Press).

Hoy, W. E. (1970). "Early Settlements on the Sonoyta River. The First Sonoyta, Santo Domingo, and Quitobaquito." MS, Western Archeological (sic) and Conservation Center, Tucson, Arizona.

Hoyt, David (1971). "Time of Decision for Cabeza Prieta." *Tucson Daily Citizen Magazine*, September 11.

Ives, Ronald L. (1935). "Geologic Verification of a Papago Legend." *Masterkey* 9, 469.

———. (1941). "The Origin of the Sonoyta Townsite, Sonora, Mexico." *American Antiquity* 7, 20.

———. (1942). "The Discovery of Pinacate Volcano." *Scientific Monthly* 54, 230-237.

———. (1951). "Recurrent Mirages at Puerto Peñasco, Sonora." *Journal Franklin Institute* 252, 285.

———. (1956). "Age of Cerro Colorado Crater, Pinacate, Sonora, Mexico." *Trans. American Geophysical Union* 38, 221.

———. (1959). "The Grave of Melchior Díaz: A Problem in Historical Sleuthing." *Kiva* 25, 2, 31.

———. (1962). "Dating of the 1746 Eruption of Tres Virgenes Volcano, Baja California del Sur, Mexico." *Bulletin of the Geological Society of America* 73, 547.

———. (1963). "The Bell of San Marcelo." *Kiva* 29, 14.

———. (1964). "The Pinacate Region, Sonora, Mexico." *Occasional Papers, California Academy of Science* No. 47 (San Francisco: California Academy of Science).

———. (1965a). "Population of the Pinacate Region 1698-1706." *Kiva*, 31, 37-45.

———. (1965b). "Lava Desert of Pinacate." *Pacific Discovery* 18.

———. (1966a). "Kino's Exploration of the Pinacate Region." *Journal of Arizona History*, 7, 59.

———, editor (1966b). "Retracing the Route of the Fages Expedition of 1781." *Arizona & the West* 8 49-70, 157-170.

———. (1984). *José Valasquez: Saga of a Borderland Soldier*. (Tucson: Southwestern Mission Research Center).

———. (1989). *Land of Lava, Ash, and Sand: The Pinacate Region of Northwestern Mexico*. Compiled by James W. Byrkit and Karen J. Dahood. (Tucson: Arizona Historial Society).

Jahns, R. H. (1955). "Collapse Depressions of the Pinacate Volcanic Field, Sonora, Mexico." In *Southern Arizona Guidebook, II*. (Tucson: Arizona Geological Society).

James, George Wharton (1907). *The Wonders of the Colorado Desert*. (Boston: Little, Brown, & Co.).

Johnson, Alfred E. (1966). "Archaeology of Sonora, Mexico." From *Handbook of Middle American Indians* 4, 26-37, edited by G. Ekholm and G. Willey.

Karns, H. J., translator. (1954). *Unknown Arizona and Sonora*, translation of *Luz de Tierra Incognita* by Juan Mateo Manje. (Tucson: Arizona Silhouettes).

Kessell, J. L. (1976). *Friars, Soldiers, and Reformers: Hispanic Arizona and the Sonoran Mission Frontier of 1967-1856*. (Tucson: University of Arizona Press).

Kelly, Allan O. (1952). "Mysterious Crater Elegante." *The Scientific Monthly*, 74, 5, May.

Kino, Eusebio F. (translated by H. E. Bolton, 1919). *Kino's Historical Memoir of Pimería Alta*. (Cleveland: A. M. Clark; reprinted 1948 Berkeley: University of California Press).

Krutch, Joseph Wood (1961). *The Forgotten Peninsula*. (New York: William Sloan Associates; reprinted in 1986 University of Arizona Press, Tucson).

Kundera, Milan (1980). *The Book of Laughter and Forgetting*. (New York: Knopf).

L'Amour, Louis (1966). *Kid Rodelo*. (New York: Bantam Books).

Lawrence, T. E. (1926, 1935). *Seven Pillars of Wisdom*. (Privately printed, 1926. Garden City, NY: Doubleday, Doran & Co., 1935).

Lease, Paul V. (1965). *Pimas, Dead Padres, and Gold*. (Menlo Park: Archivist's Press).

Lenon, Robert (1987). "The Routes of Explorers in Pimería Alta, 1687-1699." Talk at Arizona Historical Convention, Flagstaff, May 2. Privately reproduced and distributed.

Lockwood, Frank C. and D.W. Page (1930). *Tucson—The Old Pueblo*. (Phoenix: Manufacturing Statcomps; copyrighted by F.C. Lockwood).

Lopez, Barry (1987). *Crossing Open Ground*. (New York: Charles Scribner's Sons).

Lumholtz, Carl (1912). *New Trails in Mexico*. (New York: Scribner's).

Lynch, Daniel J. II (1981). *Genesis and Geochronology of Alkaline Volcanism in the Pinacate Volcanic Field, Northwestern Sonora, Mexico.* Ph.D. dissertation, University of Arizona, Tucson.

Manje, Juan Mateo (1954). *Luz de Tierra Incognita.* (Tucson: Arizona Silhouettes).

Martin, Douglas (1954). *Yuma Crossing.* (Albuquerque: University of New Mexico Press).

Martin, Paul S. and Richard G. Klein, editors (1984). *Quarternary Extinctions.* (Tucson: University of Arizona Press).

May, Larry A. (1973a). *Resource Reconnaissance of the Gran Desierto Region, Northwestern Sonora, Mexico.* M.S. thesis, University of Arizona, Tucson.

———. (1973b). "Geological Reconnaissance of the Gran Desierto Region, Northwestern Sonora, Mexico." *Journal of the Arizona Academy of Science,* 8, 158.

McClellan, Carole, and Lawrence Vogler (1977). *An Archaeological Assessment of Luke Air Force Range Located in Southwestern Arizona.* (Tucson: Arizona State Museum Archaeological Series, No. 113).

McGee, W. J. (1901). "The Old Yuma Trail." *National Geographic,* Vol. 12, March, pp. 103-107; April, pp. 129-143.

McGuire, R. H. (1982). "Problems in Culture History." In *Hohokam and Patayan,* edited by R. McGuire and M. Schiffer. (New York: Academic Press).

McGuire, R. H. and M. Schiffer, editors (1982). *Hohokam and Patayan.* (New York: Academic Press).

McKenney, Wilson (1951). "Sacred Cave of the Papagos." *Westways,* 43, No. 12, December.

Michaels, Kristin (1979). *The Magic Side of the Moon.* (New York: Signet).

Michler, Lt. N. (1857)."Report." In William H. Emory's *United States and Mexico Boundary Survey.* (reprinted in 1987, Austin: Texas Historical Association). pp. 105ff.

Momaday, N. Scott (1969). *The Way to Rainy Mountain.* (Albuquerque: University of New Mexico Press).

Morand, Anne (1983)."Introduction." In *The Art of the Yellowstone.* (Tulsa: Thomas Gilcrease Museum Association).

Mota-Padilla, Matías Angel de la (1973). *Historia de la conquista del reino de la Nueva Galicia en la América Septentrional.* (Guadalajara: Universidad de Guadalajara).

Nabhan, Gary P. (1985).*Gathering the Desert.* (Tucson: University of Arizona Press).

———. (1987).*The Desert Smells Like Rain.* (San Francisco: North Point Press).

Nichol, A. A. (1939). "O'Neill's Grave in O'Neill's Pass in the O'Neill Mountains." *Random Papers* (Casa Grande: Southwestern National Monuments, July, pp. 65-67).

Novak, Barbara and Annette Blaugrund, editors. (1980). *Next to Nature: Landscape Paintings from the National Academy of Design.* (New York: Harper and Row).

Parmenter, Ross (1966). *Explorer, Linguist and Ethnologist.* (Los Angeles: Southwest Museum).

Perrigo, Lynn I. (1960). *Our Spanish Southwest.* (Dallas: Banks Upshaw and Co.).

Pinart, Alphonse (1877, 1962)."Journey to Arizona in 1876." Originally published in French in *Bulletin de la Société de Géographie,* Ser. VI, 13, 225. Translated and published with biographical notes by H. R. Wagner (Los Angeles: Zamorano Club).

———. (1880). "Voyage en Sonora." *Bulletin de la Société de Géographie,* Ser. VI, 20, 193-244. Publication of an English translation by Dominique Spaute and William K. Hartmann, in preparation.

Polzer, S. J., Charles W. (1968a). *A Kino Guide.* (Tucson: Southwestern Mission Research Center).

———. (1968b). "Legends of Lost Missions and Mines." *The Smoke Signal,* No. 18 (Tucson: Tucson Corral of the Westerners).

Powell, Lawrence Clark (1974). *Southwest Classics.* (Tucson: University of Arizona Press).

Pumpelly, Raphael (1870). *Across America and Asia.* (New York: Leopold & Holt).

———. (1918). *My Reminiscences.* (New York: H. Holt & Co.).

Rittmann, A. (1962). *Volcanoes and their Activity.* (New York: Wiley).

Roberts, James Hall (1966). *The Burning Sky.* (New York: Morrow).

Rodack, Madelaine (1968). "Ghosts; Do not Disturb!" *Desert* 31, 4, 23.

———. (1985). "Cíbola Revisited." In *Southwestern Culture History,* edited by C. H. Lange. (Archaeological Society of New Mexico).

Rogers, Malcolm J. (1966). *Ancient Hunters of the Far West.* (San Diego: Union-Tribune Publishing).

Salvatierra, Juan María (1946). *Mision de la Baja California.* (Madrid: La Editorial Católica).

Sauer, Carl O. (1932)."The Road to Cíbola." *Ibero-Americana,* No. 3 Berkeley.

———. (1937). "The Discovery of New Mexico Reconsidered." *New Mexico Historical Review* 12, 270-287.

———. (1940). "The Credibility of the Fray Marcos Account." *New Mexico Historical Review,* 16, 233-243.

School of Renewable Natural Resources, University of Arizona (1980). "Cabeza Prieta National Wildlife Refuge Management Plan." (Unpublished).

Sedelmayr, J. (translated by Dunne, P.M. 1955). *Four Narratives 1744-51.* (Tucson: Arizona Pioneers' Historical Society).

Shaffer, Mark (1986)."Organ Pipe 'Time Bomb.'" *Arizona Republic,* March 16.

Shakel, D. W. and Karen M. Harris (1971). "Revised Minimum Age of Cerro Colorado Crater Pinacates Volcanic Field, Northwestern Sonora." *Arizona Geological Digest* IX, 2.

Sheldon, Charles (1979). *The Wilderness of Desert Bighorns and Seri Indians* (Phoenix: Arizona Desert Bighorn Sheep Society).

Simmons, Hilah L. (1966). "The Geology of the Cabeza Prieta Game Range." *Arizona Geological Society Digest,* 8, 147.

Smith, Fay Jackson (1966). "The Relación Diaria of Father Kino" (annotated translation). In *Father Kino in Arizona.* edited by F. Smith, J. Kessell, F. Fox. (Phoenix: Arizona Historical Foundation).

Stiles, Edward (1978). "Quitobaquito Spring Flows with Water—and Legends." *Tucson Citizen,* October 16.

Sykes, Godfrey (1927). "The Camino del Diablo: With Notes on a Journey in 1925." *Geographical Review* 17, 62-74.

———. (1937). "The Colorado Delta." *American Geographical Society* Special Publication No. 19.

———. (1944). *A Westerly Trend.* (Tucson: Arizona Pioneers' Historical Society).

———. (1951). "Summer Journey on the Devil's Road." *Desert* 5-6, April.

Thomas, Bob (1963). "Papagos' 'Baby Shrine' Recalls Ancient Legend." *Arizona Daily Star,* July 7, Section C, pp. 10-11.

Thoreau, Henry D. (1980). *The Natural History Essays.* (Salt Lake City: Peregrine Smith, Inc.).

Turner, Frederick (1984). "Escape from Modernism." *Harpers,* 269, 47-55, November.

Turner, H. S. (1966). *The Original Journals of Henry Smith Turner.* (Norman: University of Oklahoma Press).

United States Department of the Interior, Fish and Wildlife Service (1970). *Cabeza Prieta National Wildlife Range.* July 1970.

United States Department of the Interior (1965). *Sonoran Desert National Park, Arizona—A Proposal.* (Department of the Interior, National Park Service).

Van Dyke, John C. (1901, 1980). *The Desert.* (New York: Scribner's; reprinted in 1980, Salt Lake City: Peregrine Smith, Inc.).

Weight, H. O. (1959). *Lost Mines of Old Arizona.* (Twentynine Palms: Calico Press).

Winship, George Parker (1904). *The Journey of Coronado, 1540-1542.* (New York: A.S. Barnes and Co.).

Wood, Charles A. (1972). *Reconnaissance Geology & Geophysics of the Pinacate Craters, Sonora, Mexico.* M.S. thesis, University of Arizona, Tucson.

———. (1974). "Reconnaissance Geophysics & Geology of the Pinacate Craters, Sonora, Mexico." *Bulletin Volcanologique* 38, 149-172.

Woodin, Ann (1964). *Home is the Desert.* (New York: Collier Books).

Index